Get the eBook FREE!
(PDF, ePub, Kindle, and liveBook all included)

We believe that once you buy a book from us, you should be
able to read it in any format we have available. To get electronic
versions of this book at no additional cost to you, purchase and
then register this book at the Manning website.

Go to https://www.manning.com/freebook and follow the
instructions to complete your pBook registration.

That's it!
Thanks from Manning!

Python Workout

Python Workout

50 TEN-MINUTE EXERCISES

REUVEN LERNER

MANNING

SHELTER ISLAND

For online information and ordering of this and other Manning books, please visit
www.manning.com. The publisher offers discounts on this book when ordered in quantity.
For more information, please contact

> Special Sales Department
> Manning Publications Co.
> 20 Baldwin Road
> PO Box 761
> Shelter Island, NY 11964
> Email: orders@manning.com

Manning Publications Co.
20 Baldwin Road
PO Box 761
Shelter Island, NY 11964

Development editor:	Frances Lefkowitz
Technical development editor:	Gary Hubbard
Review editor:	Ivan Martinović
Production editor:	Lori Weidert
Copy editor:	Carl Quesnel
Proofreader:	Melody Dolab
Technical proofreader:	Ignacio Beltran Torres
Typesetter:	Dennis Dalinnik
Cover designer:	Marija Tudor

ISBN: 9781617295508
Printed in the United States of America

Dedicated to my three children, who are also my best teachers—
Atara Margalit, Shikma Bruria, and Amotz David.

brief contents

contents

preface

In many ways, learning a programming language is like learning a foreign (human) language. You can take a course, understand the subject, and even do well on the final exam. But when it comes time to actually use the language, you can find yourself flustered, unsure of just what syntax to use, or what's the most appropriate way to phrase something—let alone be unable to understand native speakers.

That's where practice comes in. Practicing a foreign language gives you greater fluency and confidence, allowing you to engage in deeper and more interesting conversations. Practicing Python allows you to solve problems more quickly and easily, while simultaneously writing more readable and maintainable code. The improvement happens over time, as you use the language in new and varied situations. It often isn't obvious that you have improved. And yet, when you look back to how you were using the language just a few months before, the difference is stark.

This book isn't meant to teach you Python. Rather, it's meant to give you the practice you need to achieve greater fluency. After going through the exercises in this book—not just skimming through the questions and peeking at the answers—you will write more readable, more idiomatic, and more maintainable Python code.

Python Workout is the result of conversations with students in my corporate Python training classes. Once the course was over, they often asked where they could get additional practice, to continue improving their skills. This book draws upon the hands-on labs that I give my students, as well as discussions that I have had with them during and after class.

The exercises are designed to help you internalize some of the core ideas in Python: core data structures, functions, comprehensions, object-oriented programming, and iterators. These might seem like simple topics, perhaps even too simple for a book of exercises. But all of Python, from the largest application to the smallest script, is based on these building blocks. Knowing them well is a crucial part of being a fluent Python developer. I often say that ignoring these building blocks in favor of more complex topics is akin to a chemistry student ignoring the elements in favor of "real" chemicals.

I can personally attest to the power of practice, not just as a Python instructor, but also as a student. For several years, I've been learning Chinese, in no small part because I travel to China every few months to teach Python courses there. Each lesson that I take, and every exercise that I do, doesn't seem to advance my fluency very much. But when I return to China after an absence of several months, I find that the practice has indeed helped, and that I'm able to communicate more easily with the locals.

I'm still far from fluent in Chinese, but I'm making progress, and I delight in looking back and seeing how far I've come. I hope and expect that *Python Workout* will do the same for you, advancing your understanding and fluency with each passing day.

acknowledgments

It might be a cliché that writing a book is a cooperative endeavor, but it also happens to be true. I thus want to thank and acknowledge a number of people, without whom this book wouldn't be possible.

First and foremost, I want to thank the thousands of students I've had the privilege of teaching over the years in my corporate Python training courses. It is thanks to their questions, suggestions, insights, and corrections that the exercises, solutions, and explanations are in their current state.

Thanks also to the many subscribers to my weekly "Better developers" newsletter (https://BetterDevelopersWeekly.com/), who often take the time to comment on and correct topics about which I've written. I've learned a great deal from them, and often put such insights to use in my teaching.

Next, Philip Guo (http://pgbovine.net/) is an assistant professor of Cognitive Science at UC San Diego. He's also the author and maintainer of the "Python Tutor" site, an invaluable tool that I often use in my courses, and that I encourage my students to use as they puzzle through their Python code. I've used many screenshots from the Python Tutor in this book, and almost every exercise solution includes a link to that site, so that you can walk through the code yourself.

Thanks to everyone who works on Python, from the core developers, to those who write and blog about the language, to those who contribute packages. The Python ecosystem is an impressive technical accomplishment, but I have also been impressed by the number of truly helpful, decent, and warm people I've met who are responsible for those accomplishments.

A host of people at Manning have contributed to the book, making it far better than anything I could have done on my own. (And there's proof; the self-published predecessor to this book wasn't nearly as good as what you're reading!) I've worked closely with a few of them, all of whom have combined skill and patience in helping this book come to life. Michael Stephens saw the promise of such an exercise-centric book and encouraged me to work with Manning. Frances Lefkowitz was not only skilled at editing the text and pointing out where it could be improved, broken up, or illustrated; she also shepherded me through the book-writing process. Gary Hubbard and Ignacio Beltran Torres both provided countless technical insights and edits, finding bugs and helping me to tighten up bad explanations. And Carl Quesnel impressed me to no end with his detailed edits of the final text.

To all the reviewers: Annette Dewind, Bill Bailey, Charles Daniels, Christoffer Fink, David Krief, David Moravec, David R. Snyder, Gary Hubbard, Geoff Craig, Glen Sirakavit, Jean-François Morin, Jeff Smith, Jens Christian B. Madsen, Jim Amrhein, Joe Justesen, Kieran Coote-Dinh, Mark Elston, Mayur Patil, Meredith Godar, Stefan Trost, Steve Love, Sushant Bhosale, Tamara L. Fultz, Tony Holdroyd, and Warren Myers, your suggestions helped make this a better book.

Finally, my family has been patient throughout my business and academic career. They were helpful and understanding as I grew my training practice, completed a PhD, and then began to travel the world teaching Python. When it comes to this book, they were actually patient twice: first when I self-published it on my website, and then again when it was upgraded, expanded, and improved (rather dramatically) to become what you're now reading. Thanks to my wife, Shira, and to my children, Atara, Shikma, and Amotz, for their understanding and appreciation.

about this book

Python Workout isn't designed to teach you Python, although I hope and expect that you'll learn quite a bit along the way. It is meant to help you improve your understanding of Python and how to use it to solve problems. You can think of it as a workbook, one whose power and learning potential depends on you. The more effort you put into this book, the more you'll get out of it.

In other words, this is a book that you should not just read or page through. For the learning to happen, you'll have to spend time answering the questions and making inevitable mistakes. There's a world of difference between reading a solution and writing the solution yourself. I hope that you'll invest time in answering the problems; I promise that it's an investment that'll repay you handily in the future.

By the time you finish *Python Workout,* you will have solved many problems having to do with core data structures, functions, comprehensions, modules, objects, and iterators. You will understand how to use them effectively and will know how to use them in various idiomatic ways. Once you've finished with these exercises, you'll find it easier to design and write Python programs for work and pleasure.

Note that it's not cheating to look for help in the Python documentation, or even on such sites as Stack Overflow (https://StackOverflow.com/). No developer can possibly remember everything that they need in their day-to-day work. I do hope that as you progress through the book, and then use Python in your career, you'll find yourself consulting such documentation less, or only for more advanced topics.

Who should read this book

This book is aimed at developers who have taken a Python course, or perhaps read an introductory book on the language. Indeed, the bulk of these exercises are aimed at people who are in my intro Python course, or who have recently finished taking it. You should already have an understanding of basic constructs, such as `if` and `for`, as well as the core data structures, such as strings, lists, tuples, and dictionaries.

But there's a difference between having a passing familiarity with these topics and knowing how to apply them to actual problems. If you can get by with Python but find yourself going to Stack Overflow many times each day, then this book will help you to become more confident and independent as you write Python code. I'd argue that if you have been using Python regularly for less than six months, then you'll gain from this book.

How this book is organized: a roadmap

This book has ten chapters, each focusing on a different aspect of Python. However, the exercises in each chapter will use techniques from other chapters. For example, nearly every exercise asks you to write a function or a class, even though functions are introduced in chapter 6 and classes are introduced in chapter 9. Think of the names as general guidelines, rather than strict rules, for what you'll be practicing and learning in each chapter.

The chapters are

1 **Numeric types**: Integers and floats—and converting between numbers and strings.
2 **Strings**: Working with strings, and seeing them not just as text, but also as sequences over which you can iterate.
3 **Lists and tuples**: Creating, modifying (in the case of lists), and retrieving from lists and tuples.
4 **Dictionaries and sets**: Exploring the different ways you can use dicts, and some of their useful methods. Also, some uses for sets, which are related to dicts.
5 **Files**: Reading from and writing to files.
6 **Functions**: Writing functions, including nested functions. Exploring Python's scoping rules.
7 **Functional programming with comprehensions**: Solving problems with list, set, and dict comprehensions.
8 **Modules and packages**: Writing and using modules in a Python program.
9 **Objects**: Creating classes, writing methods, using attributes, and understanding inheritance.
10 **Iterators and generators**: Adding the iterator protocol to classes, writing generator functions, and writing generator comprehensions.

Exercises form the main part of each chapter. For each exercise, you'll find five components:

1. **Exercise**: A problem statement for you to tackle.
2. **Working it out**: A detailed discussion of the problem and how to solve it.
3. **Solution**: The solution code, along with a link to the code on the Python Tutor (pythontutor.com) site so you can execute it. Solution code, along with test code for each solution, is also available on GitHub at https://github.com/reuven/python-workout
4. **Screencast solution**: A short video demonstration, in which I walk you through the solution in a screencast. You can watch the video to see not just the answer, but the process I go through in trying to get to that answer. If you read this book in Manning's liveBook platform, the screencast videos appear just after each solution. In the print and ebook, you'll use a link to a navigation page (https://livebook.manning.com/video/python-workout), then select the exercise by number and name.
5. **Beyond the exercise**: Three additional, related exercises. These questions are neither answered nor discussed in the book—but the code is downloadable, along with all other solution code from the book. (See the next section for details.) And you can discuss these additional exercises—and compare solutions—with other Python Workout readers in the book's online forum in Manning's liveBook platform.

Alongside the exercises are numerous sidebars, each explaining a topic that often confuses Python developers. For example, there are sidebars on f-strings, variable scoping, and what happens when you create a new object. The book also contains numerous hints, tips, and notes—all pointers meant to help you improve your Python coding fluency and to warn you away from repeating mistakes that I have made many times over the years.

About the code

This book contains a great deal of Python code. Unlike most books, the code reflects what you are supposed to write, rather than what you're supposed to read. If experience is any guide, some readers (maybe you!) will have better, more elegant, or more correct solutions than mine. If this is the case, then don't hesitate to contact me.

Solutions to all exercises, including the "beyond the exercise" questions, are available in two places: on Python Tutor (pythontutor.com), which provides an environment for you to execute the code, or on GitHub at https://github.com/reuven/python-workout, which allows you to download the code. Not only does this repository contain all the solutions, but it also includes `pytest` tests for each of them. (Unfamiliar with `pytest`? I strongly encourage you to read about it at https://pytest.org/, and to use it to check your code.)

There are some small differences between the code in the GitHub repository and what is published in the book. In particular, the solutions in the book don't include docstrings for functions, classes, and modules; the docstrings are included in the downloadable repository.

This book contains many examples of source code both in numbered listings and in line with normal text. In both cases, source code is formatted in a `fixed-width font like this` to separate it from ordinary text. Sometimes code is also in **bold** to highlight code that has changed from previous steps in the chapter, such as when a new feature adds to an existing line of code.

In many cases, the original source code has been reformatted; we've added line breaks and reworked indentation to accommodate the available page space in the book. In rare cases, even this was not enough, and listings include line-continuation markers (➡). Additionally, comments in the source code have often been removed from the listings when the code is described in the text. Code annotations accompany many of the listings, highlighting important concepts.

As I mentioned previously, purchasing this book also gives you access to screencasts of me solving each of the exercises. I hope that the combination of the solution code (in print), explanation, Python Tutor link, downloadable code, `pytest` tests, and screencasts will help you to fully understand each solution and apply its lessons to your own code.

Software/hardware requirements

First and foremost, this book requires that you have a copy of Python installed. You can download and install it most easily from https://python.org/. I suggest installing the latest version available. There are also alternative ways to install Python, including the Windows Store or Homebrew for the Mac.

This book will work with any version of Python from 3.6 and up. In a handful of places, the text describes features that are new in Python 3.7 and 3.8, but the solutions all use techniques that work with 3.6. The programs all work across operating systems, so no matter what platform you're using, the exercises in this book will work.

You don't technically need to install an editor or IDE (integrated development environment) for Python, but it'll certainly come in handy. Two of the most popular IDEs are PyCharm (from JetBrains) and VSCode (from Microsoft). Older and/or more traditional Python developers use vim or Emacs (my personal favorite). But at the end of the day, you can and should use whichever editor works best for you. Python doesn't really care what version you're using.

liveBook discussion forum

Purchase of *Python Workout* includes free access to a private web forum run by Manning Publications where you can make comments about the book, ask technical questions, and receive help from the author and from other users. To access the forum, go to https://livebook.manning.com/#!/book/python-workout/discussion. You can also

learn more about Manning's forums and the rules of conduct at https://livebook
.manning.com/#!/discussion.

Manning's commitment to our readers is to provide a venue where a meaningful
dialogue between individual readers and between readers and the author can take
place. It is not a commitment to any specific amount of participation on the part of
the author, whose contribution to the forum remains voluntary (and unpaid). We suggest you try asking the author some challenging questions lest his interest stray! The
forum and the archives of previous discussions will be accessible from the publisher's
website as long as the book is in print.

about the author

Reuven M. Lerner is a full-time Python trainer. In a given year, he teaches courses at companies in the United States, Europe, Israel, India, and China, as well as to individuals around the world, via online courses. He blogs and tweets (@reuvenmlerner) frequently about Python and is a panelist on the Business of Freelancing podcast. Reuven lives in Modi'in, Israel with his wife and three children. You can learn more about Reuven at https://lerner.co.il/.

about the cover illustration

The figure on the cover of *Python Workout* is captioned "Homme de la Terre de Feu," or "A man from the Tierra del Fuego." The illustration is taken from a collection of dress costumes from various countries by Jacques Grasset de Saint-Sauveur (1757–1810), titled *Costumes civils actuel de tous les peoples connus*, published in France in 1784. Each illustration is finely drawn and colored by hand. The rich variety of Grasset de Saint-Sauveur's collection reminds us vividly of how culturally apart the world's towns and regions were just 200 years ago. Isolated from each other, people spoke different dialects and languages. In the streets or in the countryside, it was easy to identify where they lived and what their trade or station in life was just by their dress.

The way we dress has changed since then and the diversity by region, once so rich, has faded away. It's now hard to distinguish the inhabitants of different continents, let alone different towns, regions, or countries. Perhaps we have traded cultural diversity for a more varied personal life—certainly for a more varied and fast-paced technological life.

At a time when it is hard to tell one computer book from another, Manning celebrates the inventiveness and initiative of the computer business with book covers based on the rich diversity of regional life of two centuries ago, brought back to life by Grasset de Saint-Sauveur's pictures.

Numeric types

Whether you're calculating salaries, bank interest, or cellular frequencies, it's hard to imagine a program that doesn't use numbers in one way or another. Python has three different numeric types: `int`, `float`, and `complex`. For most of us, it's enough to know about (and work with) `int` (for whole numbers) and `float` (for numbers with a fractional component).

Numbers are not only fundamental to programming, but also give us a good introduction to how a programming language operates. Understanding how variable assignment and function arguments work with integers and floats will help you to reason about more complex types, such as strings, tuples, and dicts.

This chapter contains exercises that work with numbers, as inputs and as outputs. Although working with numbers can be fairly basic and straightforward, converting between them, and integrating them with other data types, can sometimes take time to get used to.

Useful references

Table 1.1   What you need to know

Concept	What is it?	Example	To learn more
`random`	Module for generating random numbers and selecting random elements	`number = random.randint(1, 100)`	http://mng.bz/Z2wj
Comparisons	Operators for comparing values	`x < y`	http://mng.bz/oPJj
f-strings	Strings into which expressions can be interpolated	`f'It is currently {datetime.datetime .now()}'`	http://mng.bz/1z6Z and http://mng.bz/PAm2
for loops	Iterates over the elements of an iterable	`for i in range(10): print(i*i)`	http://mng.bz/Jymp
`input`	Prompts the user to enter a string, and returns a string	`input('Enter your name: ')`	http://mng.bz/wB27
`enumerate`	Helps us to number elements of iterables	`for index, item in enumerate('abc'): print(f'{index}: {item}')`	http://mng.bz/qM1K
`reversed`	Returns an iterator with the reversed elements of an iterable	`r = reversed('abcd')`	http://mng.bz/7XYx

EXERCISE 1 ■ Number guessing game

This first exercise is designed to get your fingers warmed up for the rest of the book. It also introduces a number of topics that will repeat themselves over your Python career: loops, user input, converting types, and comparing values.

More specifically, programs all have to get input to do something interesting, and that input often comes from the user. Knowing how to ask the user for input not only is useful, but allows us to think about the type of data we're getting, how to convert it into a format we can use, and what the format would be.

As you might know, Python only provides two kinds of loops: for and while. Knowing how to write and use them will serve you well throughout your Python career. The fact that nearly every type of data knows how to work inside of a for loop makes such loops common and useful. If you're working with database records, elements in an XML file, or the results from searching for text using regular expressions, you'll be using for loops quite a bit.

For this exercise

- Write a function (guessing_game) that takes no arguments.
- When run, the function chooses a random integer between 0 and 100 (inclusive).

- Then ask the user to guess what number has been chosen.
- Each time the user enters a guess, the program indicates one of the following:
  - Too high
  - Too low
  - Just right
- If the user guesses correctly, the program exits. Otherwise, the user is asked to try again.
- The program only exits after the user guesses correctly.

We'll use the randint (http://mng.bz/mBEn) function in the random module to generate a random number. Thus, you can say

```
import random
number = random.randint(10, 30)
```

and number will contain an integer from 10 to (and including) 30. We can then do whatever we want with number—print it, store it, pass it to a function, or use it in a calculation.

We'll also be prompting the user to enter text with the input function. We'll actually be using input quite a bit in this book to ask the user to tell us something. The function takes a single string as an argument, which is displayed to the user. The function then returns the string containing whatever the user entered; for example:

```
name = input('Enter your name: ')
print(f'Hello, {name}!')
```

> **NOTE** If the user simply presses Enter when presented with the input prompt, the value returned by input is an empty string, not None. Indeed, the return value from input will always be a string, regardless of what the user entered.

> **NOTE** In Python 2, you would ask the user for input using the raw_input function. Python 2's input function was considered dangerous, since it would ask the user for input and then evaluate the resulting string using the eval function. (If you're interested, see http://mng.bz/6QGG.) In Python 3, the dangerous function has gone away, and the safe one has been renamed input.

Working it out

At its heart, this program is a simple application of the comparison operators (==, <, and >) to a number, such that a user can guess the random integer that the computer has chosen. However, several aspects of this program merit discussion.

First and foremost, we use the random module to generate a random number. After importing random, we can then invoke random.randint, which takes two parameters, returning a random integer. In general, the random module is a useful tool whenever you need to choose a random value.

Note that the maximum number in random.randint is inclusive. This is unusual in Python; most of the time, such ranges in Python are exclusive, meaning that the higher number is not included.

> **TIP** The random module doesn't just generate random numbers. It also has functions to choose one or more elements from a Python sequence.

Now that the computer has chosen a number, it's the user's turn to guess what that number is. Here, we start an infinite loop in Python, which is most easily created with while True. Of course, it's important that there be a way to break out of the loop; in this case, it will be when the user correctly guesses the value of answer. When that happens, the break command is used to exit from the innermost loop.

The input (http://mng.bz/wB27) function always returns a string. This means that if we want to guess a number, we must turn the user's input string into an integer. This is done in the same way as all conversions in Python: by using the target type as a function, passing the source value as a parameter. Thus int('5') will return the integer 5, whereas str(5) will return the string '5'. You can also create new instances of more complex types by invoking the class as a function, as in list('abc') or dict([('a', 1), ('b', 2), ('c', 3)]).

In Python 3, you can't use < and > to compare different types. If you neglect to turn the user's input into an integer, the program will exit with an error, saying that it can't compare a string (i.e., the user's input) with an integer.

> **NOTE** In Python 2, it wasn't an error to compare objects of different types. But the results you would get were a bit surprising, if you didn't know what to expect. That's because Python would first compare them by type, and then compare them within that type. In other words, all integers were smaller than all lists, and all lists were smaller than all strings. Why would you ever want to use < and > on objects of different types? You probably wouldn't, and I found that this functionality confused people more than it helped them. In Python 3, you can't make such a comparison; trying to check with 1 < [10, 20, 30] will result in a TypeError exception.

In this exercise, and the rest of this book, I use *f-strings* to insert values from variables into our strings. I'm a big fan of f-strings and encourage you to try them as well. (See the sidebar discussing f-strings later in this chapter.)

Saved by the walrus

People coming to Python from other languages are often surprised to find while True loops, in which we then trap user input and break. Isn't there a better way? Some suggest using the following code:

```
while s = input('Enter thoughts:'):
    print(f'Your thoughts are: {s}')
```

This makes a lot of sense—we'll ask the user for their input and assign that to s. However, the value assigned to s will then be passed to `while`, which will evaluate it as a Boolean. If we get an empty string, then the Boolean value is `False`, and we exit from the loop.

There's just one problem with this code: it won't work. That's because assignment in Python is not an expression—that is, it doesn't return a value. If it doesn't return a value, then it can't be used in a `while` loop.

As of Python 3.8, that has changed somewhat. This version introduced the "assignment expression" operator, which looks like `:=` (a colon followed by an equal sign). But no one really calls it the "assignment expression operator"; from early on, it's been called the "walrus operator." Also from early on, this operator has been highly controversial. Some people have said that it introduced unnecessary complexity and potential bugs into the language.

Here's how the previous loop would look in Python 3.8:

```
while s := input('Enter thoughts:'):
    print(f'Your thoughts are: {s}')
```

With the walrus operator in the language, we can finally be rid of `while True` loops and their potential for havoc! But wait—don't we need to worry about the weird effects of assignment in a `while` loop's condition? Maybe, and that's part of the controversy. But I was convinced, in no small part, by the fact that regular assignment and the assignment operator are not interchangeable; where one can be used, the other cannot. I think that reduces the potential for abuse.

If you want to learn more about the walrus operator, its controversy, and why it's actually quite useful, I suggest that you watch the following talk from PyCon 2019, in which Dustin Ingram makes an effective case for it: http://mng.bz/nPxv.

You can also read more about this operator in PEP 572, where it was introduced and defined: http://mng.bz/vxOx.

Solution

```python
import random


def guessing_game():
    answer = random.randint(0, 100)

    while True:
        user_guess = int(input('What is your guess? '))

        if user_guess == answer:
            print(f'Right!  The answer is {user_guess}')
            break

        if user_guess < answer:
            print(f'Your guess of {user_guess} is too low!')
```

```
        else:
            print(f'Your guess of {user_guess} is too high!')

guessing_game()
```

You can work through a version of this code in the Python Tutor at http://mng.bz/vx1q.

> **NOTE** We're going to assume, for the purposes of this exercise, that our user will only enter valid data, namely integers. Remember that the int function normally assumes that we're giving it a decimal number, which means that its argument may contain only digits. If you really want to be pedantic, you can use the str.isdigit method (http://mng.bz/oPVN) to check that a string contains only digits. Or you can trap the ValueError exception you'll get if you run int on something that can't be turned into an integer.

Walk through your code using Python Tutor

In this book, I use many diagrams from the Python Tutor (http://mng.bz/2XJX), an amazing online resource for teaching and learning Python. (I often use it in my in-person classes.) You can enter nearly any Python code into the site and then walk through its execution, piece by piece. Most of the solutions in this book have a link pointing to the code in the Python Tutor so that you can run it without typing it into the site.

In the Python Tutor, global variables (including functions and classes) are shown in the *global frame*. Remember that if you define a variable outside a function, you've created a global variable. Any variables you create inside a function are local variables—and are shown, in the Python Tutor, inside their own shaded boxes. Simple data structures, such as integers and strings, are shown alongside the variables pointing to them, whereas lists, tuples, and dicts are shown in graphical format.

Screencast solution

Watch this short video walkthrough of the solution: https://livebook.manning.com/video/python-workout.

Beyond the exercise

You'll often be getting input from users, and because it comes as a string, you'll often need to convert it into other types, such as (in this exercise) integers. Here are some additional ideas for ways to practice this idea:

- Modify this program, such that it gives the user only three chances to guess the correct number. If they try three times without success, the program tells them that they didn't guess in time and then exits.
- Not only should you choose a random number, but you should also choose a random number base, from 2 to 16, in which the user should submit their input. If the user inputs "10" as their guess, you'll need to interpret it in the

correct number base; "10" might mean 10 (decimal), or 2 (binary), or 16 (hexadecimal).

■ Try the same thing, but have the program choose a random word from the dictionary, and then ask the user to guess the word. (You might want to limit yourself to words containing two to five letters, to avoid making it too horribly difficult.) Instead of telling the user that they should guess a smaller or larger number, have them choose an earlier or later word in the dict.

f-strings

Many people, when doing the "number guessing game" exercise, try to print a combination of a string and a number, such as "You guessed 5." They quickly discover that Python doesn't allow you to add (using +) strings and integers. How, then, can you include both types in the same line of output?

This problem has long troubled newcomers to Python from other languages. The earliest method was to use the % operator on a string:

```
'Hello, %s' % 'world'
```

While C programmers rejoiced at having something that worked like printf, everyone else found this technique to be frustrating. Among other things, % wasn't super-intuitive for new developers, forced you to use parentheses when passing more than one argument, and didn't let you reference repeated values easily.

It was thus a vast improvement when the str.format method was introduced into Python, letting us say

```
'Hello, {0}'.format('world')
```

Whereas I loved the use of str.format, many newcomers to Python found it a bit hard to use and very long. In particular, they didn't like the idea of referencing variables on the left and giving values on the right. And the syntax inside of the curly braces was unique to Python, which was frustrating for all.

Python 3.6 introduced *f-strings*, which are similar to the sort of double-quoted strings programmers in Perl, PHP, Ruby, and Unix shells have enjoyed for decades. f-strings work basically the same way as str.format but without having to pass parameters:

```
name = 'world'
f'Hello, {name}'
```

It's actually even better than that. You can put whatever expression you want inside the curly braces, and it'll be evaluated when the string is evaluated; for example

```
name = 'world'
x = 100
y = 'abcd'
f'x * 2 = {x*2}, and y.capitalize() is {y.capitalize()}'
```

(continued)

You can also affect the formatting of each data type by putting a code after a colon (`:`) inside of the curly braces. For example, you can force the string to be aligned left or right, on a field of 10 hash marks (#), with the following:

```
name = 'world'
first = 'Reuven'
last = 'Lerner'
        f'Hello, {first:#<10} {last:#>10}'
```

> The format code **#<10** means that the string should be placed, left-aligned, in a field of 10 characters, with # placed wherever the word doesn't fill it. The format code **#>10** means the same thing, but right-aligned.

I definitely encourage you to take a look at f-strings and to use them. They're one of my favorite changes to Python from the last few years.

For more information on f-strings, check the following resources:

- A comparison of Python formatting options, including f-strings: http://mng.bz/Qygm
- A long article about f-strings and how they can be used: http://mng.bz/XPAY
- The PEP in which f-strings were introduced: http://mng.bz/1z6Z

What if you're still using Python 2 and can't use f-strings? Then you can and should still use `str.format`, a string method that works approximately the same way, but with less flexibility. Plus, you have to call the method, and reference the arguments by number or name.

EXERCISE 2 ▪ Summing numbers

One of my favorite types of exercises involves reimplementing functionality that we've seen elsewhere, either inside of Python or in Unix. That's the background for this next exercise, in which you'll reimplement the `sum` (http://mng.bz/MdW2) function that comes with Python. That function takes a sequence of numbers and returns the sum of those numbers. So if you were to invoke `sum([1,2,3])`, the result would be 6.

The challenge here is to write a `mysum` function that does the same thing as the built-in `sum` function. However, instead of taking a single sequence as a parameter, it should take a variable number of arguments. Thus, although you might invoke `sum([1,2,3])`, you'd instead invoke `mysum(1,2,3)` or `mysum(10,20,30,40,50)`.

NOTE The built-in `sum` function takes an optional second argument, which we're ignoring here.

And no, you shouldn't use the built-in `sum` function to accomplish this! (You'd be amazed just how often someone asks me this question when I'm teaching courses.)

This exercise is meant to help you think about not only numbers, but also the design of functions. And in particular, you should think about the types of parameters functions can take in Python. In many languages, you can define functions multiple times, each with a different type signature (i.e., number of parameters, and parameter types). In Python, only one function definition (i.e., the last time that the function was defined) sticks. The flexibility comes from appropriate use of the different parameter types.

TIP If you're not familiar with it, you'll probably want to look into the *splat* operator (asterisk), described in this Python tutorial: http://mng.bz/aR4J.

Working it out

The mysum function is a simple example of how we can use Python's "splat" operator (aka *) to allow a function to receive any number of arguments. Because we have prefaced the name numbers with *, we're telling Python that this parameter should receive all of the arguments, and that numbers will always be a tuple.

Even if no arguments are passed to our function, numbers will still be a tuple. It'll be an empty tuple, but a tuple nonetheless.

The splat operator is especially useful when you want to receive an unknown number of arguments. Typically, you'll expect that all of the arguments will be of the same type, although Python doesn't enforce such a rule. In my experience, you'll then take the tuple (numbers, in this case) and iterate over each element with either a for loop or a list comprehension.

NOTE If you're retrieving elements from *args with numeric indexes, then you're probably doing something wrong. Use individual, named parameters if you want to pick them off one at a time.

Because we expect all of the arguments to be numeric, we set our output local variable to 0 at the start of the function, and then we add each of the individual numbers to it in a for loop. Once we have this function, we can invoke it whenever we want, on any list, set, or tuple of numbers.

While you might not use sum (or reimplement it) very often, *args is an extremely common way for a function to accept an unknown number of arguments.

Turning iterables into arguments

What if we have a list of numbers, such as [1,2,3], and wish to use mysum with it? We can't simply invoke mysum([1,2,3]); this will result in the numbers argument being a tuple whose first and only element is the list [1,2,3], which looks like this: ([1,2,3],).

Python will iterate over our one-element tuple, trying to add 0 to [1,2,3]. This will result in a TypeError exception, with Python complaining that it can't add an integer to a list.

(continued)

The solution in such a case is to preface the argument with * when we invoke the function. If we call `mysum(*[1,2,3])`, our list becomes three separate arguments, which will then allow the function to be called in the usual way.

This is generally true when invoking functions. If you have an iterable object and want to pass its elements to a function, just preface it with * in the function call.

Solution

```
def mysum(*numbers):
    output = 0
    for number in numbers:
        output += number
    return output

print(mysum(10, 20, 30, 40))
```

You can work through this code in the Python Tutor at http://mng.bz/nPQg.

Screencast solution

Watch this short video walkthrough of the solution: https://livebook.manning.com/video/python-workout.

Beyond the exercise

It's extremely common to iterate over the elements of a list or tuple, performing an operation on each element and then (for example) summing them. Here are some examples:

- The built-in version of sum takes an optional second argument, which is used as the starting point for the summing. (That's why it takes a list of numbers as its first argument, unlike our mysum implementation.) So sum([1,2,3], 4) returns 10, because 1+2+3 is 6, which would be added to the starting value of 4. Reimplement your mysum function such that it works in this way. If a second argument is not provided, then it should default to 0. Note that while you can write a function in Python 3 that defines a parameter after *args, I'd suggest avoiding it and just taking two arguments—a list and an optional starting point.
- Write a function that takes a list of numbers. It should return the average (i.e., arithmetic mean) of those numbers.
- Write a function that takes a list of words (strings). It should return a tuple containing three integers, representing the length of the shortest word, the length of the longest word, and the average word length.
- Write a function that takes a list of Python objects. Sum the objects that either are integers or can be turned into integers, ignoring the others.

EXERCISE 3 ■ Run timing

System administrators often use Python to perform a variety of tasks, including producing reports from user inputs and files. It's not unusual to report how often a particular error message has occurred, or which IP addresses have accessed a server most recently, or which usernames are most likely to have incorrect passwords. Learning how to accumulate information over time and produce some basic reports (including average times) is thus useful and important. Moreover, knowing how to work with floating-point values, and the differences between them and integers, is important.

For this exercise, then, we'll assume that you run 10 km each day as part of your exercise regime. You want to know how long, on average, that run takes.

Write a function (run_timing) that asks how long it took for you to run 10 km. The function continues to ask how long (in minutes) it took for additional runs, until the user presses Enter. At that point, the function exits—but only after calculating and displaying the average time that the 10 km runs took.

For example, here's what the output would look like if the user entered three data points:

```
Enter 10 km run time: 15
Enter 10 km run time: 20
Enter 10 km run time: 10
Enter 10 km run time: <enter>

Average of 15.0, over 3 runs
```

Note that the numeric inputs and outputs should all be floating-point values. This exercise is meant to help you practice converting inputs into appropriate types, along with tracking information over time. You'll probably be tracking data that's more sophisticated than running times and distances, but the idea of accumulating data over time is common in programs, and it's important to see how to do this in Python.

Working it out

In the previous exercise, we saw that input is a function that returns a string, based on input from the user. In this case, however, the user might provide two types of input; they might enter a number, but they also might enter the empty string.

Because empty strings, as well as the numeric 0, are considered to be False within an if statement, it's common for Python programs to use an expression as shown in the solution:

```
if not one_run:
    break
```

It's unusual, and would be a bit weird, to say

```
if len(one_run) == 0:
    break
```

Although this works, it's not considered good Python style, according to generally accepted conventions. Following these conventions can make your code more *Pythonic*, and thus more readable by other developers. In this case, using not in front of a variable that might be empty, and thus providing us with a False value in this context, is much more common.

In a real-world Python application, if you're taking input from the user and calling float (http://mng.bz/gyYR), you should probably wrap it within try (http://mng .bz/5aYl), in case the user gives you an illegal value:

```
try:
    n = float(input('Enter a number: '))
    print(f'n = {n}')
except ValueError as e:
    print('Hey! That's not a valid number!')
```

Also remember that floating-point numbers are not completely accurate. They're good enough for measuring the time it takes to run, but they're a bad idea for any sensitive measurement, such as a scientific or financial calculation.

If you didn't know this already, then I suggest you go to your local interactive Python interpreter and ask it for the value of 0.1 + 0.2. You might be surprised by the results. (You can also go to http://mng.bz/6QGD and see how this works in other programming languages.)

One common solution for this problem is to use integers. Instead of keeping track of dollars and cents (as a float), you can just keep track of cents (as an int).

Gaining control with f-strings

If you want to print a floating-point number in Python, then you might want to use an f-string. Why? Because in this way, you can specify the number of digits that will be printed out. Here's an example:

```
>>> s = 0.1 + 0.7
>>> print(s)
0.7999999999999999
```

That's probably not what you want. However, by putting s inside of an f-string, you can limit the output:

```
>>> s = 0.1 + 0.7
>>> print(f'{s:.2f}')
0.80
```

Here, I've told the f-string that I want to take the value of s and then display it as a floating-point number (f) with a maximum of two digits after the decimal point. See the reference table (table 1.1) at the start of this chapter for the full documentation on f-strings and the formatting codes you can use for different data types.

Solution

```
def run_timing():
    """Asks the user repeatedly for numeric input. Prints the average time an
    d number of runs."""

    number_of_runs = 0
    total_time = 0

    while True:
        one_run = input('Enter 10 km run time: ')

        if not one_run:
            break

        number_of_runs += 1
        total_time += float(one_run)

    average_time = total_time / number_of_runs

    print(f'Average of {average_time}, over {number_of_runs} runs')

run_timing()
```

Look, it's an infinite loop! It might seem weird to have "while True," and it's a very bad idea to have such a loop without any "break" statement to exit when a condition is reached. But as a general way of getting an unknown number of inputs from the users, I think it's totally fine.

If one_run is an empty string, stop.

You can work through this code in the Python Tutor at http://mng.bz/4Alg.

Screencast solution

Watch this short video walkthrough of the solution: https://livebook.manning.com/video/python-workout.

Beyond the exercise

Floating-point numbers are both necessary and potentially dangerous in the programming world; necessary because many things can only be represented with fractional numbers, but potentially dangerous because they aren't exact. You should thus think about when and where you use them. Here are two exercises in which you'll want to use float:

- Write a function that takes a float and two integers (before and after). The function should return a float consisting of before digits before the decimal point and after digits after. Thus, if we call the function with 1234.5678, 2 and 3, the return value should be 34.567.
- Explore the Decimal class (http://mng.bz/oPVr), which has an alternative floating-point representation that's as accurate as any decimal number can be. Write a function that takes two strings from the user, turns them into decimal instances, and then prints the floating-point sum of the user's two inputs. In other words, make it possible for the user to enter 0.1 and 0.2, and for us to get 0.3 back.

EXERCISE 4 ▪ Hexadecimal output

Loops are everywhere in Python, and the fact that most built-in data structures are iterable makes it easy to work through them, one element at a time. However, we typically iterate over an object forward, from its first element to the last one. Moreover, Python doesn't automatically provide us with the indexes of the elements. In this exercise, you'll see how a bit of creativity, along with the built-in reversed and enumerate functions, can help you to get around these issues.

Hexadecimal numbers are fairly common in the world of computers. Actually, that's not entirely true; some programmers use them all of the time. Other programmers, typically using high-level languages and doing things such as web development, barely even remember how to use them.

Now, the fact is that I barely use hexadecimal numbers in my day-to-day work. And even if I were to need them, I could use Python's built-in hex function (http://mng .bz/nPxg) and 0x prefix. The former takes an integer and returns a hex string; the latter allows me to enter a number using hexadecimal notation, which can be more convenient. Thus, 0x50 is 80, and hex(80) will return the string 0x50.

For this exercise, you need to write a function (hex_output) that takes a hex number and returns the decimal equivalent. That is, if the user enters 50, you'll assume that it's a hex number (equal to 0x50) and will print the value 80 to the screen. And no, you shouldn't convert the number all at once using the int function, although it's permissible to use int one digit at a time.

This exercise isn't meant to test your math skills; not only can you get the hex equivalent of integers with the hex function, but most people don't even need that in their day-to-day lives. However, this does touch on the conversion (in various ways) across types that we can do in Python, thanks to the fact that sequences (e.g., strings) are iterable. Consider also the built-in functions that you can use to solve this problem even more easily than if you had to write things from scratch.

> **TIP** Python's exponentiation operator is **. So the result of 2**3 is the integer 8.

Working it out

A key aspect of Python strings is that they are sequences of characters, over which we can iterate in a for (http://mng.bz/vxOJ) loop. However, for loops in Python, unlike their C counterparts, don't give us (or even use) the characters' indexes. Rather, they iterate over the characters themselves.

If we want the numeric index of each character, we can use the built-in enumerate (http://mng.bz/qM1K) function. This function returns a two-element tuple with each iteration; using Python's multiple-assignment ("unpacking") syntax, we can capture each of these values and stick them into our power and digit variables.

Here's an example of how we can use enumerate to print the first four letters of the alphabet, along with the letters' indexes in the string:

```
for index, one_letter in enumerate('abcd'):
    print(f'{index}: {one_letter}')
```

> **NOTE** Why does Python have enumerate at all? Because in many other languages, such as C, for loops iterate over sequences of numbers, which are used to retrieve elements from a sequence. But in Python, our for loops retrieve the items directly, without needing any explicit index variable. enumerate thus produces the indexes based on the elements—precisely the opposite of how things work in other languages.

You also see the use of reversed (http://mng.bz/7XYx) here, such that we start with the final digit and work our way up to the first digit. reversed is a built-in function that returns a new string whose value is the reverse of the old one. We could get the same result using slice syntax, hexnum[::-1], but I find that many people are confused by this syntax. Also, the slice returns a new string, whereas reversed returns an iterator, which consumes less memory.

We need to convert each digit of our decimal number, which was entered as a string, into an integer. We do that with the built-in int (http://mng.bz/4Ava) function, which we can think of as creating a new instance of the int class or type. We also see that int takes two arguments. The first is mandatory and is the string we want to turn into an integer. The second is optional and contains the number base. Since we're converting from hexadecimal (i.e., base 16), we pass 16 as the second argument.

Solution

```
def hex_output():
    decnum = 0
    hexnum = input('Enter a hex number to convert: ')
    for power, digit in enumerate(reversed(hexnum)):    ◀──┐
        decnum += int(digit, 16) * (16 ** power)    ◀──┐  │
    print(decnum)                                       │  │
                                                        │  │
hex_output()
```

reversed returns a new iterable, which returns another iterable's elements in reverse order. By invoking enumerate on the output from reversed, we get each element of hexnum, one at a time, along with its index, starting with 0.

Python's ** operator is used for exponentiation.

You can work through this code in the Python Tutor at http://mng.bz/Qy8e.

Screencast solution

Watch this short video walkthrough of the solution: https://livebook.manning.com/video/python-workout.

Beyond the exercise

Every Python developer should have a good understanding of the iterator protocol, which for loops and many functions use. Combining for loops with other objects, such as enumerate and slices, can help to make your code shorter and more maintainable.

- Reimplement the solution for this exercise such that it doesn't use the int function at all, but rather uses the built-in ord and chr functions to identify the character. This implementation should be more robust, ignoring characters that aren't legal for the entered number base.
- Write a program that asks the user for their name and then produces a "name triangle": the first letter of their name, then the first two letters, then the first three, and so forth, until the entire name is written on the final line.

Summary

It's hard to imagine a Python program that doesn't use numbers. Whether as numeric indexes (into a string, list, or tuple), counting the number of times an IP address appears in a log file, or calculating interest rates on bank loans, you'll be using numbers all of the time.

Remember that Python is strongly typed, meaning that integers and strings (for example) are different types. You can turn strings into integers with int, and integers into strings with str. And you can turn either of these types into a floating-point number with float.

In this chapter, we saw a few ways we can work with numbers of different types. You're unlikely to write programs that only use numbers in this way, but feeling confident about how they work and fit into the larger Python ecosystem is important.

Strings

Strings in Python are the way we work with text. Words, sentences, paragraphs, and even entire files are read into and manipulated via strings. Because so much of our work revolves around text, it's no surprise that strings are one of the most common data types.

You should remember two important things about Python strings: (1) they're immutable, and (2) in Python 3, they contain Unicode characters, encoded in UTF-8. (See the sidebars on each of these subjects.)

There's no such thing as a "character" type in Python. We can talk about a "one-character string," but that just means a string whose length is 1.

Python's strings are interesting and useful, not only because they allow us to work with text, but also because they're a Python sequence. This means that we can iterate over them (character by character), retrieve their elements via numeric indexes, and search in them with the in operator.

This chapter includes exercises designed to help you work with strings in a variety of ways. The more familiar you are with Python's string manipulation techniques, the easier it will be to work with text.

Useful references

Table 2.1 What you need to know

Concept	What is it?	Example	To learn more
in	Operator for searching in a sequence	`'a' in 'abcd'`	http://mng.bz/yy2G
Slice	Retrieves a subset of elements from a sequence	`# returns 'bdf'` `'abcdefg'[1:7:2]`	http://mng.bz/MdW7

str.split	Breaks strings apart, returning a list	`# returns ['abc',`
		`   'def', 'ghi']`
		`'abc def ghi'.split()`
			http://mng.bz/aR4z

str.join	Combines strings to create a new one	`# returns 'abc*def*ghi'`
		`'*'.join(['abc', 'def',`
		`   'ghi'])`
			http://mng.bz/gyYl

list.append	Adds an element to a list	`mylist.append('hello')`	http://mng.bz/aR7z
sorted	Returns a sorted list, based on an input sequence	`# returns [10, 20, 30]` `sorted([10, 30, 20])`	http://mng.bz/pBEG
Iterating over files	Opens a file and iterates over its lines one at a time	`for one_line in` `   open(filename):`	http://mng.bz/OMAn

EXERCISE 5 ▪ Pig Latin

Pig Latin (http://mng.bz/YrON) is a common children's "secret" language in English-speaking countries. (It's normally secret among children who forget that their parents were once children themselves.) The rules for translating words from English into Pig Latin are quite simple:

- If the word begins with a vowel (a, e, i, o, or u), add "way" to the end of the word. So "air" becomes "airway" and "eat" becomes "eatway."
- If the word begins with any other letter, then we take the first letter, put it on the end of the word, and then add "ay." Thus, "python" becomes "ythonpay" and "computer" becomes "omputercay."

(And yes, I recognize that the rules can be made more sophisticated. Let's keep it simple for the purposes of this exercise.)

For this exercise, write a Python function (`pig_latin`) that takes a string as input, assumed to be an English word. The function should return the translation of this word into Pig Latin. You may assume that the word contains no capital letters or punctuation.

This exercise isn't meant to help you translate documents into Pig Latin for your job. (If that is your job, then I really have to question your career choices.) However, it demonstrates some of the powerful techniques that you should know when working with sequences, including searches, iteration, and slices. It's hard to imagine a Python program that doesn't include any of these techniques.

Working it out

This has long been one of my favorite exercises to give students in my introductory programming classes. It was inspired by Brian Harvey, whose excellent series *Computer Science Logo Style* (http://mng.bz/gyNl), has long been one of my favorites for beginning programmers.

The first thing to consider for this solution is how we'll check to make sure that word[0], the first letter in word, is a vowel. I've often seen people start to use a loop, as in

```
starts_with_vowel = False
for vowel in 'aeiou':
    if word[0] == vowel:
        starts_with_vowel = True
        break
```

Even if that code will work, it's already starting to look a bit clumsy and convoluted.

Another solution that I commonly see is this:

```
if (word[0] == 'a' or word[0] == 'e' or
        word[0] == 'i' or word[0] == 'o' or word[0] == 'u'):
    break
```

As I like to say to my students, "Unfortunately, this code works." Why do I dislike this code so much? Not only is it longer than necessary, but it's highly repetitive. The don't repeat yourself (DRY) rule should always be at the back of your mind when writing code.

Moreover, Python programs tend to be short. If you find yourself repeating yourself and writing an unusually long expression or condition, you've likely missed a more Pythonic way of doing things.

We can take advantage of the fact that Python sees a string as a sequence, and use the built-in in operator to search for word[0] in a string containing the vowels:

```
if word[0] in 'aeiou':
```

That single line has the combined advantage of being readable, short, accurate, and fairly efficient. True, the time needed to search through a string—or any other Python sequence—rises along with the length of the sequence. But such linear time, sometimes expressed as O(n), is often good enough, especially when the strings through which we'll be searching are fairly short.

> **TIP** The in operator works on all sequences (strings, lists, and tuples) and many other Python collections. It effectively runs a for loop on the elements. Thus, using in on a dict will work but will only search through the keys, ignoring the values.

Once we've determined whether the word begins with a vowel, we can apply the appropriate Pig Latin rule.

Slices

All of Python's sequences—strings, lists, and tuples—support *slicing*. The idea is that if I say

```
s = 'abcdefgh'
print(s[2:6])        ◁— Returns "cdef"
```

I'll get all of the characters from s, starting at index 2 and until (but not including) index 6, meaning the string cdef. A slice can also indicate the step size:

```
s = 'abcdefgh'
print(s[2:6:2])      ◁— Returns "ce"
```

This code will print the string ce, since we start at index 2 (c), move forward two indexes to e, and then reach the end.

Slices are Python's way of retrieving a subset of elements from a sequence. You can even omit the starting and/or ending index to indicate that you want to start from the sequence's first element or end at its last element. For example, we can get every other character from our string with

```
s = 'abcdefgh'
print(s[::2])        ◁— Returns "aceg"
```

Solution

```
def pig_latin(word):
    if word[0] in 'aeiou':
        return f'{word}way'

    return f'{word[1:]}{word[0]}ay'


print(pig_latin('python'))
```

You can work through a version of this code in the Python Tutor at http://mng.bz/XP5M.

Screencast solution

Watch this short video walkthrough of the solution: https://livebook.manning.com/video/python-workout.

Beyond the exercise

It's hard to exaggerate just how often you'll need to work with strings in Python. Moreover, Python is often used in text analysis and manipulation. Here are some ways that you can extend the exercise to push yourself further:

- *Handle capitalized words*—If a word is capitalized (i.e., the first letter is capitalized, but the rest of the word isn't), then the Pig Latin translation should be similarly capitalized.

■ *Handle punctuation*—If a word ends with punctuation, then that punctuation should be shifted to the end of the translated word.

■ *Consider an alternative version of Pig Latin*—We don't check to see if the first letter is a vowel, but, rather, we check to see if the word contains two different vowels. If it does, we don't move the first letter to the end. Because the word "wine" contains two different vowels ("i" and "e"), we'll add "way" to the end of it, giving us "wineway." By contrast, the word "wind" contains only one vowel, so we would move the first letter to the end and add "ay," rendering it "indway." How would you check for two different vowels in the word? (Hint: sets can come in handy here.)

Immutable?

One of the most important concepts in Python is the distinction between mutable and immutable data structures. The basic idea is simple: if a data structure is immutable, then it can't be changed—ever.

For example, you might define a string and then try to change it:

```
s = 'abcd'
s[0] = '!'
```

You'll get an exception when running this code.

But this code won't work; you'll get an exception, with Python telling you that you're not allowed to modify a string.

Many data structures in Python are immutable, including such basics as integers and Boolean values. But strings are where people get tripped up most often, partly because we use strings so often, and partly because many other languages have mutable strings.

Why would Python do such a thing? There are a number of reasons, chief among which is that it makes the implementation more efficient. But it also has to do with the fact that strings are the most common type used as dict keys. If strings were mutable, they wouldn't be allowed as dict keys—or we'd have to allow for mutable keys in dicts, which would create a whole host of other issues.

Because immutable data can't be changed, we can make a number of assumptions about it. If we pass an immutable type to a function, then the function won't modify it. If we share immutable data across threads, then we don't have to worry about locking it, because it can't be changed. And if we invoke a method on an immutable type, then we get a new object back—because we can't modify immutable data.

Learning to work with immutable strings takes some time, but the trade-offs are generally worthwhile. If you find yourself needing a mutable string type, then you might want to look at StringIO (http://mng.bz/045x), which provides file-like access to a mutable, in-memory type.

Many newcomers to Python think that *immutable* is just another word for *constant*, but it isn't. Constants, which many programming languages offer, permanently connect a name with a value. In Python, there's no such thing as a constant; you can always reassign

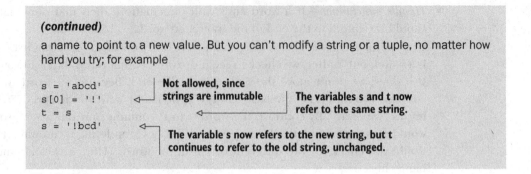

(continued)

a name to point to a new value. But you can't modify a string or a tuple, no matter how hard you try; for example

```
s = 'abcd'
s[0] = '!'        ◄─┐ Not allowed, since
                     │  strings are immutable    │ The variables s and t now
t = s           ◄────────────────────────────────┘ refer to the same string.
s = '!bcd'      ◄─┐
                  │ The variable s now refers to the new string, but t
                  │ continues to refer to the old string, unchanged.
```

EXERCISE 6 ▪ Pig Latin sentence

Now that you've successfully written a translator for a single English word, let's make things more difficult: translate a series of English words into Pig Latin. Write a function called pl_sentence that takes a string containing several words, separated by spaces. (To make things easier, we won't actually ask for a real sentence. More specifically, there will be no capital letters or punctuation.)

So, if someone were to call

```
pl_sentence('this is a test translation')
```

the output would be

```
histay isway away estay ranslationtay
```

Print the output on a single line, rather than with each word on a separate line.

This exercise might seem, at least superficially, like the previous one. But here, the emphasis is not on the Pig Latin translation. Rather, it's on the ways we typically use loops in Python, and how loops go together with breaking strings apart and putting them back together again. It's also common to want to take a sequence of strings and print them out on a single line. There are a few ways to do this, and I want you to consider the advantages and disadvantages of each one.

Working it out

The core of the solution is nearly identical to the one in the previous section, in which we translated a single word into Pig Latin. Once again, we're getting a text string as input from the user. The difference is that, in this case, rather than treating the string as a single word, we're treating it as a sentence—meaning that we need to separate it into individual words. We can do that with str.split (http://mng.bz/aR4z). str.split can take an argument, which determines which string should be used as the separator between fields.

It's often the case that you want to use any and all whitespace characters, regardless of how many there are, to split the fields. In such a case, don't pass an argument at all;

Python will then treat any number of spaces, tabs, and newlines as a single separation character. The difference can be significant:

```
s = 'abc  def  ghi'    ⌐── Two spaces separating
s.split(' ')         ◄─────── Returns ['abc', '', 'def', '', 'ghi']
s.split()          ◄──┐
                       └ Returns ['abc', 'def', 'ghi']
```

NOTE If you don't pass any arguments to `str.split`, it's effectively the same as passing `None`. You can pass any string to `str.split`, not just a single-character string. This means that if you want to split on `::`, you can do that. However, you can't split on more than one thing, saying that both `,` and `::` are field separators. To do that, you'll need to use regular expressions and the `re.split` function in the Python standard library, described here: http://mng.bz/K2RK.

Thus, we can take the user's input and break it into words—again, assuming that there are no punctuation characters—and then translate each individual word into Pig Latin. Whereas the one-word version of our program could simply print its output right away, this one needs to store the accumulated output and then print it all at once. It's certainly possible to use a string for that, and to invoke `+=` on the string with each iteration. But as a general rule, it's not a good idea to build strings in that way. Rather, you should add elements to a list using `list.append` (http://mng.bz/Mdlm) and then invoke `str.join` to turn the list's elements into a long string.

That's because strings are immutable, and `+=` on a string forces Python to create a new string. If we're adding to a string many times, then each time will trigger the creation of a new object whose contents will be larger than the previous iteration. By contrast, lists are mutable, and adding to them with `list.append` is relatively inexpensive, in both memory and computation.

Solution

```python
def pl_sentence(sentence):
    output = []
    for word in sentence.split():
        if word[0] in 'aeiou':
            output.append(f'{word}way')
        else:
            output.append(f'{word[1:]}{word[0]}ay')

    return ' '.join(output)

print(pl_sentence('this is a test'))
```

You can work through a version of this code in the Python Tutor at http://mng.bz/yydE.

Screencast solution

Watch this short video walkthrough of the solution: https://livebook.manning.com/video/python-workout.

Beyond the exercise

Splitting, joining, and manipulating strings are common actions in Python. Here are some additional activities you can try to push yourself even further:

- Take a text file, creating (and printing) a nonsensical sentence from the *n*th word on each of the first 10 lines, where *n* is the line number.
- Write a function that transposes a list of strings, in which each string contains multiple words separated by whitespace. Specifically, it should perform in such a way that if you were to pass the list ['abc def ghi', 'jkl mno pqr', 'stu vwx yz'] to the function, it would return ['abc jkl stu', 'def mno vwx', 'ghi pqr yz'].
- Read through an Apache logfile. If there is a 404 error—you can just search for ' 404 ', if you want—display the IP address, which should be the first element.

EXERCISE 7 ▪ Ubbi Dubbi

When they hear that Python's strings are immutable, many people wonder how the language can be used for text processing. After all, if you can't modify strings, then how can you do any serious work with them?

Moreover, there are times when a simple for loop, as we used with the Pig Latin examples, won't work. If we're modifying each word only once, then that's fine, but if we're potentially modifying it several times, we have to make sure that each modification won't affect future modifications.

This exercise is meant to help you practice thinking in this way. Here, you'll implement a translator from English into another secret children's language, Ubbi Dubbi (http://mng.bz/90zl). (This was popularized on the wonderful American children's program *Zoom*, which was on television when I was growing up.) The rules of Ubbi Dubbi are even simpler than those of Pig Latin, although programming a translator is more complex and requires a bit more thinking.

In Ubbi Dubbi, every vowel (a, e, i, o, or u) is prefaced with ub. Thus milk becomes mubilk (m-ub-ilk) and program becomes prubogrubam (prub-ogrub-am). In theory, you only put an ub before every vowel *sound*, rather than before each vowel. Given that this is a book about Python and not linguistics, I hope that you'll forgive this slight difference in definition.

Ubbi Dubbi is enormously fun to speak, and it's somewhat magical if and when you can begin to understand someone else speaking it. Even if you don't understand it, Ubbi Dubbi sounds extremely funny. See some YouTube videos on the subject, such as http://mng.bz/aRMY, if you need convincing.

For this exercise, you'll write a function (called ubbi_dubbi) that takes a single word (string) as an argument. It returns a string, the word's translation into Ubbi Dubbi. So if the function is called with octopus, the function will return the string uboctubopubus. And if the user passes the argument elephant, you'll output ubelubephubant.

As with the original Pig Latin translator, you can ignore capital letters, punctuation, and corner cases, such as multiple vowels combining to create a new sound. When you do have two vowels next to one another, preface each of them with ub. Thus, soap will become suboubap, despite the fact that oa combines to a single vowel sound.

Much like the "Pig Latin sentence" exercise, this brings to the forefront the various ways we often need to scan through strings for particular patterns, or translate from one Python data structure or pattern to another, and how iterations can play a central role in doing so.

Working it out

The task here is to ask the user for a word, and then to translate that word into Ubbi Dubbi. This is a slightly different task than we had with Pig Latin, because we need to operate on a letter-by-letter basis. We can't simply analyze the word and produce output based on the entire word. Moreover, we have to avoid getting ourselves into an infinite loop, in which we try to add ub before the u in ub.

The solution is to iterate over each character in word, adding it to a list, output. If the current character is a vowel, then we add ub before the letter. Otherwise, we just add the letter. At the end of the program, we join and then print the letters together. This time, we don't join the letters together with a space character (' '), but rather with an empty string (' '). This means that the resulting string will consist of the letters joined together with nothing between them—or, as we often call such collections, a *word*.

Solution

```
def ubbi_dubbi(word):
    output = []
    for letter in word:
        if letter in 'aeiou':
            output.append(f'ub{letter}')
        else:
            output.append(letter)

    return ''.join(output)

print(ubbi_dubbi('python'))
```

Why append to a list, and not to a string? To avoid allocating too much memory. For short strings, it's not a big deal. But for long loops and large strings, it's a bad idea.

You can work through this code in the Python Tutor at http://mng.bz/eQJZ.

Screencast solution

Watch this short video walkthrough of the solution: https://livebook.manning.com/video/python-workout.

Beyond the exercise

It's common to want to replace one value with another in strings. Python has a few different ways to do this. You can use str.replace (http://mng.bz/WPe0) or str.translate (http://mng.bz/8pyP), two string methods that translate strings and sets of characters, respectively. But sometimes, there's no choice but to iterate over a string, look for the pattern we want, and then append the modified version to a list that we grow over time:

- *Handle capitalized words*—If a word is capitalized (i.e., the first letter is capitalized, but the rest of the word isn't), then the Ubbi Dubbi translation should be similarly capitalized.
- *Remove author names*—In academia, it's common to remove the authors' names from a paper submitted for peer review. Given a string containing an article and a separate list of strings containing authors' names, replace all names in the article with _ characters.
- *URL-encode characters*—In URLs, we often replace special and nonprintable characters with a % followed by the character's ASCII value in hexadecimal. For example, if a URL is to include a space character (ASCII 32, aka 0x20), we replace it with %20. Given a string, URL-encode any character that isn't a letter or number. For the purposes of this exercise, we'll assume that all characters are indeed in ASCII (i.e., one byte long), and not multibyte UTF-8 characters. It might help to know about the ord (http://mng.bz/EdnJ) and hex (http://mng.bz/nPxg) functions.

EXERCISE 8 ▪ Sorting a string

If strings are immutable, then does this mean we're stuck with them forever, precisely as they are? Kind of—we can't change the strings themselves, but we can create new strings based on them, using a combination of built-in functions and string methods. Knowing how to work around strings' immutability and piece together functionality that effectively changes strings, even though they're immutable, is a useful skill to have.

In this exercise, you'll explore this idea by writing a function, strsort, that takes a single string as its input and returns a string. The returned string should contain the same characters as the input, except that its characters should be sorted in order, from the lowest Unicode value to the highest Unicode value. For example, the result of invoking strsort('cba') will be the string abc.

Working it out

The solution's implementation of strsort takes advantage of the fact that Python strings are sequences. Normally, we think of this as relevant in a for loop, in that we can iterate over the characters in a string. However, we don't need to restrict ourselves to such situations.

For example, we can use the built-in sorted (http://mng.bz/pBEG) function, which takes an iterable—which means not only a sequence, but anything over which we can iterate, such as a set of files—and returns its elements in sorted order. Invoking sorted in our string will thus do the job, in that it will sort the characters in Unicode order. However, it returns a list, rather than a string.

To turn our list into a string, we use the str.join method (http://mng.bz/gyYl). We use an empty string (' ') as the glue we'll use to join the elements, thus returning a new string whose characters are the same as the input string, but in sorted order.

Unicode

What is Unicode? The idea is a simple one, but the implementation can be extremely difficult and is confusing to many developers.

The idea behind Unicode is that we should be able to use computers to represent any character used in any language from any time. This is a very important goal, in that it means we won't have problems creating documents in which we want to show Russian, Chinese, and English on the same page. Before Unicode, mixing character sets from a number of languages was difficult or impossible.

Unicode assigns each character a unique number. But those numbers can (as you imagine) get very big. Thus, we have to take the Unicode character number (known as a *code point*) and translate it into a format that can be stored and transmitted as bytes. Python and many other languages use what's known as UTF-8, which is a *variable-length encoding*, meaning that different characters might require different numbers of bytes. Characters that exist in ASCII are encoded into UTF-8 with the same number they use in ASCII, in one byte. French, Spanish, Hebrew, Arabic, Greek, and Russian all use two bytes for their non-ASCII characters. And Chinese, as well as your childrens' emojis, are three bytes or more.

How much does this affect us? Both a lot and a little. On the one hand, it's convenient to be able to work with different languages so easily. On the other hand, it's easy to forget that there's a difference between bytes and characters, and that you sometimes (e.g., when working with files on disk) need to translate from bytes to characters, or vice versa.

For further details about characters versus strings, and the way Python stores characters in our strings, I recommend this talk by Ned Batchelder, from PyCon 2012: http://mng .bz/NKdD.

Solution

```
def strsort(a_string):
    return ''.join(sorted(a_string))

print(strsort('cbjeaf'))
```

You can work through this code in the Python Tutor at http://mng.bz/pBd0.

Screencast solution

Watch this short video walkthrough of the solution: https://livebook.manning.com/ video/python-workout.

Beyond the exercise

This exercise is designed to give you additional reminders that strings are sequences and can thus be put wherever other sequences (lists and tuples) can be used. We don't often think in terms of sorting a string, but there's no difference between running sorted on a string, a list, or a tuple. The elements (in the case of a string, the characters) are returned in sorted order.

However, sorted (http://mng.bz/pBEG) returns a list, and we wanted to get a string. We thus needed to turn the resulting list back into a string—something that str.join is designed to do. str.split (http://mng.bz/aR4z) and str.join (http://mng.bz/gyYl) are two methods with which you should become intimately familiar because they're so useful and help in so many cases.

Consider a few other variations of, and extensions to, this exercise, which also use str.split and str.join, as well as sorted:

- Given the string "Tom Dick Harry," break it into individual words, and then sort those words alphabetically. Once they're sorted, print them with commas (,) between the names.
- Which is the last word, alphabetically, in a text file?
- Which is the longest word in a text file?

Note that for the second and third challenges, you may well want to read up on the key parameter and the types of values you can pass to it. A good introduction, with examples, is here: http://mng.bz/D28E.

Summary

Python programmers are constantly dealing with text. Whether it's because we're reading from files, displaying things on the screen, or just using dicts, strings are a data type with which we're likely familiar from other languages.

At the same time, strings in Python are unusual, in that they're also sequences—and thus, thinking in Python requires that you consider their sequence-like qualities. This means searching (using in), sorting (using sorted), and using slices. It also means thinking about how you can turn strings into lists (using str.split) and turn sequences back into strings (using str.join). While these might seem like simple tasks, they crop up on a regular basis in production Python code. The fact that these data structures and methods are written in C, and have been around for many years, means they're also highly efficient—and not worth reinventing.

Lists and tuples

Consider a program that has to work with documents, keep track of users, log the IP addresses that have accessed a server, or store the names and birth dates of children in a school. In all of these cases, we're storing many pieces of information. We'll want to display, search through, extend, and modify this information.

These are such common tasks that every programming language supports *collections*, data structures designed for handling such cases. Lists and tuples are Python's built-in collections. Technically, they differ in that lists are mutable, whereas tuples are immutable. But in practice, lists are meant to be used for sequences of the same type, whereas tuples are meant for sequences of different types.

For example, a series of documents, users, or IP addresses would be best stored in a list—because we have many objects of the same type. A record containing someone's name and birth date would be best stored in a tuple, because the name and birth date are of different types. A bunch of such name-birth date tuples, however, could be stored in a list, because it would contain a sequence of tuples—and the tuples all would be of the same type.

Because they're mutable, lists support many more methods and operators. After all, there's not much you can do with a tuple other than pass it, retrieve its elements, and make some queries about its contents. Lists, by contrast, can be extended, contracted, and modified, as well as searched, sorted, and replaced. So you can't add a person's shoe size to the name-birth date tuple you've created for them. But you can add a bunch of additional name-birth date tuples to the list you've created, as well as remove elements from that list if they're no longer students in the school.

Learning to distinguish between when you would use lists versus when you would use tuples can take some time. If the distinction isn't totally clear to you just yet, it's not your fault!

Lists and tuples are both Python *sequences*, which means that we can run for loops on them, search using the in operator, and retrieve from them, both using individual indexes and with slices. The third sequence type in Python is the string, which we looked at in the previous chapter. I find it useful to think of the sequences in this way.

Table 3.1 Sequence comparison

Type	Mutable?	Contains	Syntax	Retrieval
str	No	One-element strings	s = 'abc'	s[0] # returns 'a'
list	Yes	Any Python type	mylist = [10, 20, 30, 40, 50]	mylist[2] # returns 30
tuple	No	Any Python type	t = (100, 200, 300, 400, 500)	t[3] # returns 400

In this chapter, we'll practice working with lists and tuples. We'll see how to create them, modify them (in the case of lists), and use them to keep track of our data. We'll also use *list comprehensions*, a syntax that's confusing to many but which allows us to take one Python iterable and create a new list based on it. We'll talk about comprehensions quite a bit in this chapter and the following ones; if you're not familiar or comfortable with them, look at the references provided in table 3.2.

Table 3.2 What you need to know

Concept	What is it?	Example	To learn more
list	Ordered, mutable sequence	[10, 20, 30]	http://mng.bz/NKAD
tuple	Ordered, immutable sequence	(3, 'clubs')	http://mng.bz/D2VE
List comprehensions	Returns a list based on an iterable	# returns ['10', '20', '30] [str(x) for x in [10, 20, 30]]	http://mng.bz/OMpO

range	Returns an iterable sequence of integers	# every 3rd integer, from 10 until (and not including) 50
		numbers = range(10, 50, 3)
			http://mng.bz/B2DJ

operator.itemgetter	Returns a function that operates like square brackets	# final('abcd') == 'd'
		final = operator.itemgetter(-1)
			http://mng.bz/dyPQ

Table 3.2 What you need to know *(continued)*

Concept	What is it?	Example	To learn more
collections .Counter	Subclass of dict useful for counting items in an iterable	```# roughly the same as {'a':2, 'b':2, 'c':1, 'd':1} c = collections .Counter('abcdab')```	http://mng.bz/rrBX
max	Built-in function returning the largest element of an iterable	```# returns 30 max([10, 20, 30])```	http://mng.bz/Vgq5
str.format	String method returning a new string based on a template (similar to f-strings)	```# returns 'x = 100, y = [10, 20, 30]' 'x = {0}, y = {1}' .format(100, [10, 20, 30])```	http://mng.bz/Z2eZ

EXERCISE 9 ▪ First-last

For many programmers coming from a background in Java or C#, the dynamic nature of Python is quite strange. How can a programming language fail to police which type can be assigned to which variable? Fans of dynamic languages, such as Python, respond that this allows us to write generic functions that handle many different types.

Indeed, we need to do so. In many languages, you can define a function multiple times, as long as each definition has different parameters. In Python, you can only define a function once—or, more precisely, defining a function a second time will overwrite the first definition—so we need to use other techniques to work with different types of inputs.

In Python, you can write a single function that works with many types, rather than many nearly identical functions, each for a specific type. Such functions demonstrate the elegance and power of dynamic typing.

The fact that sequences—strings, lists, and tuples—all implement many of the same APIs is not an accident. Python encourages us to write generic functions that can apply to all of them. For example, all three sequence types can be searched with in, can return individual elements with an index, and can return multiple elements with a slice.

We'll practice these ideas with this exercise. Write a function, firstlast, that takes a sequence (string, list, or tuple) and returns the first and last elements of that sequence, in a two-element sequence of the same type. So firstlast('abc') will return the string ac, while firstlast([1,2,3,4]) will return the list [1,4].

Working it out

This exercise is as tricky as it is short. However, I believe it helps to demonstrate the difference between retrieving an individual element from a sequence and a slice from that sequence. It also shows the power of a dynamic language; we don't need to define several different versions of firstlast, each handling a different type. Rather, we can define a single function that handles not only the built-in sequences, but also any new types we might define that can handle indexes and slices.

One of the first things that Python programmers learn is that they can retrieve an element from a sequence—a string, list, or tuple—using square brackets and a numeric index. So you can retrieve the first element of s with s[0] and the final element of s with s[-1].

But that's not all. You can also retrieve a *slice*, or a subset of the elements of the sequence, by using a colon inside the square brackets. The easiest and most obvious way to do this is something like s[2:5], which means that you want a string whose content is from s, starting at index 2, up to but not including index 5. (Remember that in a slice, the final number is always "up to but not including.")

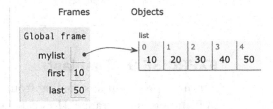

```
1  mylist = [10, 20, 30, 40, 50]
2
3  first = mylist[0]
⟹ 4  last = mylist[-1]
```

Edit this code

Figure 3.1   Individual elements (from the Python Tutor)

When you retrieve a single element from a sequence (figure 3.1), you can get any type at all. String indexes return one-character strings, but lists and tuples can contain anything. By contrast, when you use a slice, you're guaranteed to get the same type back—so a slice of a tuple is a tuple, regardless of the size of the slice or the elements it contains. And a slice of a list will return a list. In figures 3.2 and 3.3 from the Python Tutor, notice that the data structures are different, and thus the results of retrieving from each type will be different.

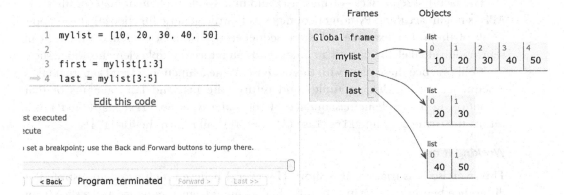

Figure 3.2   Retrieving slices from a list (from the Python Tutor)

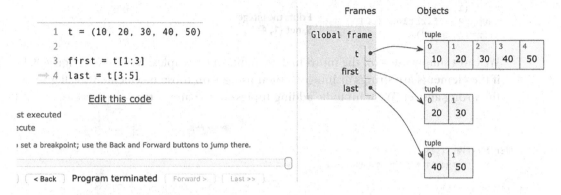

Figure 3.3   Retrieving slices from a tuple (from the Python Tutor)

Staying in bounds

When retrieving a single index, you can't go beyond the bounds:

```
s = 'abcd'
s[5]    # raises an IndexError exception
```

However, when retrieving with a slice, Python is more forgiving, ignoring any index beyond the data structure's boundaries:

```
s = 'abcd'
s[3:100]    # returns 'd'
```

In figures 3.2 and 3.3, there is no index 5. And yet, Python forgives us, showing the data all the way to the end. We just as easily could have omitted the final number.

Given that we're trying to retrieve the first and last elements of sequence and then join them together, it might seem reasonable to grab them both (via indexes) and then add them together:

```
# not a real solution!
def firstlast(sequence):
    return sequence[0] + sequence[-1]
```

But this is what really happens (figure 3.4):

```
def firstlast(sequence):          ⟵          Not a real solution!
    return sequence[0] + sequence[-1]

t1 = ('a', 'b', 'c')                        Prints the string
output1 = firstlast(t1)          ⟵          'ac', not ('a', 'c')
print(output1)
```

```
t2 = (1,2,3,4)
output2 = firstlast(t2)
print(output2)
```

**Prints the integer
5, not (1, 4)**

We can't simply use + on the individual elements of our tuples. As we see in figure 3.4, if the elements are strings or integers, then using + on those two elements will give us the wrong answer. We want to be adding tuples—or whatever type sequence is.

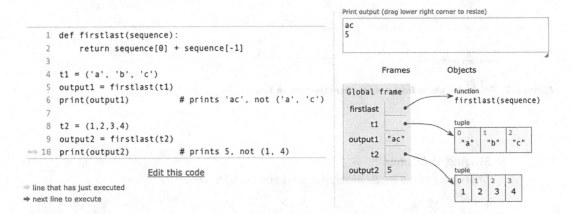

Figure 3.4   Naive, incorrect adding of slices (from the Python Tutor)

The easiest way to do that is to use a slice, using s[:1] to get the first element and s[-1:] to get the final element (figure 3.5). Notice that we have to say s[-1:] so that the sequence will start with the element at -1 and end at the end of the sequence itself.

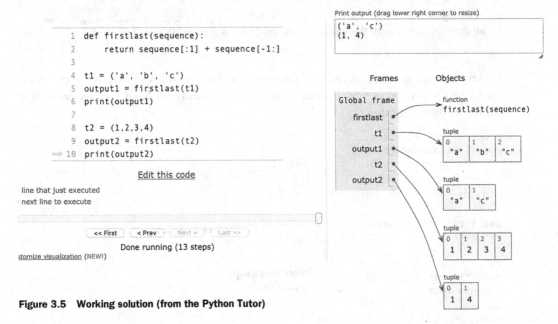

Figure 3.5   Working solution (from the Python Tutor)

The bottom line is that when you retrieve a slice from an object *x*, you get back a new object of the same type as *x*. But if you retrieve an individual element from *x*, you'll get whatever was stored in *x*—which might be the same type as *x*, but you can't be sure.

Solution

```
def firstlast(sequence):
    return sequence[:1] + sequence[-1:]      ◁──┐  In both cases, we're using
                                                 │  slices, not indexes.
print(firstlast('abcd'))
```

You can work through this code in the Python Tutor at http://mng.bz/RAPP.

Screencast solution

Watch this short video walkthrough of the solution: https://livebook.manning.com/video/python-workout.

Beyond the exercise

One of these techniques involves taking advantage of Python's dynamic typing; that is, while data is strongly typed, variables don't have any types. This means that we can write a function that expects to take any indexable type (i.e., one that can get either a single index or a slice as an argument) and then return something appropriate. This is a common technique in Python, one with which you should become familiar and comfortable; for example

- Don't write one function that squares integers, and another that squares floats. Write one function that handles all numbers.
- Don't write one function that finds the largest element of a string, another that does the same for a list, and a third that does the same for a tuple. Write just one function that works on all of them.
- Don't write one function to find the largest word in a file that works on files and another that works on the io.StringIO (http://mng.bz/PAOP) file simulator used in testing. Write one function that works on both.

Slices are a great way to get at just part of a piece of data. Whether it's a substring or part of a list, slices allow you to grab just part of any sequence. I'm often asked by students in my courses how they can iterate over just the final *n* elements of a list. When I remind them that they can do this with the slice mylist[-3:] and a for loop, they're somewhat surprised and embarrassed that they didn't think of this first; they were sure that it must be more difficult than that.

Here are some ideas for other tasks you can try, using indexes and slices:

1 Write a function that takes a list or tuple of numbers. Return a two-element list, containing (respectively) the sum of the even-indexed numbers and the sum of the odd-indexed numbers. So calling the function as even_odd_sums([10, 20, 30, 40, 50, 60]), you'll get back [90, 120].

2 Write a function that takes a list or tuple of numbers. Return the result of alternately adding and subtracting numbers from each other. So calling the function as plus_minus([10, 20, 30, 40, 50, 60]), you'll get back the result of 10+20-30+40-50+60, or 50.

3 Write a function that partly emulates the built-in zip function (http://mng.bz/ Jyzv), taking any number of iterables and returning a list of tuples. Each tuple will contain one element from each of the iterables passed to the function. Thus, if I call myzip([10, 20,30], 'abc'), the result will be [(10, 'a'), (20, 'b'), (30, 'c')]. You can return a list (not an iterator) and can assume that all of the iterables are of the same length.

Are lists arrays?

Newcomers to Python often look for the array type. But for Python developers, lists are the typical go-to data type for anyone needing an array or array-like structure.

Now, lists aren't arrays: arrays have a fixed length, as well as a type. And while you could potentially argue that Python's lists handle only one type, namely anything that inherits from the built-in object class, it's definitely not true that lists have a fixed length. Exercise 9 demonstrates that pretty clearly, but doesn't use the list.append or list.remove methods.

> **NOTE** Python does have an array type in the standard library (http://mng .bz/wBlQ), and data scientists commonly use NumPy arrays (http://mng.bz/ qMX2). For the most part, though, we don't need or use arrays in Python. They don't align with the language's dynamic nature. Instead, we normally use lists and tuples.

Behind the scenes, Python lists are implemented as arrays of pointers to Python objects. But if arrays are of fixed size, how can Python use them to implement lists? The answer is that Python allocates some extra space in its list array, such that we can add a few items to it. But at a certain point, if we add enough items to our list, these spare locations will be used up, thus forcing Python to allocate a new array and move all of the pointers to that location. This is done for us automatically and behind the scenes, but it shows that adding items to a list isn't completely free of computational overhead. You can see this in action using sys.getsizeof (http://mng.bz/7Xzy), which shows the number of bytes needed to store a list (or any other data structure):

```
>>> import sys
>>> mylist = []
>>> for i in range(25):
...     l = len(mylist)
...     s = sys.getsizeof(mylist)
...     print(f'len = {l}, size = {s}')
...     mylist.append(i)
```

Running this code gives us the following output:

```
len = 0, size = 64
len = 1, size = 96
```

```
len = 2, size = 96
len = 3, size = 96
len = 4, size = 96
len = 5, size = 128
len = 6, size = 128
len = 7, size = 128
len = 8, size = 128
len = 9, size = 192
len = 10, size = 192
len = 11, size = 192
len = 12, size = 192
len = 13, size = 192
len = 14, size = 192
len = 15, size = 192
len = 16, size = 192
len = 17, size = 264
len = 18, size = 264
len = 19, size = 264
len = 20, size = 264
len = 21, size = 264
len = 22, size = 264
len = 23, size = 264
len = 24, size = 264
```

As you can see, then, the list grows as necessary but always has some spare room, allowing it to avoid growing if you're just adding a handful of elements.

NOTE Different versions of Python, as well as different operating systems and platforms, may allocate memory differently than what I've shown here.

How much do you need to care about this in your day-to-day Python development? As with all matters of memory allocation and Python language implementation, I think of this as useful background knowledge, either for when you're in a real bind when optimizing, or just for a better sense of and appreciation for how Python does things.

But if you're worried on a regular basis about the size of your data structures, or the way Python is allocating memory behind the scenes, then I'd argue that you're probably worrying about the wrong things—or you're using the wrong language for the job at hand. Python is a fantastic language for many things, and its garbage collector works well enough most of the time. But you don't have fine-tuned control over the garbage collector, and Python largely assumes that you'll outsource control to the language.

EXERCISE 10 ▪ Summing anything

You've seen how you can write a function that takes a number of different types. You've also seen how you can write a function that returns different types, using the argument that the function received.

In this exercise, you'll see how you can have even more flexibility experimenting with types. What happens if you're running methods not on the argument itself, but on elements within the argument? For example, what if you want to sum the elements of a list—regardless of whether those elements are integers, floats, strings, or even lists?

This challenge asks you to redefine the mysum function we defined in chapter 1, such that it can take any number of arguments. The arguments must all be of the same type and know how to respond to the + operator. (Thus, the function should work with numbers, strings, lists, and tuples, but not with sets and dicts.)

> **NOTE** Python 3.9, which is scheduled for release in the autumn of 2020, will apparently include support for | on dicts. See PEP 584 (http://mng.bz/mB42) for more details.

The result should be a new, longer sequence of the type provided by the parameters. Thus, the result of mysum('abc', 'def') will be the string abcdef, and the result of mysum([1,2,3], [4,5,6]) will be the six-element list [1,2,3,4,5,6]. Of course, it should also still return the integer 6 if we invoke mysum(1,2,3).

Working through this exercise will give you a chance to think about sequences, types, and how we can most easily create return values of different types from the same function.

Working it out

This new version of mysum is more complex than the one we saw previously. It still accepts any number of arguments, which are put into the items tuple thanks to the "splat" (*) operator.

> **TIP** While we traditionally call the "takes any number of arguments" parameter *args, you can use any name you want. The important part is the *, not the name of the parameter; it still works the same way and is always a tuple.

The first thing we do is check to see if we received any arguments. If not, we return items, an empty tuple. This is necessary because the rest of the function requires that we know the type of the passed arguments, and that we have an element at index 0. Without any arguments, neither will work.

Notice that we don't check for an empty tuple by comparing it with () or checking that its length is 0. Rather, we can say if not items, which asks for the Boolean value of our tuple. Because an empty Python sequence is False in a Boolean context, we get False if args is empty and True otherwise.

In the next line, we grab the first element of items and assign it to output (figure 3.6). If it's a number, output will be a number; if it's a string, output will be a string; and so on. This gives us the base value to which we'll add (using +) each of the subsequent values in items.

Once that's in place, we do what the original version of mysum did—but instead of iterating over all of items, we can now iterate over items[1:] (figure 3.7), meaning all of the elements except for the first one. Here, we again see the value of Python's slices and how we can use them to solve problems.

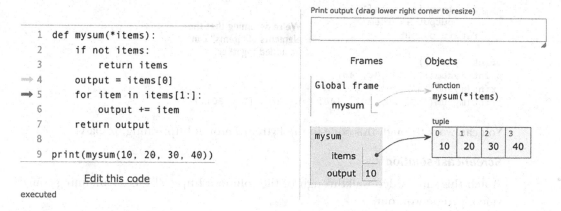

Figure 3.6   After assigning the first element to output (from the Python Tutor)

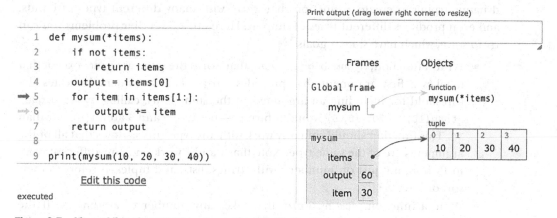

Figure 3.7   After adding elements to output (from the Python Tutor)

You can think of this implementation of mysum as the same as our original version, except that instead of adding each element to 0, we're adding each one to items[0].

But wait, what if the person passed us only a single argument, and thus args doesn't contain anything at index 1? Fortunately, slices are forgiving and allow us to specify indexes beyond the sequence's boundaries. In such a case, we'll just get an empty sequence, over which the for loop will run zero times. This means we'll just get the value of items[0] returned to us as output.

Solution

```
def mysum(*items):
    if not items:
        return items
    output = items[0]
```

In Python, everything is considered "True" in an "if," except for "None," "False," 0, and empty collections. So if the tuple "items" is empty, we'll just return an empty tuple.

```
    for item in items[1:]:
        output += item                We're assuming that the
    return output                     elements of "items" can
                                      be added together.
print(mysum())
print(mysum(10, 20, 30, 40))
print(mysum('a', 'b', 'c', 'd'))
print(mysum([10, 20, 30], [40, 50, 60], [70, 80]))
```

You can work through this code in the Python Tutor at http://mng.bz/5aA1.

Screencast solution

Watch this short video walkthrough of the solution: https://livebook.manning.com/video/python-workout.

Beyond the exercise

This exercise demonstrates some of the ways we can take advantage of Python's dynamic typing to create a function that works with many different types of inputs, and even produces different types of outputs. Here are a few other problems you can try to solve, which have similar goals:

- Write a function, `mysum_bigger_than`, that works the same as `mysum`, except that it takes a first argument that precedes `*args`. That argument indicates the threshold for including an argument in the sum. Thus, calling `mysum_bigger_than(10, 5, 20, 30, 6)` would return 50—because 5 and 6 aren't greater than 10. This function should similarly work with any type and assumes that all of the arguments are of the same type. Note that > and < work on many different types in Python, not just on numbers; with strings, lists, and tuples, it refers to their sort order.

- Write a function, `sum_numeric`, that takes any number of arguments. If the argument is or can be turned into an integer, then it should be added to the total. Arguments that can't be handled as integers should be ignored. The result is the sum of the numbers. Thus, `sum_numeric(10, 20, 'a', '30', 'bcd')` would return 60. Notice that even if the string 30 is an element in the list, it's converted into an integer and added to the total.

- Write a function that takes a list of dicts and returns a single dict that combines all of the keys and values. If a key appears in more than one argument, the value should be a list containing all of the values from the arguments.

EXERCISE 11 ▪ Alphabetizing names

Let's assume you have phone book data in a list of dicts, as follows:

```
PEOPLE = [{'first':'Reuven', 'last':'Lerner',
    'email':'reuven@lerner.co.il'},
  {'first':'Donald', 'last':'Trump',
```

```
    'email':'president@whitehouse.gov'},
  {'first':'Vladimir', 'last':'Putin',
    'email':'president@kremvax.ru'}
  ]
```

First of all, if these are the only people in your phone book, then you should rethink whether Python programming is truly the best use of your time and connections. Regardless, write a function, `alphabetize_names`, that assumes the existence of a `PEOPLE` constant defined as shown in the code. The function should return the list of dicts, but sorted by last name and then by first name.

> **NOTE** Python doesn't really have constants; with the exception of some internal types and data structures, every variable, function, and attribute can always be modified. That said, variables defined outside of any function are generally referred to as "constants" and are defined in ALL CAPS.

You can solve this exercise several ways, but all will require using the `sorted` method that you saw in the last chapter, along with a function passed as an argument to its `key` parameter. You can read more about `sorted` and how to use it, including custom sorts with `key`, at http://mng.bz/D28E. One of the options for solving this exercise involves `operator.itemgetter`, about which you can read here: http://mng.bz/dyPQ.

Working it out

While Python's data structures are useful by themselves, they become even more powerful and useful when combined together. Lists of lists, lists of tuples, lists of dicts, and dicts of dicts are all quite common. Learning to work with these structures is an important part of being a fluent Python programmer. This exercise shows how you can not only store data in such structures, but also retrieve, manipulate, sort, and format it.

The solution I propose has two parts. In the first part, we sort our data according to the criteria I proposed, namely last name and then first name. The second part of the solution addresses how we'll print output to the end user.

Let's take the second problem first. We have a list of dicts. This means that when we iterate over our list, `person` is assigned a dict in each iteration. The dict has three keys: `first`, `last`, and `email`. We'll want to use each of these keys to display each phone-book entry.

We could thus say:

```
for person in people:
    print(f'{person["last"]}, {person["first"]}: {person["email"]}')
```

So far, so good. But we still haven't covered the first problem, namely sorting the list of dicts by last name and then first name. Basically, we want to tell Python's sort facility that it shouldn't compare dicts. Rather, it should compare the `last` and `first` values from within each dict.

In other words, we want

```
{'first':'Vladimir', 'last':'Putin', 'email':'president@kremvax.ru'}
```

to become

```
['Putin', 'Vladimir']
```

We can do this by taking advantage of the key parameter to sorted. The value passed to that parameter must be a function that takes a single argument. The function will be invoked once per element, and the function's return value will be used to sort the values.

Thus, we can sort elements of a list by saying

```
mylist = ['abcd', 'efg', 'hi', 'j']
mylist = sorted(mylist, key=len)
```

After executing this code, mylist will now be sorted in increasing order of length, because the built-in len function (http://mng.bz/oPmr) will be applied to each element before it's compared with others. In the case of our alphabetizing exercise, we could write a function that takes a dict and returns the sort of list that's necessary:

```
def person_dict_to_list(d):
    return [d['last'], d['first']]
```

We could then apply this function when sorting our list:

```
print(sorted(people, key=person_dict_to_list))
```

Following that, we could then iterate over the now-sorted list and display our people.

But wait a second—why should we write a special-purpose function (person_dict _to_list) that'll only be used once? Surely there must be a way to create a temporary, inline function. And indeed there is, with lambda (http://mng.bz/GVy8), which returns a new, anonymous function. With lambda, we end up with the following solution:

```
for p in sorted(people,
            key=lambda x: [x['last'], x['first']]):
    print(f'{p["last"]}, {p["first"]}: {p["email"]}')
```

Many of the Python developers I meet are less than thrilled to use lambda. It works but makes the code less readable and more confusing to many. (See the sidebar for more thoughts on lambda.)

Fortunately, the operator module has the itemgetter function. itemgetter takes any number of arguments and returns a function that applies each of those arguments in square brackets. For example, if I say

```
s = 'abcdef'
t = (10, 20, 30, 40, 50, 60)
```

```
get_2_and_4 = operator.itemgetter(2, 4)
print(get_2_and_4(s))
print(get_2_and_4(t))
```
←─┐ **Notice that itemgetter returns a function.**
←─┐ **Returns the tuple ('c', 'e')**
Returns the tuple (30, 50)

If we invoke itemgetter('last', 'first'), we'll get a function we can apply to each of our person dicts. It'll return a tuple containing the values associated with last and first.

In other words, we can just write:

```
from operator import itemgetter
for p in sorted(people,
                key=itemgetter('last', 'first')):
    print(f'{p["last"]}, {p["first"]}: {p["email"]}')
```

Solution

```
import operator

PEOPLE = [{'first': 'Reuven', 'last': 'Lerner',
           'email': 'reuven@lerner.co.il'},
          {'first': 'Donald', 'last': 'Trump',
           'email': 'president@whitehouse.gov'},
          {'first': 'Vladimir', 'last': 'Putin',
           'email': 'president@kremvax.ru'}
          ]

def alphabetize_names(list_of_dicts):
    return sorted(list_of_dicts,
        key=operator.itemgetter('last', 'first'))

print(alphabetize_names(PEOPLE))
```

←─ **The "key" parameter to "sorted" gets a function, whose result indicates how we'll sort.**

You can work through this code in the Python Tutor at http://mng.bz/Yr6Q.

Screencast solution

Watch this short video walkthrough of the solution: https://livebook.manning.com/ video/python-workout.

Beyond the exercise

Learning to sort Python data structures, and particularly combinations of Python's built-in data structures, is an important part of working with Python. It's not enough to use the built-in sorted function, although that's a good part of it; understanding how sorting works, and how you can use the key parameter, is also essential. This exercise has introduced this idea, but consider a few more sorting opportunities:

- Given a sequence of positive and negative numbers, sort them by absolute value.
- Given a list of strings, sort them according to how many vowels they contain.
- Given a list of lists, with each list containing zero or more numbers, sort by the sum of each inner list's numbers.

What is lambda?

Many Python developers ask me just what `lambda` is, what it does, and where they might want to use it.

The answer is that `lambda` returns a function object, allowing us to create an anonymous function. And we can use it wherever we might use a regular function, without having to "waste" a variable name.

Consider the following code:

```
glue = '*'
s = 'abc'
print(glue.join(s))
```

This code prints `a*b*c`, the string returned by calling `glue.join` on `s`. But why do you need to define either `glue` or `s`? Can't you just use strings without any variables? Of course you can, as you see here:

```
print('*'.join('abc'))
```

This code produces the same result as we had before. The difference is that instead of using variables, we're using literal strings. These strings are created when we need them here, and go away after our code is run. You could say that they're *anonymous strings*. Anonymous strings, also known as *string literals*, are perfectly normal and natural, and we use them all of the time.

Now consider that when we define a function using `def`, we're actually doing two things: we're both creating a function object and assigning that function object to a variable. We call that variable a function, but it's no more a function than `x` is an integer after we say that `x=5`. Assignment in Python always means that a name is referring to an object, and functions are objects just like anything else in Python.

For example, consider the following code:

```
mylist = [10, 20, 30]

def hello(name):
    return f'Hello, {name}'
```

If we execute this code in the Python tutor, we can see that we've defined two variables (figure 3.8). One (`mylist`) points to an object of type `list`. The second (`hello`) points to a function object.

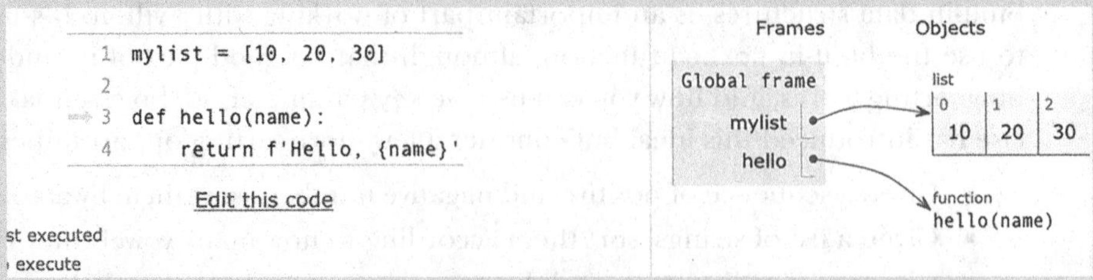

Figure 3.8 Both `mylist` and `hello` point to objects (from the Python Tutor).

Because functions are objects, they can be passed as arguments to other functions. This seems weird at first, but you quickly get used to the idea of passing around all objects, including functions.

For example, I'm going to define a function (`run_func_with_world`) that takes a function as an argument. It then invokes that function, passing it the string `world` as an argument:

```
def hello(name):
    return f'Hello, {name}'

def run_func_with_world(func):
    return func('world')

print(run_func_with_world(hello))
```

Notice that we're now passing `hello` as an argument to the function `run_func_with_world` (figure 3.9). As far as Python is concerned, this is totally reasonable and normal.

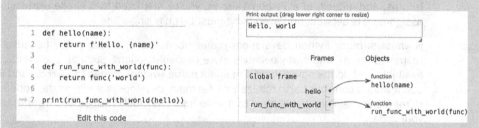

Figure 3.9   Calling `hello` from another function (from the Python Tutor)

In many instances we'll want to write a function that takes another function as an argument. One such example is `sorted`.

What does this have to do with `lambda`? Well, we can always create a function using `def`— but then we find ourselves creating a new variable. And for what? So that we can use it once? Ignoring environmental concerns, you probably don't want to buy metal forks, knives, and spoons for a casual picnic; rather, you can just buy plasticware. In the same way, if I only need a function once, then why would I define it formally and give it a name?

This is where `lambda` enters the picture; it lets us create an anonymous function, perfect for passing to other functions. It goes away, removed from memory as soon as it's no longer needed.

If we think of `def` as both (a) creating a function object and then (b) defining a variable that refers to that object, then we can think of `lambda` as doing just the first of these two tasks. That is, `lambda` creates and returns a function object. The code that I wrote in which I called `run_func_with_world` and passed it `hello` as an argument could be rewritten using `lambda` as follows:

```
def run_func_with_world(f):
    return f('world')

print(run_func_with_world(lambda name: f'Hello, {name}'))
```

(continued)

Here (figure 3.10), I've removed the definition of `hello`, but I've created an anonymous function that does the same thing, using `lambda`.

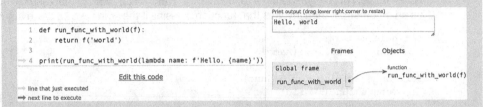

Figure 3.10   Calling an anonymous function from a function (from the Python Tutor)

To create an anonymous function with `lambda`, use the reserved world `lambda` and then list any parameters before a colon. Then write the one-line expression that the `lambda` returns. And indeed, in a Python `lambda`, you're restricted to a single expression—no assignment is allowed, and everything must be on a single line.

Nowadays, many Python developers prefer not to use `lambda`, partly because of its restricted syntax, and partly because more readable options, such as `itemgetter`, are available and do the same thing. I'm still a softie when it comes to `lambda` and like to use it when I can—but I also realize that for many developers it makes the code harder to read and maintain. You'll have to decide just how much `lambda` you want to have in your code.

EXERCISE 12 ▪ Word with most repeated letters

Write a function, `most_repeating_word`, that takes a sequence of strings as input. The function should return the string that contains the greatest number of repeated letters. In other words

- For each word, find the letter that appears the most times.
- Find the word whose most-repeated letter appears more than any other.

That is, if words is set to

```
words = ['this', 'is', 'an', 'elementary', 'test', 'example']
```

then your function should return elementary. That's because

- this has no repeating letters.
- is has no repeating letters.
- an has no repeating letters.
- elementary has one repeating letter, e, which appears three times.
- test has one repeating letter, t, which appears twice.
- example has one repeating letter, e, which appears twice.

So the most common letter in elementary appears more often than the most common letters in any of the other words. (If it's a tie, then any of the appropriate words can be returned.)

You'll probably want to use Counter, from the collections module, which is perfect for counting the number of items in a sequence. More information is here: http://mng.bz/rrBX. Pay particular attention to the most_common method (http://mng.bz/vxlJ), which will come in handy here.

Working it out

This solution combines a few of my favorite Python techniques into a short piece of code:

- Counter, a subclass of dict defined in the collections module, which makes it easy to count things
- Passing a function to the key parameter in max

For our solution to work, we'll need to find a way to determine how many times each letter appears in a word. The easiest way to do that is Counter. It's true that Counter inherits from dict and thus can do anything that a dict can do. But we normally build an instance of Counter by initializing it on a sequence; for example

```
>>> Counter('abcabcabbbc')
Counter({'a': 3, 'b': 5, 'c': 3})
```

We can thus feed Counter a word, and it'll tell us how many times each letter appears in that word. We could, of course, iterate over the resulting Counter object and grab the letter that appears the most times. But why work so hard when we can invoke Counter.most_common?

```
>>> Counter('abcabcabbbc').most_common()
[('b', 5), ('a', 3), ('c', 3)]
```
⟵ **Shows how often each item appears in the string, from most common to least common, in a list of tuples**

The result of invoking Counter.most_common is a list of tuples, with the names and values of the counter's values in descending order. So in the Counter.most_common example, we see that b appears five times in the input, a appears three times, and c also appears three times. If we were to invoke most_common with an integer argument n, we would only see the n most common items:

```
>>> Counter('abcabcabbbc').most_common(1)
[('b', 5)]
```
⟵ **Only shows the most common item, and its count**

This is perfect for our purposes. Indeed, I think it would be useful to wrap this up into a function that'll return the number of times the most frequently appearing letter is in the word:

```
def most_repeating_letter_count(word):
    return Counter(word).most_common(1)[0][1]
```

The (1) [0] [1] at the end looks a bit confusing. It means the following:

1 We only want the most commonly appearing letter, returned in a one-element list of tuples.

2 We then want the first element from that list, a tuple.

3 We then want the count for that most common element, at index 1 in the tuple.

Remember that we don't care which letter is repeated. We just care how often the most frequently repeated letter is indeed repeated. And yes, I also dislike the multiple indexes at the end of this function call, which is part of the reason I want to wrap this up into a function so that I don't have to see it as often. But we can call most_common with an argument of 1 to say that we're only interested in the highest scoring letter, then that we're interested in the first (and only) element of that list, and then that we want the second element (i.e., the count) from the tuple.

To find the word with the greatest number of matching letters, we'll want to apply most_repeating_letter_count to each element of WORDS, indicating which has the highest score. One way to do this would be to use sorted, using most_repeating _letter_count as the key function. That is, we'll sort the elements of WORDS by number of repeated letters. Because sorted returns a list sorted from lowest to highest score, the final element (i.e., at index –1) will be the most repeating word.

But we can do even better than that: The built-in max function takes a key function, just like sorted, and returns the element that received the highest score. We can thus save ourselves a bit of coding with a one-line version of most_repeating_word:

```
def most_repeating_word(words):
    return max(words,
               key=most_repeating_letter_count)
```

Solution

```
from collections import Counter
import operator

WORDS = ['this', 'is', 'an',
         'elementary', 'test', 'example']

def most_repeating_letter_count(word):
    return Counter(word).most_common(1)[0][1]

def most_repeating_word(words):
    return max(words,
               key-most_repeating_letter_count (1) {0}{1}

print(most_repeating_word(WORDS))
```

What letter appears the most times, and how many times does it appear?

Counter.most_common returns a list of two-element tuples (value and count) in descending order.

Just as you can pass key to sorted, you can also pass it to max and use a different sort method.

You can work through this code in the Python Tutor at http://mng.bz/MdjW.

Screencast solution

Watch this short video walkthrough of the solution: https://livebook.manning.com/video/python-workout.

Beyond the exercise

Sorting, manipulating complex data structures, and passing functions to other functions are all rich topics deserving of your attention and practice. Here are a few things you can do to go beyond this exercise and explore these ideas some more:

- Instead of finding the word with the greatest number of repeated letters, find the word with the greatest number of repeated vowels.
- Write a program to read /etc/passwd on a Unix computer. The first field contains the username, and the final field contains the user's *shell*, the command interpreter. Display the shells in decreasing order of popularity, such that the most popular shell is shown first, the second most popular shell second, and so forth.
- For an added challenge, after displaying each shell, also show the usernames (sorted alphabetically) who use each of those shells.

EXERCISE 13 ■ Printing tuple records

A common use for tuples is as records, similar to a struct in some other languages. And of course, displaying those records in a table is a standard thing for programs to do. In this exercise, we'll do a bit of both—reading from a list of tuples and turning them into formatted output for the user.

For example, assume we're in charge of an international summit in London. We know how many hours it'll take each of several world leaders to arrive:

```
PEOPLE = [('Donald', 'Trump', 7.85),
          ('Vladimir', 'Putin', 3.626),
          ('Jinping', 'Xi', 10.603)]
```

The planner for this summit needs to have a list of the world leaders who are coming, along with the time it'll take for them to arrive. However, this travel planner doesn't need the degree of precision that the computer has provided; it's enough for us to have two digits after the decimal point.

For this exercise, write a Python function, format_sort_records, that takes the PEOPLE list and returns a formatted string that looks like the following:

```
Trump     Donald    7.85
Putin     Vladimir  3.63
Xi        Jinping   10.60
```

Notice that the last name is printed before the first name (taking into account that Chinese names are generally shown that way), followed by a decimal-aligned indication of how long it'll take for each leader to arrive in London. Each name should be printed in a 10-character field, and the time should be printed in a 5-character field, with one space character of padding between each of the columns. Travel time should display only two digits after the decimal point, which means that even though the input for Xi Jinping's flight is 10.603 hours, the value displayed should be 10.60.

Working it out

Tuples are often used in the context of structured data and database records. In particular, you can expect to receive a tuple when you retrieve one or more records from a relational database. You'll then need to retrieve the individual fields using numeric indexes.

This exercise had several parts. First of all, we needed to sort the people in alphabetical order according to last name and first name. I used the built-in sorted function to sort the tuples, using a similar algorithm to what we used with the list of dicts in an earlier exercise. The for loop thus iterated over each element of our sorted list, getting a tuple (which it called person) in each iteration. You can often think of a dict as a list of tuples, especially when iterating over it using the items method (figure 3.11).

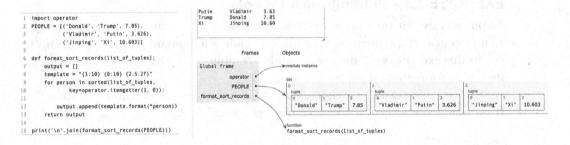

Figure 3.11 Iterating over our list of tuples (from the Python Tutor)

The contents of the tuple then needed to be printed in a strict format. While it's often nice to use f-strings, str.format (http://mng.bz/Z2eZ) can still be useful in some circumstances. Here, I take advantage of the fact that person is a tuple, and that *person, when passed to a function, becomes not a tuple, but the elements of that tuple. This means that we're passing three separate arguments to str.format, which we can access via {0}, {1}, and {2}.

In the case of the last name and first name, we wanted to use a 10-character field, padding with space characters. We can do that in str.format by adding a colon (:) character after the index we wish to display. Thus, {1:10} tells Python to display the item with index 1, inserting spaces if the data contains fewer than 10 characters. Strings are left aligned by default, such that the names will be displayed flush left within their columns.

The third column is a bit trickier, in that we wanted to display only two digits after the decimal point, a maximum of five characters, to have the travel-time decimal aligned, and (as if that weren't enough) to pad the column with space characters.

In str.format (and in f-strings), each type is treated differently. So if we simply give {2:10} as the formatting option for our floating-point numbers (i.e., person[2]), the number will be right-aligned. We can force it to be displayed as a floating-point number if we put an f at the end, as in {2:10f}, but that will just fill with zeros after the decimal point. The specifier for producing two digits after the decimal point, with a maximum of five digits total, would be {5.2f}, which produces the output we wanted.

Solution

```
import operator
PEOPLE = [('Donald', 'Trump', 7.85),
          ('Vladimir', 'Putin', 3.626),
          ('Jinping', 'Xi', 10.603)]

def format_sort_records(list_of_tuples):
    output = []
    template = '{1:10} {0:10} {2:5.2f}'
    for person in sorted(list_of_tuples,
            key=operator.itemgetter(1, 0)):

        output.append(template.format(*person))
    return output

print('\n'.join(format_sort_records(PEOPLE)))
```

> You can use operator.itemgetter with any data structure that takes square brackets. You can also pass it more than one argument, as seen here.

You can work through this code in the Python Tutor at http://mng.bz/04KW.

Screencast solution

Watch this short video walkthrough of the solution: https://livebook.manning.com/video/python-workout.

Beyond the exercise

Here are some ideas you can use to extend this exercise and learn more about similar data structures:

- If you find tuples annoying because they use numeric indexes, you're not alone! Reimplement this exercise using namedtuple objects (http://mng.bz/gyWl), defined in the collections module. Many people like to use named tuples because they give the right balance between readability and efficiency.
- Define a list of tuples, in which each tuple contains the name, length (in minutes), and director of the movies nominated for best picture Oscar awards last year. Ask the user whether they want to sort the list by title, length, or director's name, and then present the list sorted by the user's choice of axis.

- Extend this exercise by allowing the user to sort by two or three of these fields, not just one of them. The user can specify the fields by entering them separated by commas; you can use `str.split` to turn them into a list.

Summary

In this chapter, we explored a number of ways we can use lists and tuples and manipulate them within our Python programs. It's hard to exaggerate just how common lists and tuples are, and how familiar you should be with them. To summarize, here are some of the most important points to remember about them:

- Lists are mutable and tuples are immutable, but the real difference between them is how they're used: lists are for sequences of the same type, and tuples are for records that contain different types.
- You can use the built-in `sorted` function to sort either lists or tuples. You'll get a list back from your call to `sorted`.
- You can modify the sort order by passing a function to the `key` parameter. This function will be invoked once for each element in the sequence, and the output from the function will be used in ordering the elements.
- If you want to count the number of items contained in a sequence, try using the `Counter` class from the `collections` module. It not only lets us count things quickly and easily, and provides us with a `most_common` method, but also inherits from `dict`, giving us all of the dict functionality we know and love.

Dictionaries and sets

Dictionaries (http://mng.bz/5aAz), or *dicts*, are one of Python's most powerful and important data structures. You may recognize them from other programming languages, in which they can be known as "hashes," "associative arrays," "hash maps," or "hash tables."

In a dict, we don't enter individual elements, as in a list or tuple. Rather, we enter pairs of data, with the first item known as the *key* and the second item known as the *value*. Whereas the index in a string, list, or tuple is always an integer, and always starts with 0, dict keys can come from a wide variety of Python types—typically integers or strings.

This seemingly small difference, that we can use arbitrary keys to locate our values, rather than using integer indexes, is actually crucial. Many programming tasks involve name-value pairs—such as usernames/user IDs, IP addresses/hostnames, and email addresses/encrypted passwords. Moreover, much of the Python language itself is implemented using dicts. So knowing how dicts work, and how to better use them, will give you insights into the actual implementation of Python.

I use dicts in three main ways:

- *As small databases, or records*—It's often convenient to use dicts for storing name-value pairs. We can load a configuration file into Python as a dict, retrieving the values associated with the configuration options. We can store information about a file, or a user's preference, or a variety of other things with standard names and unknown values. When used this way, you define a dict once, often at the top of a program, and it doesn't change.
- *For storing closely related names and values*—Rather than creating a number of separate variables, you can create a dict with several key-value pairs. I do this

when I want to store (for example) several pieces of information about a website, such as its URL, my username, and the last date I visited. Sure, you could use several variables to keep track of this information, but a dict lets you manage it more easily—as well as pass it to a function or method all at once, via a single variable.

- *For accumulating information over time*—If you're keeping track of which errors have occurred in your program, and how many times each error has happened, a dict can be a great way to do this. You can also use one of the classes that inherit from dict, such as Counter or defaultdict, both defined in the collections module (http://mng.bz/6Qwy). When used this way, a dict grows over time, adding new key-value pairs and updating the values as the program executes.

You'll undoubtedly find additional ways to use dicts in your programs, but these are the three that occur most often in my work.

Hashing and dicts

From what I've written so far, it might sound like any Python object can be used as the key or value in a dict. But that's not true. While absolutely anything can be stored in a Python value, only *hashable* types, meaning those on which we can run the hash function, can be used as keys. This same hash function ensures that a dict's keys are unique, and that searching for a key can be quite fast.

What's a hash function? Why does Python use one? And how does it affect what we do?

The basic idea is as follows. Let's assume that you have a building with 26 offices. If a visitor comes looking to meet with a Ms. Smith, how can they know where to find her? Without a receptionist or office directory, the visitor will need to go through the offices, one by one, looking for Ms. Smith's office.

This is the way that we search through a string, list, or tuple in Python. The time it takes to find a value in such a sequence is described in computer science literature as O(n). This means that as the sequence gets longer, finding what you're looking for takes proportionally more time.

Now let's reimagine our office environment. There's still no directory or receptionist, but there is a sign saying that if you're looking for an employee, then just go to the office whose number matches the first letter of their last name—using the scheme a=1, b=2, c=3, and so forth.

Since the visitor wants to find Ms. Smith, they calculate that S is the 19th letter in the English alphabet, go to room 19, and are delighted to find that she's there. If the visitor were looking for Mr. Jones, of course, they would instead go to room 10, since J is the 10th letter of the alphabet.

This sort of search, as you can see, doesn't require much time at all. Indeed, it doesn't matter whether our company has two employees or 25 employees, or even 250 employees—as the company grows, visitors can still find our employees' offices in the same amount of time. This is known in the programming world as O(1), or *constant time*, and it's pretty hard to beat.

Of course, there is a catch: what if we have two people whose last names both begin with "S"? We can solve this problem a few different ways. For example, we can use the first two letters of the last name, or have all of the people whose names begin with "S" share an office. Then we have to search through all of the people in a given office, which typically won't be too terrible.

The description I've given you here is a simplified version of a hash function. Such functions are used in a variety of places in the programming world. For example, they're especially popular for cryptography and security, because while their mapping of inputs to outputs is deterministic, it's virtually impossible to calculate without using the hash function itself. They're also central to how Python's dicts work.

A dict entry consists of a key-value pair. The key is passed to Python's hash function, which returns the location at which the key-value pair should be stored. So if you say d['a'] = 1, then Python will execute hash('a') and use the result to store the key-value pair. And when you ask for the value of d['a'], Python can invoke hash('a') and immediately check in the indicated memory slot whether the key-value pair is there. Dicts are called *mappings* in the Python world, because the hash function *maps* our key to an integer, which we can then use to store our key-value pairs.

I'm leaving out a number of details here, including the significant behind-the-scenes changes that occurred in Python 3.6. These changes guaranteed that key-value pairs will be stored (and retrieved) in chronological order and reduced memory usage by about one third. But this mental model should help to explain how dicts accomplish search times of O(1) (constant time), regardless of how many key-value pairs are added, and why they're used not only by Python developers, but by the language itself. You can learn more about this new implementation in a great talk by Raymond Hettinger at http://mng.bz/oPmM.

The hash function explains why Python's dicts

- always store key-value pairs together
- guarantee very fast lookup for keys
- ensure key uniqueness
- don't guarantee anything regarding value lookup

As for why lists and other mutable built-in types are seen as "unhashable" in Python, the reason is simple: if the key changes, the output from running hash on it will change too. That means the key-value pair might be in the dict but not be findable. To avoid such trouble, Python ensures that our keys can't change. The terms *hashable* and *immutable* aren't the same, but there's a great deal of overlap—and when you're starting off with the language, it's not worth worrying about the differences very much.

Sets

Closely related to dicts are sets (http://mng.bz/vxlM), which you can think of as dicts without values. (I often joke that this means sets are actually immoral dicts.) Sets are extremely useful when you need to look something up in a large collection, such as filenames, email addresses, or postal codes, because searching is O(1), just as in a dict. I've also increasingly found myself using sets to remove duplicate values from an input list—such as IP addresses in a log file, or the license plate numbers of vehicles that have passed through a parking garage entrance in a given day.

In this chapter, you'll use dicts and sets in a variety of ways to solve problems. It's safe to say that nearly every Python program uses dicts, or perhaps an alternative dict such as `defaultdict` from the `collections` module.

Table 4.1   What you need to know

Concept	What is it?	Example	To learn more
`input`	Prompts the user to enter a string, and returns a string.	`input('Enter your name: ')`	http://mng.bz/wB27
`dict`	Python's dict type for storing key-value pairs. `dict` can also be used to create a new dict.	`d = {'a':1, 'b':2}` or `d = dict'a', 1), ('b', 2`	http://mng.bz/5aAz
`d[k]`	Retrieves the value associated with key k in dict d.	`x = d[k]`	http://mng.bz/5aAz
`dict.get`	Just like `d[k]`, except that it returns `None` (or the second, optional argument) if k isn't in d.	`x = d.get(k)` or `x = d.get(k, 10)`	http://mng.bz/4AeV
`dict.items`	Returns an iterator that returns a key-value pair (as a tuple) with each iteration.	`for key, value in d.items():`	http://mng.bz/4AeV
`set`	Python's set type for storing unique, hashable items. `set` can also be used to create a new set.	`s = {1,2,3} # creates a 3-element set`	http://mng.bz/K2eE
`set.add`	Adds one item to a set.	`s.add(10)`	http://mng.bz/yyzq
`set.update`	Adds the elements of one or more iterables to a set.	`s.update([10, 20, 30, 40, 50])`	http://mng.bz/MdOn
`str.isdigit`	Returns `True` if all of the characters in a string are digits 0-9.	`'12345'.isdigit() # returns True`	http://mng.bz/oPVN

EXERCISE 14 ■ Restaurant

One common use for dicts is as a small database within our program. We set up the dict at the top of the program, and then reference it throughout the program.

For example, you might set up a dict of months, with the month names as keys and numbers as values. Or perhaps you'll have a dict of users, with user IDs as the keys and email addresses as the values.

In this exercise, I want you to create a new constant dict, called MENU, representing the possible items you can order at a restaurant. The keys will be strings, and the values will be prices (i.e., integers). You should then write a function, restaurant, that asks the user to enter an order:

- If the user enters the name of a dish on the menu, the program prints the price and the running total. It then asks the user again for their order.
- If the user enters the name of a dish not on the menu, the program scolds the user (mildly). It then asks the user again for their order.
- If the user enters an empty string, the program stops prompting and prints the total amount.

For example, a session with the user might look like this:

```
Order: sandwich
sandwich costs 10, total is 10
Order: tea
tea costs 7, total is 17
Order: elephant
Sorry, we are fresh out of elephant today.
Order: <enter>
Your total is 17
```

Note that you can always check to see if a key is in a dict with the in operator. That returns True or False.

Working it out

In this exercise, the dict is defined once and remains constant throughout the life of the program. Sure, we could have used a list of lists, or even a list of tuples, but when we have name-value pairs, it's more natural for us to stick them into a dict, then retrieve items from the dict via the keys.

So, what's happening in this program? First, we set up our dict (menu) with its keys and values. We also set up total so that we can add to it later on. We then ask the user to enter a string. We invoke strip on the user's string so that if they enter a bunch of space characters (but nothing else), we'll treat that as an empty string too.

If we get empty input from the user, we break out of the loop. As always, we check for an empty string not with an explicit if order == ' ', or even checking len(order) == 0, but rather with if not order, as per Python's conventions.

But if the user gave us a string, then we'll look for it in the dict. The in operator checks if the string exists there; if so, we can retrieve the price and add it to total.

If order isn't empty, but it's not a key in menu, we tell the user that the product isn't in stock.

On the one hand, this use of dicts isn't very advanced or difficult to understand. On the other hand, it allows us to work with our data in a fairly straightforward way, taking advantage of the fast search that dicts provide and using the associated data within our programs.

Solution

```python
MENU = {'sandwich': 10, 'tea': 7, 'salad': 9}        ◄─┐  Defines a constant dict with
                                                        item names (strings) and
def restaurant():          Keeps asking the user for    prices (integers)
    total = 0              input, until an explicit
    while True:            "break" from the loop
        order = input('Order: ').strip()        ◄──────  Gets the user's input, and uses
                                                          str.strip to remove leading and
        if not order:    ◄─┐                              trailing whitespace
            break           If "order" is an empty string,
                            break out of the loop.

        if order in MENU:        ◄─┐
            price = MENU[order]     If "order" is a defined menu item,
            total += price          then get its price and add to total.
            print(f'{order} is {price}, total is {total}')

        else:                                        ◄──  If "order" is neither
            print(f'We are fresh out of {order} today')   empty nor in the dict,
                                                          then we don't serve
    print(f'Your total is {total}')                      this item.

restaurant()
```

You can work through this code in the Python Tutor at http://mng.bz/jgPV.

Screencast solution

Watch this short video walkthrough of the solution: https://livebook.manning.com/video/python-workout.

Beyond the exercise

It might, at first, seem weird to think of a key-value store (like a dict) as a database. But it turns out that examples abound of where and how you can use such a data structure. Here are some additional practice questions you can use to improve your skills in this area:

- Create a dict in which the keys are usernames and the values are passwords, both represented as strings. Create a tiny login system, in which the user must enter a username and password. If there is a match, then indicate that the user has successfully logged in. If not, then refuse them entry. (Note: This is a nice little exercise, but please *never* store unencrypted passwords. It's a major security risk.)

- Define a dict whose keys are dates (represented by strings) from the most recent week and whose values are temperatures. Ask the user to enter a date, and display the temperature on that date, as well as the previous and subsequent dates, if available.

- Define a dict whose keys are names of people in your family, and whose values are their birth dates, as represented by Python date objects (http://mng.bz/ jggr). Ask the user to enter the name of someone in your family, and have the program calculate how many days old that person is.

EXERCISE 15 ▪ Rainfall

Another use for dicts is to accumulate data over the life of a program. In this exercise, you'll use a dict for just that.

Specifically, write a function, get_rainfall, that tracks rainfall in a number of cities. Users of your program will enter the name of a city; if the city name is blank, then the function prints a report (which I'll describe) before exiting.

If the city name isn't blank, then the program should also ask the user how much rain has fallen in that city (typically measured in millimeters). After the user enters the quantity of rain, the program again asks them for a city name, rainfall amount, and so on—until the user presses Enter instead of typing the name of a city.

When the user enters a blank city name, the program exits—but first, it reports how much total rainfall there was in each city. Thus, if I enter

```
Boston
5
New York
7
Boston
5
[Enter; blank line]
```

the program should output

```
Boston: 10
New York: 7
```

The order in which the cities appear is not important, and the cities aren't known to the program in advance.

Working it out

This program uses dicts in a classic way, as a tiny database of names and values that grows over the course of the program. In the case of this program, we use the rainfall dict to keep track of the cities and the amount of rain that has fallen there to date.

We use an infinite loop, which is most easily accomplished in Python with while True. Only when the program encounters break will it exit from the loop.

At the top of each loop, we get the name of the city for which the user is reporting rainfall. As we've already seen, Python programmers typically don't check to see if a string is empty by checking its length. Rather, they check to see if the string contains a `True` or `False` value in a Boolean context. If a string is empty, then it will be `False` in the `if` statement. Our statement `if not city_name` means, "If the `city_name` variable contains a `False` value," or, in simpler terms, "if `city_name` is empty."

Let's walk through the execution of this program with the examples provided earlier in this section and see how the program works. When the user is asked for input the first time, the user is presented with a prompt (figure 4.1). The `rainfall` dict has already been defined, and we're looking to populate it with a key-value pair.

```
 1  def get_rainfall():
 2      rainfall = {}
 3      while True:
 4          city_name = input('Enter city name: ')
 5          if not city_name:
 6              break
 7
 8          mm_rain = input('Enter mm rain: ')
 9          rainfall[city_name] = rainfall.get(city_name,
10                          0) + int(mm_rain)
11
12      for city, rain in rainfall.items():
13          print(f'{city}: {rain}')
14
15  get_rainfall()
```

```
Frames                    Objects

Global frame              function
                          get_rainfall()
get_rainfall

                          empty dict
get_rainfall

    rainfall
```

Figure 4.1   Asking the user for the first input

After entering a city name (`Boston`), we enter the amount of rain that fell (5). Because this is the first time that `Boston` has been listed as a city, we add a new key-value pair to `rainfall`. We do this by assigning the key `Boston` and the value 5 to our dict (figure 4.2).

Notice that this code uses `dict.get` with a default, to either get the current value associated with `Boston` (if there is one) or 0 (if there isn't). The first time we ask about a city, there's no key named `Boston`, and certainly no previous rainfall.

There are two parts to this exercise that often surprise or frustrate new Python programmers. The first is that `input` (http://mng.bz/wB27) returns a string. This is fine when the user enters a city but not as good when the user enters the amount of rain that fell. Storing the rainfall as a string works relatively well when a city is entered only once. However, if a city is entered more than once, the program will find itself having to add (with the + operator) two strings together. Python will happily do this, but the result will be a newly concatenated string, rather than the value of the added integers.

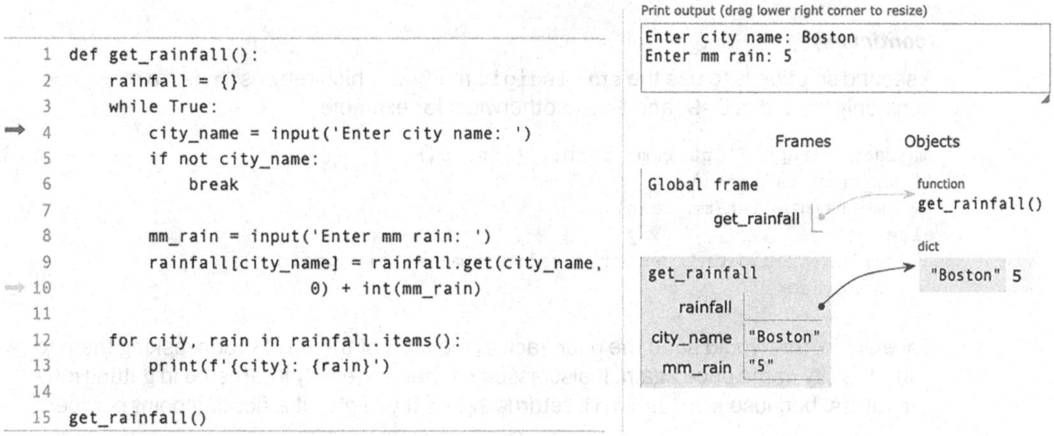

```
 1  def get_rainfall():
 2      rainfall = {}
 3      while True:
→4          city_name = input('Enter city name: ')
 5          if not city_name:
 6              break
 7
 8          mm_rain = input('Enter mm rain: ')
 9          rainfall[city_name] = rainfall.get(city_name,
→10                      0) + int(mm_rain)
 11
 12     for city, rain in rainfall.items():
 13         print(f'{city}: {rain}')
 14
 15  get_rainfall()
```

Enter city name: Boston
Enter mm rain: 5

Frames   Objects

Global frame   function
    get_rainfall   get_rainfall()

                                dict
get_rainfall

    rainfall   "Boston" 5

    city_name "Boston"

    mm_rain   "5"

Figure 4.2   After adding the key-value pair to the dict

For this reason, we invoke int on mm_rain, such that we get an integer. If you want, you could replace int with float, and thus get a floating-point value back. Regardless, it's important that if you use input to get input from the user, and if you want to use a numeric value rather than a string, you must convert it.

Trapping input errors

My solution deliberately doesn't check to see if the user's input can be turned into an integer. This means that if the user enters a string containing something other than the digits 0–9, the call to int will return an error. I didn't want to complicate the solution code too much.

If you do want to trap such errors, then you have two basic options. One is to wrap the call to int inside of a try block. If the call to int fails, you can catch the exception; for example

```
try:
    mm_rain = int(input('Enter mm rain: '))
except ValueError:
    print('You didn't enter a valid integer; try again.')
    continue

rainfall[city_name] = rainfall.get(city_name, 0) + mm_rain
```

In this code, we let the user enter whatever they want. If we encounter an error (exception) when converting, we send the user back to the start of our while loop, when we ask for the city name. A slightly more complex implementation would have the user simply reenter the value of mm_rain.

(continued)

A second solution is to use the `str.isdigit` method, which returns `True` if a string contains only the digits 0–9, and `False` otherwise; for example

```
mm_rain = input('Enter mm rain: ').strip()
if mm_rain.isdigit():
    mm_rain = int(mm_rain)
else:
    print('You didn't enter a valid number; try again.')
    continue
```

Once again, this would send the user back to the start of the `while` loop, asking them to enter the city name once again. It also assumes that we're only interested in getting integer values, because `str.isdigit` returns `False` if you give it a floating point number.

You might have noticed that Python's strings have three methods with similar names: `isdigit`, `isdecimal`, and `isnumeric`. In most cases, the three are interchangeable. However, you can learn more about how they're different at http://mng.bz/eQDv.

The second tricky part of this exercise is that you must handle the first time a city is named (i.e., before the city's name is a key in `rainfall`), as well as subsequent times.

The first time that someone enters `Boston` as a city name, we'll need to add the key-value pair for that city and its rainfall into our dict. The second time that someone enters `Boston` as a city name, we need to add the new value to the existing one.

One simple solution to this problem is to use the `dict.get` method with two arguments. With one argument, `dict.get` either returns the value associated with the named key or `None`. But with two arguments, `dict.get` returns either the value associated with the key or the second argument (figure 4.3).

```
 1  def get_rainfall():
 2      rainfall = {}
 3
 4      while True:
 5          city_name = input('Enter city name: ')
 6          if not city_name:
 7              break
 8
 9          mm_rain = input('Enter mm rain: ')
10          rainfall[city_name] = rainfall.get(city_name,
11                      0) + int(mm_rain)
12
13      for city, rain in rainfall.items():
14          print(f'{city}: {rain}')
15
16  get_rainfall()
```

Print output (drag lower right corner to resize)
```
Enter city name: Boston
Enter mm rain: 5
Enter city name: Boston
Enter mm rain: 7
```

Figure 4.3 Adding to an existing name-value pair

Thus, when we call `rainfall.get(city_name, 0)`, Python checks to see if `city_name` already exists as a key in `rainfall`. If so, then the call to `rainfall.get` will return the value associated with that key. If `city_name` is not in `rainfall`, we get 0 back.

An alternative solution would use the `defaultdict` (http://mng.bz/pBy8), a class defined in the `collections` (http://mng.bz/6Qwy) module that allows you to define a dict that works just like a regular one—until you ask it for a key that doesn't exist. In such cases, `defaultdict` invokes the function with which it was defined; for example

```
from collections import defaultdict
rainfall = defaultdict(int)          ←    defaultdict(int) means that if we say rainfall[k]
rainfall['Boston'] += 30                  and k isn't in rainfall, the int function will execute
rainfall                # defaultdict(<type 'int'>, {'Boston': 30})   without any arguments, giving us the int 0 back.

rainfall['Boston'] += 30

rainfall                # defaultdict(<type 'int'>, {'Boston': 60})
```

Solution

```
def get_rainfall():                  We don't know what cities the user
    rainfall = {}           ←        will enter, so we create an empty
                                     dict, ready to be filled.

    while True:
        city_name = input('Enter city name: ')
        if not city_name:                                 If you're from the United States,
            break                                         then you might be surprised to
                                                          hear that other countries measure
        mm_rain = input('Enter mm rain: ')     ←          rainfall in millimeters.
        rainfall[city_name] = rainfall.get(city_name,
                    0) + int(mm_rain)     ←
                                                 The first time we encounter a city,
    for city, rain in rainfall.items():          we'll add 0 to its current rainfall.
        print(f'{city}: {rain}')                 Any subsequent time, we'll add the
                                                 current rainfall to the previously
get_rainfall()                                   stored rainfall. dict.get makes this
                                                 possible.
```

You can work through this code in the Python Tutor at http://mng.bz/WPzd.

Screencast solution

Watch this short video walkthrough of the solution: https://livebook.manning.com/video/python-workout.

Beyond the exercise

It's pretty standard to use dicts to keep track of accumulated values (such as the number of times something has happened, or amounts of money) associated with arbitrary values. The keys can represent what you're tracking, and the values can track data having to do with the key. Here are some additional things you can do:

- Instead of printing just the total rainfall for each city, print the total rainfall and the average rainfall for reported days. Thus, if you were to enter 30, 20, and 40 for Boston, you would see that the total was 90 and the average was 30.
- Open a log file from a Unix/Linux system—for example, one from the Apache server. For each response code (i.e., three-digit code indicating the HTTP request's success or failure), store a list of IP addresses that generated that code.
- Read through a text file on disk. Use a dict to track how many words of each length are in the file—that is, how many three-letter words, four-letter words, five-letter words, and so on. Display your results.

EXERCISE 16 ▪ Dictdiff

Knowing how to work with dicts is crucial to your Python career. Moreover, once your learn how to use `dict.get` effectively, you'll find that your code is shorter, more elegant, and more maintainable.

Write a function, `dictdiff`, that takes two dicts as arguments. The function returns a new dict that expresses the difference between the two dicts.

If there are no differences between the dicts, `dictdiff` returns an empty dict. For each key-value pair that differs, the return value of `dictdiff` will have a key-value pair in which the value is a list containing the values from the two different dicts. If one of the dicts doesn't contain that key, it should contain `None`. The following provides some examples:

```
d1 = {'a':1, 'b':2, 'c':3}
d2 = {'a':1, 'b':2, 'c':4}
print(dictdiff(d1, d1))
print(dictdiff(d1, d2))
```
Prints "{}", because we're comparing d1 with itself

Prints "{'c': [3, 4]}", because d1 contains c:3 and d2 contains c:4

```
d3 = {'a':1, 'b':2, 'd':3}
d4 = {'a':1, 'b':2, 'c':4}
print(dictdiff(d3, d4))
```
Prints "{'c': [None, 4], 'd': [3, None]}", because d4 has c:4 and d3 has d:3

```
d5 = {'a':1, 'b':2, 'd':4}
print(dictdiff(d1, d5))
```
Prints "{'c': [3, None], 'd': [None, 4]}", because d1 has c:3 and d5 has d:4

Working it out

Let's start by thinking about the overall design of this program:

- We create an empty output dict.
- We go through each of the keys in `first` and `second`.
- For each key, we check if the key also exists in the other dict.
- If the key exists in both, then we check if the values are the same.
- If the values are the same, then we do nothing to `output`.
- If the values are different, then we add a key-value pair to `output`, with the currently examined key and a list of the values from `first` and `second`.
- If the key doesn't exist in one dict, then we use `None` as the value.

This all sounds good, but there's a problem with this approach: it means that we're going through each of the keys in first and then each of the keys in second. Given that at least some keys will hopefully overlap, this sounds like an inefficient approach. It would be better and smarter for us to collect all of the keys from first and second, put them into a set (thus ensuring that each appears only once), and then iterate over them.

It turns out that dict.keys() returns a special object of type dict_keys. But that object implements several of the same methods available on sets, including | (union) and & (intersection)! The result is a set containing the unique keys from both dicts together:

```
all_keys = first.keys() | second.keys()
```

> **NOTE** In Python 2, dict.keys and many similar methods returned lists, which support the + operator. In Python 3, almost all such methods were modified to return iterators. When the returned result is small, there's almost no difference between the implementations. But when the returned result is large, there's a big difference, and most prefer to use an iterator. Thus, the behavior in Python 3 is preferable, even if it's a bit surprising for people moving from Python 2.

Because a set is effectively a dict without values, we know for sure that by putting these lists into our all_keys set, we'll only pass through each key once. Rather than checking whether a key exists in each dict, and then retrieving its value, and then checking whether the values are the same, I used the dict.get (http://mng.bz/4AeV) method. This saves us from getting a KeyError exception. Moreover, if one of the dicts lacks the key in question, we get None back. We can use that not only to check whether the dicts are the same, but also to retrieve the values.

Now let's walk through each of the examples I gave as part of the problem description and see what happens:

```
d1 = {'a':1, 'b':2, 'c':3}
print(dictdiff(d1, d1))
```

We see this example in figure 4.4. In this figure, we see that the local variables first and second both point to the same dict, d1.

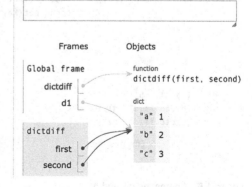

```
→  1  def dictdiff(first, second):
   2      output = {}
   3      all_keys = first.keys() | second.keys()
   4
   5      for key in all_keys:
   6          if first.get(key) != second.get(key):
   7              output[key] = [first.get(key),
   8                             second.get(key)]
   9      return output
  10
  11  d1 = {'a':1, 'b':2, 'c':3}
→ 12  print(dictdiff(d1, d1))
```

Figure 4.4 Taking the diff of d1 and itself

When we iterate over the combined set of keys (figure 4.5), we're actually iterating over the keys of d1. Because we never find any differences, the return value (output) is {}, the empty dict.

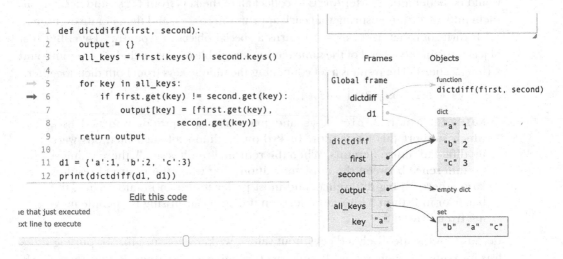

```
 1  def dictdiff(first, second):
 2      output = {}
 3      all_keys = first.keys() | second.keys()
 4
 5      for key in all_keys:
 6          if first.get(key) != second.get(key):
 7              output[key] = [first.get(key),
 8                             second.get(key)]
 9      return output
10
11  d1 = {'a':1, 'b':2, 'c':3}
12  print(dictdiff(d1, d1))
```

Edit this code

Frames   Objects

Global frame   function
    dictdiff   dictdiff(first, second)
    d1   dict
                          "a" 1
dictdiff   "b" 2
    first   "c" 3
    second
    output   empty dict
    all_keys   set
    key   "a"   "b"   "a"   "c"
```

le that just executed
xt line to execute

**Figure 4.5   Iterating over the keys of** d1

When we compare d1 and d2, we see that first and second point to two different dicts (figure 4.6). They also have the same keys, but different values for the c key. We can see in figure 4.7 how our output dict gets a new key-value pair, representing the c key's different values.

```
 1  def dictdiff(first, second):
 2      output = {}
 3      all_keys = first.keys() | second.keys()
 4
 5      for key in all_keys:
 6          if first.get(key) != second.get(key):
 7              output[key] = [first.get(key),
 8                             second.get(key)]
 9      return output
10
11
12
13  d1 = {'a':1, 'b':2, 'c':3}
14  d2 = {'a':1, 'b':2, 'c':4}
15  print(dictdiff(d1, d1))
16  print(dictdiff(d1, d2))
```

Edit this code

Frames   Objects

Global frame   function
    dictdiff   dictdiff(first, second)
    d1   dict
    d2   "a" 1
                          "b" 2
                          "c" 3

                      dict
                          "a" 1
                          "b" 2
                          "c" 4

at just executed

Figure 4.6   Comparing d1 **and** d2
```

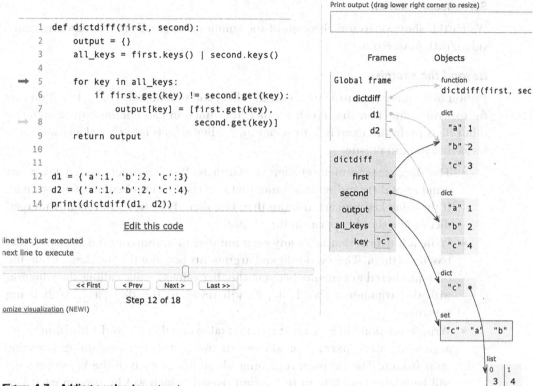

```
    1  def dictdiff(first, second):
    2      output = {}
    3      all_keys = first.keys() | second.keys()
    4
➡   5      for key in all_keys:
    6          if first.get(key) != second.get(key):
    7              output[key] = [first.get(key),
➡   8                             second.get(key)]
    9      return output
   10
   11
   12  d1 = {'a':1, 'b':2, 'c':3}
   13  d2 = {'a':1, 'b':2, 'c':4}
   14  print(dictdiff(d1, d2))
```

Edit this code

line that just executed
next line to execute

[<< First] [< Prev] [Next >] [Last >>]

Step 12 of 18

omize visualization (NEW!)

Figure 4.7 Adding a value to output

When we compare d3 and d4, we can see how things get more complex. Our output dict will now have two key-value pairs, and each value will be (as specified) a list. In this way, you can see how we build our dict from nothing to become a report describing the differences between the two arguments.

Solution

```
def dictdiff(first, second):
    output = {}
    all_keys = first.keys() | second.keys()      ◁── Gets all keys from both first
                                                      and second, without repeats
    for key in all_keys:
        if first.get(key) != second.get(key):
            output[key] = [first.get(key),        ◁── Takes advantage of the fact
                           second.get(key)]            that dict.get returns None
    return output                                      when a key doesn't exist


d1 = {'a':1, 'b':2, 'c':3}
d2 = {'a':1, 'b':2, 'd':4}
print(dictdiff(d1, d2))
```

You can work through this code in the Python Tutor at http://mng.bz/8prW.

Screencast solution

Watch this short video walkthrough of the solution: https://livebook.manning.com/video/python-workout.

Beyond the exercise

Python functions can return any object they like, and that includes dicts. It's often useful to write a function that creates a dict; the function can combine or summarize other dicts (as in this exercise), or it can turn other objects into dicts. Here are some ideas that you can pursue:

- The `dict.update` method merges two dicts. Write a function that takes any number of dicts and returns a dict that reflects the combination of all of them. If the same key appears in more than one dict, then the most recently merged dict's value should appear in the output.
- Write a function that takes any even number of arguments and returns a dict based on them. The even-indexed arguments become the dict keys, while the odd-numbered arguments become the dict values. Thus, calling the function with the arguments ('a', 1, 'b', 2) will result in the dict {'a':1, 'b':2} being returned.
- Write a function , `dict_partition`, that takes one dict (d) and a function (f) as arguments. `dict_partition` will return two dicts, each containing key-value pairs from d. The decision regarding where to put each of the key-value pairs will be made according to the output from f, which will be run on each key-value pair in d. If f returns `True`, then the key-value pair will be put in the first output dict. If f returns `False`, then the key-value pair will be put in the second output dict.

EXERCISE 17 ■ How many different numbers?

In my consulting work, I'm sometimes interested in finding error messages, IP addresses, or usernames in a log file. But if a message, address, or username appears twice, then there's no added benefit. I'd thus like to ensure that I'm looking at each value once and only once, without the possibility of repeats.

In this exercise, you can assume that your Python program contains a list of integers. We want to print the number of different integers contained within that list. Thus, consider the following:

```
numbers = [1, 2, 3, 1, 2, 3, 4, 1]
```

With the definition provided, running `len(numbers)` will return 7, because the list contains seven elements. How can we get a result of 4, reflecting the fact that the list contains four different values? Write a function, called `how_many_different_numbers`, that takes a single list of integers and returns the number of different integers it contains.

Working it out

A set, by definition, contains unique elements—just as a dict's keys are guaranteed to be unique. Thus, if you ever have a list of values from which you want to remove all of the duplicates, you can just create a set. You can create the set as in the solution code

```
unique_numbers = set(numbers)
```

or you can do so by creating an empty set, and then adding new elements to it:

```
numbers = [1, 2, 3, 1, 2, 3, 4, 1]
unique_numbers = set()
for number in numbers:
    unique_numbers.add(number)
```

This example uses set.add, which adds one new element to a set. You can add items en masse with set.update, which takes an iterable as an argument:

```
numbers = [1, 2, 3, 1, 2, 3, 4, 1]
unique_numbers = set()
unique_numbers.update(numbers)    ◁—
```
You can only use set.update with an iterable. Think of it as shorthand for running a for loop on each of the elements of numbers, invoking set.add on the current iteration's item.

Finally, you might be tempted to use the curly-brace syntax for sets:

```
numbers = [1, 2, 3, 1, 2, 3, 4, 1]
unique_numbers = {numbers}    ◁—┘  Doesn't work!
```

This code won't work, because Python thinks you want to add the list numbers to the set as a single element. And just as lists can't be dict keys, they also can't be elements in a set.

But of course, we don't want to add numbers. Rather, we want to add the elements from within numbers. Here we can use the * (splat) operator, but in a slightly different way than we've seen before:

```
numbers = [1, 2, 3, 1, 2, 3, 4, 1]
unique_numbers = {*numbers}
```

This tells Python that it should take the elements of numbers and feed them (in a sort of for loop) to the curly braces. And indeed, this works just fine.

Is it better to use set without the *, or {} with the *? That's a judgment call. I'm partial to the curly braces and *, but I also understand that * can be confusing to many people and might make your code less readable/maintainable to newcomers.

Solution

```
def how_many_different_numbers(numbers):
    unique_numbers = set(numbers)     ◁—
    return len(unique_numbers)
```
Invokes set on numbers, thus returning a set with the unique elements from numbers

```
print(how_many_different_numbers([1, 2, 3, 1,
      2, 3, 4, 1]))
```

You can work through this code in the Python Tutor at http://mng.bz/EdQD.

Screencast solution

Watch this short video walkthrough of the solution: https://livebook.manning.com/video/python-workout.

Beyond the exercise

Whenever I hear the word *unique* or *different* in a project's specification, I think of sets, because they automatically enforce uniqueness and work with a sequence of values. So if you have a sequence of usernames, dates, IP addresses, e-mail addresses, or products and want to reduce that to a sequence containing the same data, but with each item appearing only once, then sets can be extremely useful.

Here are some things you can try to work with sets even more:

- Read through a server (e.g., Apache or nginx) log file. What were the different IP addresses that tried to access your server?
- Reading from that same server log, what response codes were returned to users? The 200 code represents "OK," but there are also 403, 404, and 500 errors. (Regular expressions aren't required here but will probably help.)
- Use `os.listdir` (http://mng.bz/YreB) to get the names of files in the current directory. What file extensions (i.e., suffixes following the final . character) appear in that directory? It'll probably be helpful to use `os.path.splitext` (http://mng.bz/GV4v).

Summary

Dicts are, without a doubt, the most versatile and important data structure in the Python world. Learning to use them effectively and efficiently is a crucial part of becoming a fluent developer. In this chapter, we practiced several ways to use them, including tracking counts of elements and storing data we got from the user. We also saw that you can use `dict.get` to retrieve from a dict without having to fear that the key doesn't exist.

When working with dicts, remember

- The keys must be hashable, such as a number or string.
- The values can be anything at all, including another dict.
- The keys are unique.
- You can iterate over the keys in a `for` loop or comprehension.

5
Files

Files are an indispensable part of the world of computers, and thus of programming. We read data from files, and write to files. Even when something isn't really a file—such as a network connection—we try to use an interface similar to files because they're so familiar.

To normal, everyday users, there are different types of files—Word, Excel, Power-Point, and PDF, among others. To programmers, things are both simpler and more complicated. They're simpler in that we see files as data structures to which we can write strings, and from which we can read strings. But files are also more complicated, in that when we read the string into memory, we might need to parse it into a data structure.

Working with files is one of the easiest and most straightforward things you can do in Python. It's also one of the most common things that we need to do, since programs that don't interact with the filesystem are rather boring.

In this chapter, we'll practice working with files—reading from them, writing to them, and manipulating the data that they contain. Along the way, you'll get used to some of the paradigms that are commonly used when working with Python files, such as iterating over a file's contents and writing to files in a with block.

In some cases, we'll work with data formatted as CSV (comma-separated values) or JSON (JavaScript object notation), two common formats that modules in Python's standard library handle. If you've forgotten the basics of CSV or JSON, I have some short reminders in this chapter.

After this chapter, you'll not only be more comfortable working with files, you'll also better understand how you can translate from in-memory data structures (e.g., lists and dicts) to on-disk data formats (e.g., CSV and JSON) and back. In this way, files make it possible for you to keep data structures intact—even when the program isn't running or when the computer is shut down—or even to transfer such data structures to other computers.

Table 5.1   What you need to know

Concept	What is it?	Example	To learn more
Files	Overview of working with files in Python	`f = open('/etc/passwd')`	http://mng.bz/D22R
`with`	Puts an object in a *context manager*; in the case of a file, ensures it's flushed and closed by the end of the block	`with open ('file.text') as f:`	http://mng.bz/6QJy
Context manager	Makes your own objects work in `with` statements	`with MyObject() as m:`	http://mng.bz/B221
`set.update`	Adds elements to a set	`s.update([10, 20, 30])`	http://mng.bz/MdOn
`os.stat`	Retrieves information (size, permissions, type) about a file	`os.stat('file.txt')`	http://mng.bz/dyyo
`os.listdir`	Returns a list of files in a directory	`os.listdir('/etc/')`	http://mng.bz/YreB
`glob.glob`	Returns a list of files matching a pattern	`glob.glob('/etc/*.conf')`	http://mng.bz/044N
Dict comprehension	Creates a dict based on an iterator	`{word : len(word)` `for word in 'ab cde'.split()}`	http://mng.bz/Vggy
`str.split`	Breaks strings apart, returning a list	`# Returns ['ab', 'cd', 'ef']` `'ab cd ef'.split()`	http://mng.bz/aR4z
`hashlib`	Module with cryptographic functions	`import hashlib`	http://mng.bz/NK2x
`csv`	Module for working with CSV files	`x = csv.reader(f)`	http://mng.bz/xWWd
`json`	Module for working with JSON	`json.loads(json_string)`	http://mng.bz/AAAo

EXERCISE 18 ■ Final line

It's very common for new Python programmers to learn how they can iterate over the lines of a file, printing one line at a time. But what if I'm not interested in each line, or even in most of the lines? What if I'm only interested in a single line—the final line of the file?

Now, retrieving the final line of a file might not seem like a super useful action. But consider the Unix head and tail utilities, which show the first and last lines of a file, respectively—and which I use all the time to examine files, particularly log files and configuration files. Moreover, knowing how to read specific parts of a file, as opposed to the entire thing, is a useful and practical skill to have.

In this exercise, write a function (get_final_line) that takes a filename as an argument. The function should return that file's final line on the screen.

Working it out

The solution code uses a number of common Python idioms that I'll explain here. And along the way, you'll see how using these idioms leads not just to more readable code, but also to more efficient execution.

Depending on which arguments you use when calling it, the built-in open function can return a number of different objects, such as TextIOWrapper or BufferedReader. These objects all implement the same API for working with files and are thus described in the Python world as "file-like objects." Using such an object allows us to paper over the many different types of filesystems out there and just think in terms of "a file." Such an object also allows us to take advantage of whatever optimizations, such as buffering, the operating system might be using.

Here's how open is usually invoked:

```
f = open(filename)
```

In this case, filename is a string representing a valid file name. When we invoke open with just one argument, it should be a filename. The second, optional, argument is a string that can include multiple characters, indicating whether we want to read from, write to, or append to the file (using r, w, or a), and whether the file should be read by character (the default) or by bytes (the b option, in which case we'll use rb, wb, or ab). (See the sidebar about the b option and reading the file in byte, or binary, mode.) I could thus more fully write the previous line of code as

```
f = open(filename, 'r')
```

Because we read from files more often than we write to them, r is the default value for the second argument. It's quite usual for Python programs not to specify r if reading from a file.

As you can see here, we've put the resulting object into the variable f. And because file-like objects are all iterable, returning one line per iteration, it's typical to then say this:

```
for current_line in f:
    print(current_line)
```

But if you're just planning to iterate over f once, then why create it as a variable at all? We can avoid the variable definition and simply iterate over the file object that open returned:

```
for current_line in open(filename):
    print(current_line)
```

With each iteration over a file-like object, we get the next line from the file, up to and including the \n newline character. Thus, in this code, line is always going to be a string that always contains a single \n character at the end of it. A blank line in a file will contain just the \n newline character.

In theory, files should end with an \n, such that you'll never finish the file in the middle of a line. In practice, I've seen many files that don't end with an \n. Keep this in mind whenever you're printing out a file; assuming that a file will always end with a newline character can cause trouble.

What about closing the file? This code will work, printing the length of each line in a file. However, this sort of code is frowned upon in the Python world because it doesn't explicitly close the file. Now, when it comes to reading from files, it's not *that* big of a deal, especially if you're only opening a small number of them at a time. But if you're writing to files, or if you're opening many files at once, you'll want to close them—both to conserve resources and to ensure that the file has been closed for good.

The way to do that is with the with construct. I could rewrite the previous code as follows:

```
with open(filename) as f:
    for one_line in f:
        print(len(one_line))
```

Instead of opening the file and assigning the file object to f directly, we've opened it within the context of with, assigned it to f as part of the with statement, and then opened a block.

There's more detail about this in the sidebar about with and "context managers," but you should know that this is the standard Pythonic way to open a file—in no small part because it guarantees that the file has been closed by the end of the block.

Binary mode using b

What happens if you open a nontext file, such as a PDF or a JPEG, with open and then try to iterate over it, one line at a time?

First, you'll likely get an error right away. That's because Python expects the contents of a file to be valid UTF-8 formatted Unicode strings. Binary files, by definition, don't use Unicode. When Python tries to read a non-Unicode string, it'll raise an exception, complaining that it can't define a string with such content.

To avoid that problem, you can and should open the file in *binary* or *bytes* mode, adding a b to r, w, or a in the second argument to open; for example

```
for current_line in open(filename, 'rb'):    ←┐  Opens the file in "r" (read)
    print(current_line)    ←┐                  └─ and "b" (binary) mode
                            │  The type of current_line here is bytes, similar
                            │  to a string but without Unicode characters.
```

Now you won't be constrained by a lack of Unicode characters.

But wait. Remember that with each iteration, Python will return everything up to and including the next \n character. In a binary file, such a character won't appear at the end of every line, because there are no lines to speak of. Without such a character, what you get back from each iteration will probably be nonsense.

The bottom line is that if you're reading from a binary file, you shouldn't forget to use the b flag. But when you do that, you'll find that you don't want to read the file per line anyway. Instead, you should be using the read method to retrieve a fixed number of bytes. When read returns 0 bytes, you'll know that you're at the end of the file; for example

```
with open(filename, 'rb') as f:    ←┐  Uses "with", in a "context
    while True:                      │  manager," to open the file
        one_chunk = f.read(1000)    ←┐
        if not one_chunk:            │  Reads up to 1,000 bytes and
            break                    │  returns them as a bytes object
        print(f'This chunk contains {len(one_chunk)} bytes')
```

In this particular exercise, you were asked to print the final line of a file. One way to do so might look like the following code:

```
for current_line in open(filename):
    pass

print(current_line)
```

This trick works because we iterate over the lines of the file and assign current_line in each iteration—but we don't actually do anything in the body of the for loop. Rather, we use pass, which is a way of telling Python to do nothing. (Python requires that we have at least one line in an indented block, such as the body of a for loop.)

The reason that we execute this loop is for its side effect—namely, the fact that the final value assigned to `current_line` remains in place after the loop exits.

However, looping over the rows of a file just to get the final one strikes me as a bit strange, even if it works. My preferred solution, shown in figure 5.1, is to iterate over each line of the file, getting the current line but immediately assigning it to `final_line`.

```
 1  from io import StringIO
 2
 3  fakefile = StringIO('''
 4  nobody:*:-2:-2::0:0:Unprivileged User:/var/empty:/usr/bin/false
 5  root:*:0:0::0:0:System Administrator:/var/root:/bin/sh
 6  daemon:*:1:1::0:0:System Services:/var/root:/usr/bin/false
 7  ''')
 8
 9  def get_final_line(filename):
10      final_line = ''
11      for current_line in fakefile:
12          final_line = current_line
13      return final_line
14
15  print(get_final_line('/etc/passwd'))
```

Figure 5.1   Immediately before printing the final line

When we exit from the loop, `final_line` will contain whatever was in the most recent line. We can thus print it out afterwards.

Normally, `print` adds a newline after printing something to the screen. However, when we iterate over a file, each line already ends with a newline character. This can lead to doubled whitespace between printed output. The solution is to stop `print` from displaying anything by overriding the default \n value in the end parameter. By passing end='', we tell `print` to add '', the empty string, after printing `final_line`. For further information about the arguments you can pass to print, take a look here: http://mng.bz/RAAZ.

Solution

```
def get_final_line(filename):
    final_line = ''
    for current_line in open(filename):    ◁——  Iterates over each line of the file.
        final_line = current_line                You don't need to declare a
    return final_line                            variable; just iterate directly
                                                 over the result of open.

print(get_final_line('/etc/passwd'))
```

You can work through a version of this code in the Python Tutor at http://mng.bz/ D24g.

Simulating files in Python Tutor

Philip Guo's Python Tutor site (http://mng.bz/2XJX), which I use for diagrams and also to allow you to experiment with the book's solutions, doesn't support files. This is understandable—a free server system that lets people run arbitrary code is hard enough to create and support. Allowing people to work with arbitrary files would add plenty of logistical and security problems.

However, there is a solution: StringIO (http://mng.bz/PAOP). StringIO objects are what Python calls "file-like objects." They implement the same API as file objects, allowing us to read from them and write to them just like files. Unlike files, though, StringIO objects never actually touch the filesystem.

StringIO wasn't designed for use with the Python Tutor, although it's a great workaround for the limitations there. More typically, I see (and use) StringIO in automated tests. After all, you don't really want to have a test touch the filesystem; that would make things run much more slowly. Instead, you can use StringIO to simulate a file.

If you're doing any software testing, you should take a serious look at StringIO, part of the Python standard library. You can load it with

```
from io import StringIO
```

When we're looking at files, the versions of code that you'll see in Python Tutor thus will be slightly different from the ones in the book itself. However, they should work the same way, allowing you to explore the code visually. Unfortunately, exercises that involve directory listings can't be papered over as easily, and thus lack any Python Tutor link.

Screencast solution

Watch this short video walkthrough of the solution: https://livebook.manning.com/video/python-workout.

Beyond the exercise

Iterating over files, and understanding how to work with the content as (and after) you iterate over them, is an important skill to have when working with Python. It is also important to understand how to turn the contents of a file into a Python data structure—something we'll look at several more times in this chapter. Here are a few ideas for things you can do when iterating through files in this way:

- Iterate over the lines of a text file. Find all of the words (i.e., non-whitespace surrounded by whitespace) that contain only integers, and sum them.
- Create a text file (using an editor, not necessarily Python) containing two tab-separated columns, with each column containing a number. Then use Python to read through the file you've created. For each line, multiply each first number by the second, and then sum the results from all the lines. Ignore any line that doesn't contain two numeric columns.
- Read through a text file, line by line. Use a dict to keep track of how many times each vowel (a, e, i, o, and u) appears in the file. Print the resulting tabulation.

EXERCISE 19 ▪ /etc/passwd to dict

It's both common and useful to think of files as sequences of strings. After all, when you iterate over a file object, you get each of the file's lines as a string, one at a time. But it often makes more sense to turn a file into a more complex data structure, such as a dict.

In this exercise, write a function, passwd_to_dict, that reads from a Unix-style "password file," commonly stored as /etc/passwd, and returns a dict based on it. If you don't have access to such a file, you can download one that I've uploaded at http://mng.bz/2XXg.

Here's a sample of what the file looks like:

```
nobody:*:-2:-2::0:0:Unprivileged User:/var/empty:/usr/bin/false
root:*:0:0::0:0:System Administrator:/var/root:/bin/sh
daemon:*:1:1::0:0:System Services:/var/root:/usr/bin/false
```

Each line is one user record, divided into colon-separated fields. The first field (index 0) is the username, and the third field (index 2) is the user's unique ID number. (In the system from which I took the /etc/passwd file, nobody has ID -2, root has ID 0, and daemon has ID 1.) For our purposes, you can ignore all but these two fields.

Sometimes, the file will contain lines that fail to adhere to this format. For example, we generally ignore lines containing nothing but whitespace. Some vendors (e.g., Apple) include comments in their /etc/passwd files, in which the line starts with a # character.

The function passwd_to_dict should return a dict based on /etc/passwd in which the dict's keys are usernames and the values are the users' IDs.

Some help from string methods

The string methods str.startswith, str.endswith, and str.strip are helpful when doing this kind of analysis and manipulation.

For example, str.startswith returns True or False, depending on whether the string starts with a string:

```
s = 'abcd'
s.startswith('a')      # returns True
s.startswith('abc')    # returns True
s.startswith('b')      # returns False
```

Similarly, str.endswith tells us whether a string ends with a particular string:

```
s = 'abcd'
s.endswith('d')      # returns True
s.endswith('cd')     # returns True
s.endswith('b')      # returns False
```

str.strip removes the whitespace—the space character, as well as \n, \r, \t, and even \v—on either side of the string. The str.lstrip and str.rstrip methods only remove whitespace on the left and right, respectively. All of these methods return strings:

```
s = '  \t\t\ta  b  c  \t\t\n'
s.strip()    # returns 'a  b  c'
s.lstrip()   # returns 'a  b  c  \t\t\n'
s.rstrip()   # returns '  \t\t\ta  b  c'
```

Working it out

Once again, we're opening a text file and iterating over its lines, one at a time. Here, we assume that we know the file's format, and that we can extract fields from within each record.

In this case, we're splitting each line across the : character, using the str.split method. str.split always returns a list of strings, although the length of that list depends on the number of times that : occurs in the string. In the case of /etc/passwd, we will assume that any line containing : is a legitimate user record and thus has all of the necessary fields.

However, the file might contain comment lines beginning with #. If we were to invoke str.split (http://mng.bz/aR4z) on those lines, we'd get back a list, but one containing only a single element—leading to an IndexError exception if we tried to retrieve user_info[2].

It's thus important that we ignore those lines that begin with #. Fortunately, we can use a str.startswith (http://mng.bz/PAAw) method. Specifically, I identify and discard comment and blank lines using this code:

```
if not line.startswith(('#', '\n')):
```

The invocation of str.startswith passes it a tuple of two strings. str.startswith will return True if either of the strings in that tuple are found at the start of the line. Because every line contains a newline, including blank lines, we could say that a line that starts with \n is a blank line.

Assuming that it has found a user record, our program then adds a new key-value pair to users. The key is user_info[0], and the value is user_info[2]. Notice how we can use user_info[0] as the name of a key; as long as the value of that variable contains a string, we may use it as a dict key.

I use with (http://mng.bz/lGG2) here to open the file, thus ensuring that it's closed when the block ends. (See the sidebar about with and context managers.)

Solution

```
def passwd_to_dict(filename):
    users = {}
    with open(filename) as passwd:
        for line in passwd:
            if not line.startswith(('#', '\n')):       # Ignores comment
                user_info = line.split(':')            #   and blank lines
                                                       # Turns the line into a
                                                       #   list of strings
```

```
        users[user_info[0]] = int(user_info[2])
    return users

print(passwd_to_dict('/etc/passwd'))
```

You can work through a version of this code in the Python Tutor at http://mng.bz/lGWR.

Screencast solution

Watch this short video walkthrough of the solution: https://livebook.manning.com/video/python-workout.

Beyond the exercise

At a certain point in your Python career, you'll stop seeing files as sequences of characters on a disk, and start seeing them as raw material you can transform into Python data structures. Our programs have more semantic power with structured data (e.g., dicts) than strings. We can similarly do more and think in deeper ways if we read a file into a data structure rather than just into a string.

For example, imagine a CSV file in which each line contains the name of a country and its population. Reading this file as a string, it would be possible—but frustrating—to compare the populations of France and Thailand. But reading this file into a dict, it would be trivial to make such a comparison.

Indeed, I'm a particular fan of reading files into dicts, in no small part because many file formats lend themselves to this sort of translation—but you can also use more complex data structures. Here are some additional exercises you can try to help you see that connection and make the transformation in your code:

- Read through /etc/passwd, creating a dict in which user login shells (the final field on each line) are the keys. Each value will be a list of the users for whom that shell is defined as their login shell.
- Ask the user to enter integers, separated by spaces. From this input, create a dict whose keys are the factors for each number, and the values are lists containing those of the users' integers that are multiples of those factors.
- From /etc/passwd, create a dict in which the keys are the usernames (as in the main exercise) and the values are themselves dicts with keys (and appropriate values) for user ID, home directory, and shell.

`with` **and context managers**

As we've seen, it's common to open a file as follows:

```
with open('myfile.txt', 'w') as f:
    f.write('abc\n')
    f.write('def\n')
```

Most people believe, correctly, that using `with` ensures that the file, f, will be flushed and closed at the end of the block. (You thus don't have to explicitly call f.close() to ensure the contents will be flushed.) But because with is overwhelmingly used with files, many developers believe that there's some inherent connection between with and files. The truth is that with is a much more general Python construct, known as a *context manager*.

The basic idea is as follows:

 1 You use with, along with an object and a variable to which you want to assign the object.
 2 The object should know how to behave inside of the context manager.
 3 When the block starts, with turns to the object. If a __enter__ method is defined on the object, then it runs. In the case of files, the method is defined but does nothing other than return the file object itself. Whatever this method returns is assigned to the as variable at the end of the with line.
 4 When the block ends, with once again turns to the object, executing its __exit__ method. This method gives the object a chance to change or restore whatever state it was using.

It's pretty obvious, then, how with works with files. Perhaps the __enter__ method isn't important and doesn't do much, but the __exit__ method certainly is important and does a lot—specifically in flushing and closing the file. If you pass two or more objects to with, the __enter__ and __exit__ methods are invoked on each of them, in turn.

Other objects can and do adhere to the context manager protocol. Indeed, if you want, you can write your own classes such that they'll know how to behave inside of a with statement. (Details of how to do so are in the "What you need to know" table at the start of the chapter.)

Are context managers only used in the case of files? No, but that's the most common case by far. Two other common cases are (1) when processing database transactions and (2) when locking certain sections in multi-threaded code. In both situations, you want to have a section of code that's executed within a certain context—and thus, Python's context management, via with, comes to the rescue.

If you want to learn more about context managers, here's a good article on the subject: http://mng.bz/B221.

EXERCISE 20 ■ Word count

Unix systems contain many utility functions. One of the most useful to me is wc (http://mng.bz/Jyyo), the word count program. If you run wc against a text file, it'll count the characters, words, and lines that the file contains.

The challenge for this exercise is to write a wordcount function that mimics the wc Unix command. The function will take a filename as input and will print four lines of output:

 1 Number of characters (including whitespace)
 2 Number of words (separated by whitespace)
 3 Number of lines
 4 Number of unique words (case sensitive, so "NO" is different from "no")

I've placed a test file (wcfile.txt) at http://mng.bz/B2ml. You may download and use that file to test your implementation of wc. Any file will do, but if you use this one, your results will match up with mine. That file's contents look like this:

```
This is a test file.

It contains 28 words and 20 different words.

It also contains 165 characters.

It also contains 11 lines.

It is also self-referential.

Wow!
```

This exercise, like many others in this chapter, tries to help you see the connections between text files and Python's built-in data structures. It's very common to use Python to work with log files and configuration files, collecting and reporting that data in a human-readable format.

Working it out

This program demonstrates a number of Python's capabilities that many programmers use on a daily basis. First and foremost, many people who are new to Python believe that if they have to measure four aspects of a file, then they should read through the file four times. That might mean opening the file once and reading through it four times, or even opening it four separate times. But it's more common in Python to loop over the file once, iterating over each line and accumulating whatever data the program can find from that line.

How will we accumulate this data? We could use separate variables, and there's nothing wrong with that. But I prefer to use a dict (figure 5.2), since the counts are closely related, and because it also reduces the code I need to produce a report.

So, once we're iterating over the lines of the file, how can we count the various elements? Counting lines is the easiest part: each iteration goes over one line, so we can simply add 1 to counts['lines'] at the top of the loop.

Next, we want to count the number of characters in the file. Since we're already iterating over the file, there's not that much work to do. We get the number of characters in the current line by calculating len(one_line), and then adding that to counts['characters'].

Many people are surprised that this includes whitespace characters, such as spaces and tabs, as well as newlines. Yes, even an "empty" line contains a single newline character. But if we didn't have newline characters, then it wouldn't be obvious to the computer when it should start a new line. So such characters are necessary, and they take up some space.

Next, we want to count the number of words. To get this count, we turn one_line into a list of words, invoking one_line.split. The solution invokes split without any

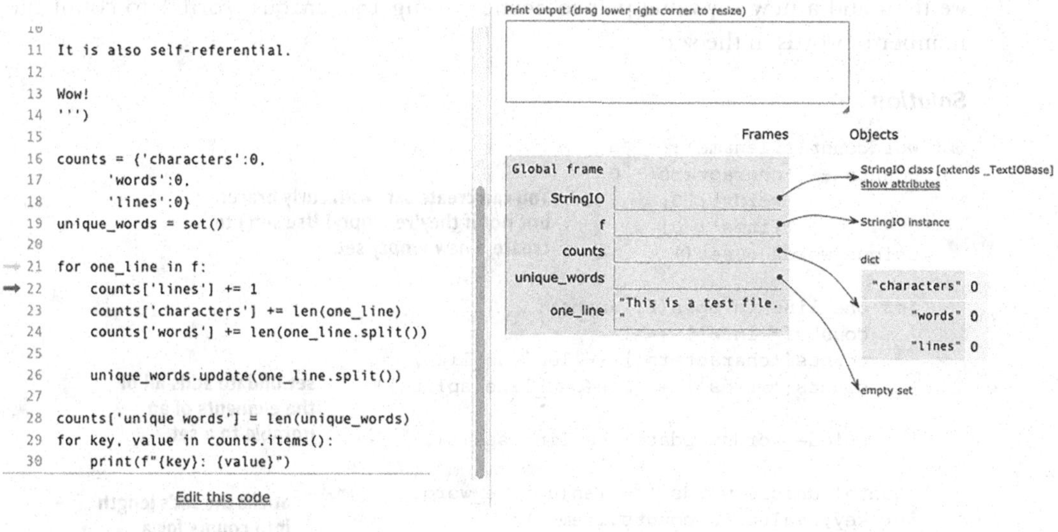

```
10
11  It is also self-referential.
12
13  Wow!
14  ''')
15
16  counts = {'characters':0,
17           'words':0,
18           'lines':0}
19  unique_words = set()
20
→ 21  for one_line in f:
➡ 22      counts['lines'] += 1
  23      counts['characters'] += len(one_line)
  24      counts['words'] += len(one_line.split())
  25
  26      unique_words.update(one_line.split())
  27
  28  counts['unique words'] = len(unique_words)
  29  for key, value in counts.items():
  30      print(f"{key}: {value}")
```

Edit this code

Print output (drag lower right corner to resize)

Frames | Objects

Global frame
StringIO → StringIO class [extends _TextIOBase] show attributes
f → StringIO instance
counts
unique_words → dict
one_line → "This is a test file."
"characters" 0
"words" 0
"lines" 0
empty set

Figure 5.2 Initialized counts in the dict

arguments, which causes it to use all whitespace—spaces, tabs, and newlines—as delimiters. The result is then put into counts['words'].

The final item to count is unique words. We could, in theory, use a list to store new words. But it's much easier to let Python do the hard work for us, using a set to guarantee the uniqueness. Thus, we create the unique_words set at the start of the program, and then use unique_words.update (http://mng.bz/MdOn) to add all of the words in the current line into the set (figure 5.3). For the report to work on our dict,

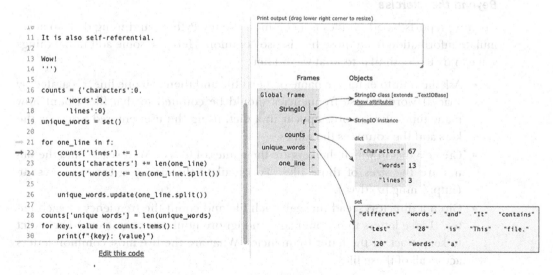

Figure 5.3 The data structures, including unique words, after several lines

we then add a new key-value pair to `counts`, using `len(unique_words)` to count the number of words in the set.

Solution

```
def wordcount(filename):
    counts = {'characters': 0,
              'words': 0,
              'lines': 0}                    ┌─ You can create sets with curly braces,
    unique_words = set()         ◄───┘  but not if they're empty! Use set() to
                                             create a new empty set.

    for one_line in open(filename):
        counts['lines'] += 1
        counts['characters'] += len(one_line)
        counts['words'] += len(one_line.split())      ┐ set.update adds all of
                                                        │ the elements of an
        unique_words.update(one_line.split())  ◄──┘ iterable to a set.

    counts['unique words'] = len(unique_words)   ◄─┐
    for key, value in counts.items():                │ Sticks the set's length
        print(f'{key}: {value}')                     │ into counts for a
                                                      │ combined report

wordcount('wcfile.txt')
```

You can work through a version of this code in the Python Tutor at http://mng.bz/ MdZo.

Screencast solution

Watch this short video walkthrough of the solution: https://livebook.manning.com/ video/python-workout.

Beyond the exercise

Creating reports based on files is a common use for Python, and using dicts to accumulate information from those files is also common. Here are some additional things you can try to do, similar to what we did here:

- Ask the user to enter the name of a text file and then (on one line, separated by spaces) words whose frequencies should be counted in that file. Count how many times those words appear in a dict, using the user-entered words as the keys and the counts as the values.
- Create a dict in which the keys are the names of files on your system and the values are the sizes of those files. To calculate the size, you can use `os.stat` (http://mng.bz/dyyo).
- Given a directory, read through each file and count the frequency of each letter. (Force letters to be lowercase, and ignore nonletter characters.) Use a dict to keep track of the letter frequencies. What are the five most common letters across all of these files?

EXERCISE 21 ■ Longest word per file

So far, we've worked with individual files. Many tasks, however, require you to analyze data in multiple files—such as all of the files in a dict. This exercise will give you some practice working with multiple files, aggregating measurements across all of them.

In this exercise, write two functions. find_longest_word takes a filename as an argument and returns the longest word found in the file. The second function, find_all_longest_words, takes a directory name and returns a dict in which the keys are filenames and the values are the longest words from each file.

If you don't have any text files that you can use for this exercise, you can download and use a zip file I've created from the five most popular books at Project Gutenberg (https://gutenberg.org/). You can download the zip file from http://mng.bz/rrWj.

> **NOTE** There are several ways to solve this problem. If you already know how to use comprehensions, and particularly dict comprehensions, then that's probably the most Pythonic approach. But if you aren't yet comfortable with them, and would prefer not to jump to read about them in chapter 7, then no worries—you can use a traditional for loop, and you'll be just fine.

Working it out

In this case, you're being asked to take a directory name and then find the longest word in each plain-text file in that directory. As noted, your function should return a dict in which the dict's keys are the filenames and the dict's values are the longest words in each file.

Whenever you hear that you need to transform a collection of inputs into a collection of outputs, you should immediately think about comprehensions—most commonly list comprehensions, but set comprehensions and dict comprehensions are also useful. In this case, we'll use a dict comprehension—which means that we'll create a dict based on iterating over a source. The source, in our case, will be a list of filenames. The filenames will also provide the dict keys, while the values will be the result of passing the filenames to a function.

In other words, our dict comprehension will

1 Iterate over the list of files in the named directory, putting the filename in the variable filename.
2 For each file, run the function find_longest_word, passing filename as an argument. The return value will be a string, the longest string in the file.
3 Each filename-longest word combination will become a key-value pair in the dict we create.

How can we implement find_longest_word? We could read the file's entire contents into a string, turn that string into a list, and then find the longest word in the list with sorted. Although this will work well for short files, it'll use a lot of memory for even medium-sized files.

My solution is thus to iterate over every line of a file, and then over every word in the line. If we find a word that's longer than the current `longest_word`, we replace the old word with the new one. When we're done iterating over the file, we can return the longest word that we found.

Note my use of `os.path.join` (http://mng.bz/oPPM) to combine the directory name with a filename. You can think of `os.path.join` as a filename-specific version of `str.join`. It has additional advantages, as well, such as taking into account the current operating system. On Windows, `os.path.join` will use backslashes, whereas on Macs and Unix/Linux systems, it'll use a forward slash.

Solution

```
import os

def find_longest_word(filename):
    longest_word = ''
    for one_line in open(filename):
        for one_word in one_line.split():
            if len(one_word) > len(longest_word):
                longest_word = one_word
    return longest_word

def find_all_longest_words(dirname):
    return {filename:
            find_longest_word(os.path.join(dirname,
                                           filename))      ◁── Gets the filename and its full path
            for filename in os.listdir(dirname)            ◁── Iterates over all of the files in dirname
            if os.path.isfile(os.path.join(dirname,
                                           filename))}      ◁── We're only interested in files, not directories or special files.

print(find_all_longest_words('.'))
```

Because these functions work with directories, there is no Python Tutor link.

Screencast solution

Watch this short video walkthrough of the solution: https://livebook.manning.com/video/python-workout.

Beyond the exercise

You'll commonly produce reports about files and file contents using dicts and other basic data structures in Python. Here are a few possible exercises to practice these ideas further:

- Use the `hashlib` module in the Python standard library, and the `md5` function within it, to calculate the MD5 hash for the contents of every file in a user-specified directory. Then print all of the filenames and their MD5 hashes.
- Ask the user for a directory name. Show all of the files in the directory, as well as how long ago the directory was modified. You will probably want to use a

combination of `os.stat` and the Arrow package on PyPI (http://mng.bz/nPPK) to do this easily.

■ Open an HTTP server's log file. (If you lack one, then you can read one from me at http://mng.bz/vxxM.) Summarize how many requests resulted in numeric response codes—202, 304, and so on.

Directory listings

For a language that claims "there's one way to do it," Python has too many ways to list files in a directory. The two most common are `os.listdir` and `glob.glob`, both of which I've mentioned in this chapter. A third way is to use `pathlib`, which provides us with an object-oriented API to the filesystem.

The easiest and most standard of these is `os.listdir`, a function in the `os` module. It returns a list of strings, the names of files in the directory; for example

```
filenames = os.listdir('/etc/')
```

The good news is that it's easy to understand and work with `os.listdir`. The bad news is that it returns a list of filenames without the directory name, which means that to open or work with the files, you'll need to add the directory name at the beginning—ideally with `os.path.join`, which works cross-platform.

The other problem with `os.listdir` is that you can't filter the filenames by a pattern. You get everything, including subdirectories and hidden files. So if you want just all of the `.txt` files in a directory, `os.listdir` won't be enough.

That's where the `glob` module comes in. It lets you use patterns, sometimes known as *globbing*, to describe the files that you want. Moreover, it returns a list of strings—with each string containing the complete path to the file. For example, I can get the full paths of the configuration files in `/etc/` on my computer with

```
filenames = glob.glob('/etc/*.conf')
```

I don't need to worry about other files or subdirectories in this case, which makes it much easier to work with. For a long time, `glob.glob` was thus my go-to function for finding files.

Then there's `pathlib`, a module that comes with the Python standard library and makes things easier in many ways. You start by creating a `pathlib.Path` object, which represents a file or directory:

```
import pathlib
p = pathlib.Path('/etc/')
```

Once you have this `Path` object, you can do lots of things with it that previously required separate functions—including the ones I've just described. For example, you can get an iterator that returns files in the directory with `iterdir`:

```
for one_filename in p.iterdir():
    print(one_filename)
```

> **(continued)**
>
> In each iteration, you don't get a string, but rather a `Path` object (or more specifically, on my Mac I get a `PosixPath` object). Having a full-fledged `Path` object, rather than a string, allows you to do lots more than just print the filename; you can open and inspect the file as well.
>
> If you want to get a list of files matching a pattern, as I did with `glob.glob`, you can use the `glob` method:
>
> ```
> for one_filename in p.glob('*.conf'):
>     print(one_filename)
> ```
>
> `pathlib` is a great addition to recent Python versions. If you have a chance to use it, you should do so; I've found that it clarifies and shortens quite a bit of my code. A good introduction to `pathlib` is here: http://mng.bz/4AAV.

EXERCISE 22 ■ Reading and writing CSV

In a CSV file, each record is stored on one line, and fields are separated by commas. CSV is commonly used for exchanging information, especially (but not only) in the world of data science. For example, a CSV file might contain information about different vegetables:

```
lettuce,green,soft
carrot,orange,hard
pepper,green,hard
eggplant,purple,soft
```

Each line in this CSV file contains three fields, separated by commas. There aren't any headers describing the fields, although many CSV files do have them.

Sometimes, the comma is replaced by another character, so as to avoid potential ambiguity. My personal favorite is to use a TAB character (\t in Python strings).

Python comes with a `csv` module (http://mng.bz/Qyyj) that handles writing to and reading from CSV files. For example, you can write to a CSV file with the following code:

```
import csv

with open('/tmp/stuff.csv', 'w') as f:
    o = csv.writer(f)
    o.writerow(range(5))
    o.writerow(['a', 'b', 'c', 'd', 'e'])
```

Creates a csv.writer object, wrapping our file-like object "f"

Writes the integers from 0-4 to the file, separated by commas

Writes this list of strings as a record to the CSV file, separated by commas

Not all CSV files necessarily look like CSV files. For example, the standard Unix /etc/passwd file, which contains information about users on a system (but no longer users' passwords, despite its name), separates fields with : characters.

For this exercise, create a function, passwd_to_csv, that takes two filenames as arguments: the first is a passwd-style file to read from, and the second is the name of a file in which to write the output.

The new file's contents are the username (index 0) and the user ID (index 2). Note that a record may contain a comment, in which case it will not have anything at index 2; you should take that into consideration when writing the file. The output file should use TAB characters to separate the elements.

Thus, the input will look like this

```
root:*:0:0::0:0:System Administrator:/var/root:/bin/sh
daemon:*:1:1::0:0:System Services:/var/root:/usr/bin/false
# I am a comment line
_ftp:*:98:-2::0:0:FTP Daemon:/var/empty:/usr/bin/false
```

and the output will look like this:

```
root    0
daemon  1
_ftp    98
```

Notice that the comment line in the input file is not placed in the output file. You can assume that any line with at least two colon-separated fields is legitimate.

How Python handles end of lines and newlines on different OSs

Different operating systems have different ways of indicating that we've reached the end of the line. Unix systems, including the Mac, use ASCII 10 (line feed, or LF). Windows systems use two characters, namely ASCII 13 (carriage return, or CR) + ASCII 10. Old-style Macs used just ASCII 13.

Python tries to bridge these gaps by being flexible, and making some good guesses, when it reads files. I've thus rarely had problems using Python to read text files that were created using Windows. By the same token, my students (who typically use Windows) generally have no problem reading the files that I've created on the Mac. Python figures out what line ending is being used, so we don't need to provide any more hints. And inside of the Python program, the line ending is symbolized by \n.

Writing to files, in contrast, is a bit trickier. Python will try to use the line ending appropriate for the operating system. So if you're writing to a file on Windows, it'll use CR+LF (sometimes shown as \r\n). If you're writing to a file on a Unix machine, then it'll just use LF.

This typically works just fine. But sometimes, you'll find yourself seeing too many or too few newlines when you read from a file. This might mean that Python has guessed incorrectly, or that the file used a few different line endings, confusing Python's guessing algorithm.

In such cases, you can pass a value to the newline parameter in the open function, used to open files. You can try to explicitly use newline='\n' to force Unix-style newlines, or newline='\r\n' to force Windows-style newlines. If this doesn't fix the problem, you might need to examine the file further to see how it was defined.

For a complete introduction to working with CSV files in Python, check out http://mng.bz/XPP6/.

Working it out

The solution program uses a number of aspects of Python that are useful when working with files. We've already seen and discussed with earlier in this chapter. Here, you can see how you can use with to open two separate files, or generally to define any number of objects. As soon as our block exits, both of the files are automatically closed.

We define two variables in the with statement, for the two files with which we'll be working. The passwd file is opened for reading from /etc/passwd. The output file is opened for writing, and writes to /tmp/output.csv. Our program will act as a go-between, translating from the input file and placing a reformatted subset into the output file.

We do this by creating one instance of csv.reader, which wraps passwd. However, because /etc/passwd uses colons (:) to delimit fields, we must tell this to csv.reader. Otherwise, it'll try to use commas, which will likely lead to an error—or, worse yet, not lead to an error, despite parsing the file incorrectly. Similarly, we define an instance of csv.writer, wrapping our output file and indicating that we want to use \t as the delimiter.

Now that we have our objects in place for reading and writing CSV data, we can run through the input file, writing a row (line) to the output file for each of those inputs. We take the username (from index 0) and the user ID (from index 2), create a tuple, and pass that tuple to csv.writerow. Our csv.writer object knows how to take our fields and print them to the file, separated by \t.

Perhaps the trickiest thing here is to ensure we don't try to transform lines that contain comments—that is, those which begin with a hash (#) character. There are a number of ways to do this, but the method that I've employed here is simply to check the number of fields we got for the current input line. If there's only one field, then it must be a comment line, or perhaps another type of malformed line. In such a case, we ignore the line altogether. Another good technique would be to check for # at the start of the line, perhaps using str.startswith.

Solution

```python
import csv

def passwd_to_csv(passwd_filename, csv_filename):
    with open(passwd_filename) as passwd,
         open(csv_filename, 'w') as output:
        infile = csv.reader(passwd,
                    delimiter=':')
        outfile = csv.writer(output,
                    delimiter='\t')
        for record in infile:
            if len(record) > 1:
                outfile.writerow((record[0], record[2]))
```

Fields in the input file are separated by colons (":").

Fields in the output file are separated by tabs ("\t").

Because we can't write to files on the Python Tutor, there is no link for this exercise.

Screencast solution

Watch this short video walkthrough of the solution: https://livebook.manning.com/video/python-workout.

Beyond the exercise

CSV files are extremely useful and common, and the csv module that comes with Python works with them very well. If you need something more advanced, then you might want to look into pandas (http://mng.bz/yyyq), which handles a wide array of CSV variations, as well as many other formats.

Here are several additional exercises you can try to improve your facility with CSV files:

- Extend this exercise by asking the user to enter a space-separated list of integers, indicating which fields should be written to the output CSV file. Also ask the user which character should be used as a delimiter in the output file. Then read from /etc/passwd, writing the user's chosen fields, separated by the user's chosen delimiter.

- Write a function that writes a dict to a CSV file. Each line in the CSV file should contain three fields: (1) the key, which we'll assume to be a string, (2) the value, and (3) the type of the value (e.g., str or int).

- Create a CSV file, in which each line contains 10 random integers between 10 and 100. Now read the file back, and print the sum and mean of the numbers on each line.

EXERCISE 23 ▪ JSON

JSON (described at http://json.org/) is a popular format for data exchange. In particular, many web services and APIs send and receive data using JSON.

JSON-encoded data can be read into a very large number of programming languages, including Python. The Python standard library comes with the json module (http://mng.bz/Mddn), which can be used to turn JSON-encoded strings into Python objects, and vice versa. The json.load method reads a JSON-encoded string from a file and returns a combination of Python objects.

In this exercise, you're analyzing test data in a high school. There's a scores directory on the filesystem containing a number of files in JSON format. Each file represents the scores for one class. Write a function, print_scores, that takes a directory name as an argument and prints a summary of the student scores it finds.

If you're trying to analyze the scores from class 9a, they'd be in a file called 9a.json that looks like this:

```
[{"math" : 90, "literature" : 98, "science" : 97},
 {"math" : 65, "literature" : 79, "science" : 85},
```

```
  {"math" : 78, "literature" : 83, "science" : 75},
  {"math" : 92, "literature" : 78, "science" : 85},
  {"math" : 100, "literature" : 80, "science" : 90}
]
```

The directory may also contain files for 10th grade (10a.json, 10b.json, and 10c.json) and other grades and classes in the high school. Each file contains the JSON equivalent of a list of dicts, with each dict containing scores for several different school subjects.

> **NOTE** Valid JSON uses double quotes ("), not single quotes ('). This can be surprising and frustrating for Python developers to discover.

Your function should print the highest, lowest, and average test scores for each subject in each class. Given two files (9a.json and 9b.json) in the scores directory, we would see the following output:

```
scores/9a.json
    science: min 75, max 97, average 86.4
    literature: min 78, max 98, average 83.6
    math: min 65, max 100, average 85.0
scores/9b.json
    science: min 35, max 95, average 82.0
    literature: min 38, max 98, average 72.0
    math: min 38, max 100, average 77.0
```

You can download a zipfile with these JSON files from http://mng.bz/Vg1x.

Working it out

In many languages, the first response to this kind of problem would be "Let's create our own class!" But in Python, while we can (and often do) create our own classes, it's often easier and faster to make use of built-in data structures—lists, tuples, and dicts.

In this particular case, we're reading from a JSON file. JSON is a data representation, much like XML; it isn't a data type per se. Thus, if we want to create JSON, we must use the json module to turn our Python data into JSON-formatted strings. And if we want to read from a JSON file, we must read the contents of the file, as strings, into our program, and then turn it into Python data structures.

In this exercise, though, you're being asked to work on multiple files in one directory. We know that the directory is called scores and that the files all have a .json suffix. We could thus use os.listdir on the directory, filtering (perhaps with a list comprehension) through all of those filenames such that we only work on those ending with .json.

However, this seems like a more appropriate place to use glob (http://mng .bz/044N), which takes a Unix-style filename pattern with (among others) * and ? characters and returns a list of those filenames that match the pattern. Thus, by invoking glob.glob('scores/*.json'), we get all of the files ending in .json within the scores directory. We can then iterate over that list, assigning the current filename (a string) to `filename`.

Next, we create a new entry in our `scores` dict, which is where we'll store the scores. This will actually be a dict of dicts, in which the first level will be the name of the file—and thus the class—from which we've read the data. The second-level keys will be the subjects; the dict's values will be a list of scores, from which we can then calculate the statistics we need. Thus, once we've defined `filename`, we immediately add the filename as a key to `scores`, with a new empty dict as the value.

Sometimes, you'll need to read each line of a file into Python and then invoke `json.loads` to turn that line into data. In our case, however, the file contains a single JSON array. We must thus use `json.load` to read from the file object `infile`, which turns the contents of the file into a Python list of dicts.

Because `json.load` returns a list of dicts, we can iterate over it. Each test result is placed in the `result` variable, which is a dict, in which the keys are the subjects and the values are the scores. Our goal is to reveal some statistics for each of the subjects in the class, which means that while the input file reports scores on a per-student basis, our report will ignore the students in favor of the subjects.

Given that `result` is a dict, we can iterate over its key-value pairs with `result.items()`, using parallel assignment to iterate over the key and value (here called `subject` and `score`). Now, we don't know in advance what subjects will be in our file, nor do we know how many tests there will be. As a result, it's easiest for us to store our scores in a list. This means that our `scores` dict will have one top-level key for each filename, and one second-level key for each subject. The second-level value will be a list, to which we'll then append with each iteration through the JSON-parsed list.

We'll want to add our score to the list:

```
scores[filename][subject]
```

Before we can do that, we need to make sure the list exists. One easy way to do this is with `dict.setdefault`, which assigns a key-value pair to a dict, but only if the key doesn't already exist. In other words, `d.setdefault(k, v)` is the same as saying

```
if k not in d:
    d[k] = v
```

We use `dict.setdefault` (http://mng.bz/aRRB) to create the list if it doesn't yet exist. In the next line, we add the score to the list for this subject, in this class.

When we've completed our initial `for` loop, we have all of the scores for each class. We can then iterate over each class, printing the name of the class.

Then, we iterate over each subject for the class. We once again use the method `dict.items` to return a key-value pair—in this case, calling them `subject` (for the name of the class) and `subject_scores` (for the list of scores for that subject). We then use an f-string to produce some output, using the built-in `min` (http://mng.bz/gyyE)

and max (http://mng.bz/Vgq5) functions, and then combining sum (http://mng.bz/
eQQv) and len to get the average score.

While this program reads from a file containing JSON and then produces output
on the user's screen, it could just as easily read from a network connection containing
JSON, and/or write to a file or socket in JSON format. As long as we use built-in and
standard Python data structures, the json module will be able to take our data and
turn it into JSON.

Solution

```python
import json
import glob


def print_scores(dirname):

    scores = {}

    for filename in glob.glob(f'{dirname}/*.json'):
        scores[filename] = {}

        with open(filename) as infile:
            for result in json.load(infile):
                for subject, score in result.items():
                    scores[filename].setdefault(subject,
                                                [])
                    scores[filename][subject].append(score)

    for one_class in scores:
        print(one_class)
        for subject, subject_scores in scores[one_class].items():
            min_score = min(subject_scores)
            max_score = max(subject_scores)
            average_score = (sum(subject_scores) /
                             len(subject_scores))

            print(subject)
            print(f'\tmin {min_score}')
            print(f'\tmax {max_score}')
            print(f'\taverage {average_score}')
```

Reads from the file infile
and turns it from JSON
into Python objects

Makes sure that
subject exists as a key
in scores[filename]

Summarizes the scores

Because these functions work with directories, there is no Python Tutor link.

Screencast solution

Watch this short video walkthrough of the solution: https://livebook.manning.com/
video/python-workout.

Beyond the exercise

Here are some more tasks you can try that use JSON:

- Convert /etc/passwd from a CSV-style file into a JSON-formatted file. The JSON file will contain the equivalent of a list of Python tuples, with each tuple representing one line from the file.
- For a slightly different challenge, turn each line in the file into a Python dict. This will require identifying each field with a unique column or key name. If you're not sure what each field in /etc/passwd does, you can give it an arbitrary name.
- Ask the user for the name of a directory. Iterate through each file in that directory (ignoring subdirectories), getting (via os.stat) the size of the file and when it was last modified. Create a JSON-formatted file on disk listing each filename, size, and modification timestamp. Then read the file back in, and identify which files were modified most and least recently, and which files are largest and smallest, in that directory.

EXERCISE 24 ■ Reverse lines

In many cases, we want to take a file in one format and save it to another format. In this function, we do a basic version of this idea. The function takes two arguments: the names of the input file (to be read from) and the output file (which will be created).

For example, if a file looks like

```
abc def
ghi jkl
```

then the output file will be

```
fed cba
lkj ihg
```

Notice that the newline remains at the end of the string, while the rest of the characters are all reversed.

Transforming files from one format into another and taking data from one file and creating another one based on it are common tasks. For example, you might need to translate dates to a different format, move timestamps from Eastern Daylight Time into Greenwich Mean Time, or transform prices from euros into dollars. You might also want to extract only some data from an input file, such as for a particular date or location.

Working it out

This solution depends not only on the fact that we can iterate over a file one line at a time, but also that we can work with more than one object in a with statement. Remember that with takes one or more objects and allows us to assign variables to them. I particularly like the fact that when I want to read from one file and write to another, I can just use `with` to open one for reading, open a second for writing, and then do what I've shown here.

I then read through each line of the input file. I then reverse the line using Python's slice syntax—remember that `s[::-1]` means that we want all of the elements of `s`, from the start to the end, but I use a step size of –1, which returns a reversed version of the string.

Before we can reverse the string, however, we first want to remove the newline character that's the final character in the string. So we first run `str.rstrip()` on the current line, and then we reverse it. We then write it to the output file, adding a newline character so we'll actually descend by one line.

The use of `with` guarantees that both files will be closed when the block ends. When we close a file that we opened for writing, it's automatically flushed, which means we don't need to worry about whether the data has actually been saved to disk.

I should note that people often ask me how to read from and write to the same file. Python does support that, with the `r+` mode. But I find that this opens the door to many potential problems because of the chance you'll overwrite the wrong character, and thus mess up the format of the file you're editing. I suggest that people use this sort of read-from-one, write-to-the-other code, which has roughly the same effect, without the potential danger of messing up the input file.

Solution

```
def reverse_lines(infilename, outfilename):
    with open(infilename) as infile, open(outfilename, 'w') as outfile:
        for one_line in infile:
            outfile.write(f'{one_line.rstrip()[::-1]}\n')
```

str.rstrip removes all whitespace
from the right side of a string.

Because these functions work with directories, there is no Python Tutor link.

Screencast solution

Watch this short video walkthrough of the solution: https://livebook.manning.com/video/python-workout.

Beyond the exercise

Here are some more exercise ideas for translating files from one format to another using `with` and this kind of technique:

- "Encrypt" a text file by turning all of its characters into their numeric equivalents (with the built-in `ord` function) and writing that file to disk. Now "decrypt" the file (using the built-in `chr` function), turning the numbers back into their original characters.

- Given an existing text file, create two new text files. The new files will each contain the same number of lines as the input file. In one output file, you'll write all of the vowels (a, e, i, o, and u) from the input file. In the other, you'll write all of the consonants. (You can ignore punctuation and whitespace.)
- The final field in /etc/passwd is the *shell*, the Unix command interpreter that's invoked when a user logs in. Create a file, containing one line per shell, in which the shell's name is written, followed by all of the usernames that use the shell; for example

```
/bin/bash:root, jci, user, reuven, atara
/bin/sh:spamd, gitlab
```

Summary

It's almost impossible to imagine writing programs without using files. And while there are many different types of files, Python is especially well suited for working with text files—especially, but not only, including log files and configuration files, as well those formatted in such standard ways as JSON and CSV.

It's important to remember a few things when working with files:

- You will typically open files for either reading or writing.
- You can (and should) iterate over files one line at a time, rather than reading the whole thing into memory at once.
- Using with when opening a file for writing ensures that the file will be flushed and closed.
- The csv module makes it easy to read from and write to CSV files.
- The json module's dump and load functions allow us to move between Python data structures and JSON-formatted strings.
- Reading from files into built-in Python data types is a common and powerful technique.

Functions 6

Functions are one of the cornerstones of programming—but not because there's a technical need for them. We could program without functions, if we really had to. But functions provide a number of great benefits.

First, they allow us to avoid repetition in our code. Many programs have instructions that are repeated: asking a user to log in, reading data from a particular type of configuration file, or calculating the length of an MP3, for example. While the computer won't mind (or even complain) if the same code appears in multiple places, we—and the people who have to maintain the code after we're done with it—will suffer and likely complain. Such repetition is hard to remember and keep track of. Moreover, you'll likely find that the code needs improvement and maintenance; if it occurs multiple times in your program, then you'll need to find and fix it each of those times.

As mentioned in chapter 2, the maxim "don't repeat yourself" (DRY) is a good thing to keep in mind when programming. And writing functions is a great way to apply the phrase, "DRY up your code."

A second benefit of functions is that they let us (as developers) think at a higher level of abstraction. Just as you can't drive if you're constantly thinking about what your car's various parts are doing, you can't program if you're constantly thinking about all of the parts of your program and what they're doing. It helps, semantically and cognitively, to wrap functionality into a named package, and then to use that name to refer to it.

In natural language, we create new verbs all of the time, such as *programming* and *texting*. We don't have to do this; we could describe these actions using many more words, and with much more detail. But doing so becomes tedious and draws attention away from the point that we're making. Functions are the verbs of programming; they let us define new actions based on old ones, and thus let us think in more sophisticated terms.

For all of these reasons, functions are a useful tool and are available in all programming languages. But Python's functions add a twist to this: they're objects, meaning that they can be treated as data. We can store functions in data structures and retrieve them from there as well. Using functions in this way seems odd to many newcomers to Python, but it provides a powerful technique that can reduce how much code we write and increase our flexibility.

Moreover, Python doesn't allow for multiple definitions of the same function. In some languages, you can define a function multiple times, each time having a different signature. So you could, for example, define the function once as taking a single string argument, a second time as taking a list argument, a third time as taking a dict argument, and a fourth time as taking three float arguments.

In Python, this functionality doesn't exist; when you define a function, you're assigning to a variable. And just as you can't expect that x will simultaneously contain the values 5 and 7, you similarly can't expect that a function will contain multiple implementations.

The way that we get around this problem in Python is with flexible parameters. Between default values, variable numbers of arguments (*args), and keyword arguments (**kwargs), we can write functions that handle a variety of situations.

You've already written a number of functions as you've progressed through this book, so the purpose of this chapter isn't to teach you how to write functions. Rather, the goal is to show you how to use various function-related techniques. This will allow you not only to write code once and use it numerous times, but also to build up a hierarchy of new verbs, describing increasingly complex and higher level tasks.

Table 6.1 What you need to know

Concept	What is it?	Example	To learn more
def	Keyword for defining functions and methods	def double(x): return x * 2	http://mng.bz/xW46
global	In a function, indicates a variable must be global	global x	http://mng.bz/mBNP
nonlocal	In a nested function, indicates a variable is local to the enclosing function	nonlocal x	http://mng.bz/5apz
operator module	Collection of methods that implement built-in operators	operator.add(2,4)	http://mng.bz/6QAy

Default parameter values

Let's say that I can write a simple function that returns a friendly greeting:

```
def hello(name):
    return f'Hello, {name}!'
```

This will work fine if I provide a value for name:

```
>>> hello('world')
'Hello, world!'
```

But what if I don't?

```
>>> hello()
Traceback (most recent call last):
  File "<stdin>", line 1, in <module> TypeError: hello() missing 1 requi
    red positional argument: 'name'
```

In other words, Python knows that the function takes a single argument. So if you call the function with one argument, you're just fine. Call it with no arguments (or with two arguments, for that matter), and you'll get an error message.

How does Python know how many arguments the function should take? It knows because the function object, which we created when we defined the function with def, keeps track of that sort of thing. Instead of invoking the function, we can look inside the function object. The __code__ attribute (see figure 6.1) contains the core of the function, including the bytecodes into which your function was compiled. Inside that object are a number of hints that Python keeps around, including this one:

```
>>> hello.__code__.co_argcount
1
```

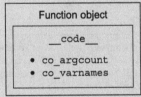

Figure 6.1   **A function object, along with its __code__ section**

In other words, when we define our function with a parameter, the function object keeps track of that in co_argcount. And when we invoke the function, Python compares the number of arguments with co_argcount. If there's a mismatch, then we get an error, as we saw a little earlier. However, there's still a way that we can define the function such that an argument is optional—we can add a default value to the parameter:

```
def hello(name='world'):
    return f'Hello, {name}!'
```

When we run the function now, Python gives us more slack. If we pass an argument, then that value is assigned to the name parameter. But if we don't pass an argument, then the string `world` is assigned to `name`, as per our default (see table 6.2). In this way, we can call our function with either no arguments or one argument; however, two arguments aren't allowed.

Table 6.2 Calling `hello`

Call	Value of name	Return value
`hello()`	world, thanks to the default	`Hello, world!`
`hello('out there')`	out there	`Hello, out there!`
`hello('a', 'b')`	Error: Too many arguments	No return value

NOTE Parameters with defaults must come after those without defaults.

WARNING Never use a mutable value, such as a list or dict, as a parameter's default value. You shouldn't do so because default values are stored and reused across calls to the function. This means that if you modify the default value in one call, that modification will be visible in the next call. Most code checkers and IDEs will warn you about this, but it's important to keep in mind.

EXERCISE 25 ■ XML generator

Python is often used not just to parse data, but to format it as well. In this exercise, you'll write a function that uses a combination of different parameters and parameter types to produce a variety of outputs.

Write a function, `myxml`, that allows you to create simple XML output. The output from the function will always be a string. The function can be invoked in a number of ways, as shown in table 6.3.

Table 6.3 Calling `myxml`

Call	Return value
`myxml('foo')`	`<foo></foo>`
`myxml('foo', 'bar')`	`<foo>bar</foo>`
`myxml('foo', 'bar', a=1, b=2, c=3)`	`<foo a="1" b="2" c="3">bar</foo>`

Notice that in all cases, the first argument is the name of the tag. In the latter two cases, the second argument is the content (text) placed between the opening and closing tags. And in the third case, the name-value pairs will be turned into attributes inside of the opening tag.

Working it out

Let's start by assuming that we only want our function to take a single argument, the name of the tag. That would be easy to write. We could say

```
def myxml(tagname):
    return f'<{tagname}></{tagname}>'
```

If we decide we want to pass a second (optional) argument, this will fail. Some people thus assume that our function should take *args, meaning any number of arguments, all of which will be put in a tuple. But, as a general rule, *args is meant for situations in which you don't know how many values you'll be getting and you want to be able to accept any number.

My general rule with *args is that it should be used when you'll put its value into a for loop, and that if you're grabbing elements from *args with numeric indexes, then you're probably doing something wrong.

The other option, though, is to use a default. And that's what I've gone with. The first parameter is mandatory, but the second is optional. If I make the second one (which I call content here) an empty string, then I know that either the user passes content or the content is empty. In either case, the function works. I can thus define it as follows:

```
def myxml(tagname, content=''):
    return f'<{tagname}>{content}</{tagname}>'
```

But what about the key-value pairs that we can pass, and which are then placed as attributes in the opening tag?

When we define a function with **kwargs, we're telling Python that we might pass any name-value pair in the style name=value. These arguments aren't passed in the normal way but are treated separately, as *keyword arguments*. They're used to create a dict, traditionally called kwargs, whose keys are the keyword names and whose values are the keyword values. Thus, we can say

```
def myxml(tagname, content='', **kwargs):
    attrs = ''.join([f' {key}="{value}"'
                     for key, value in kwargs.items()])
    return f'<{tagname}{attrs}>{content}</{tagname}>'
```

As you can see, I'm not just taking the key-value pairs from **kwargs and putting them into a string. I first have to take that dict and turn it into name-value pairs in XML format. I do this with a list comprehension, running on the dict. For each key-value pair, I create a string, making sure that the first character in the string is a space, so we don't bump up against the tagname in the opening tag.

There's a lot going on in this code, and it uses a few common Python paradigms. Understanding that, it's probably useful to go through it, step by step, just to make things clearer:

1 In the body of myxml, we know that tagname will be a string (the name of the tag), content will be a string (whatever content should go between the tags), and kwargs will be a dict (with the attribute name-value pairs).

2 Both content and kwargs might be empty, if the user didn't pass any values for those parameters.

3 We use a list comprehension to iterate over kwargs.items(). This will provide us with one key-value pair in each iteration.

4 We use the key-value pair, assigned to the variables key and value, to create a string of the form key="value". We get one such string for each of the attribute key-value pairs passed by the user.

5 The result of our list comprehension is a list of strings. We join these strings together with str.join, with an empty string between the elements.

6 Finally, we return the combination of the opening tag (with any attributes we might have gotten), the content, and the closing tag.

Solution

The function has one mandatory parameter, one with a default, and "**kwargs".

Uses a list comprehension to create a string from kwargs

Returns the XML-formatted string

```
def myxml(tagname, content='', **kwargs):
    attrs = ''.join([f' {key}="{value}"'
                     for key, value in kwargs.items()])
    return f'<{tagname}{attrs}>{content}</{tagname}>'

print(myxml('tagname', 'hello', a=1, b=2, c=3))
```

You can work through a version of this code in the Python Tutor at http://mng.bz/OMoK.

Screencast solution

Watch this short video walkthrough of the solution: https://livebook.manning.com/video/python-workout.

Beyond the exercise

Learning to work with functions, and the types of parameters that you can define, takes some time but is well worthwhile. Here are some exercises you can use to sharpen your thinking when it comes to function parameters:

- Write a copyfile function that takes one mandatory argument—the name of an input file—and any number of additional arguments: the names of files to which the input should be copied. Calling copyfile('myfile.txt', 'copy1.txt', 'copy2.txt', 'copy3.txt') will create three copies of myfile.txt: one each in copy1.txt, copy2.txt, and copy3.txt.

- Write a "factorial" function that takes any number of numeric arguments and returns the result of multiplying them all by one another.

- Write an `anyjoin` function that works similarly to `str.join`, except that the first argument is a sequence of any types (not just of strings), and the second argument is the "glue" that we put between elements, defaulting to " " (a space). So `anyjoin([1,2,3])` will return `1 2 3`, and `anyjoin('abc', pass:'**')` will return `pass:a**b**c`.

Variable scoping in Python

Variable scoping is one of those topics that many people prefer to ignore—first because it's dry, and then because it's obvious. The thing is, Python's scoping is very different from what I've seen in other languages. Moreover, it explains a great deal about how the language works, and why certain decisions were made.

The term *scoping* refers to the visibility of variables (and all names) from within the program. If I set a variable's value within a function, have I affected it outside of the function as well? What if I set a variable's value inside a `for` loop?

Python has four levels of scoping:

- Local
- Enclosing function
- Global
- Built-ins

These are known by the abbreviation LEGB. If you're in a function, then all four are searched, in order. If you're outside of a function, then only the final two (globals and built-ins) are searched. Once the identifier is found, Python stops searching.

That's an important consideration to keep in mind. If you haven't defined a function, you're operating at the global level. Indentation might be pervasive in Python, but it doesn't affect variable scoping at all.

But what if you run `int('s')`? Is `int` a global variable? No, it's in the built-ins namespace. Python has very few reserved words; many of the most common types and functions we run are neither globals nor reserved keywords. Python searches the builtins namespace after the global one, before giving up on you and raising an exception.

What if you define a global name that's identical to one in built-ins? Then you have effectively *shadowed* that value. I see this all the time in my courses, when people write something like

```
sum = 0
for i in range(5):
    sum += i
print(sum)

print(sum([10, 20, 30]))

TypeError: 'int' object is not callable
```

(continued)

Why do we get this weird error? Because in addition to the sum function defined in built-ins, we have now defined a global variable named sum. And because globals come before built-ins in Python's search path, Python discovers that sum is an integer and refuses to invoke it.

It's a bit frustrating that the language doesn't bother to check or warn you about redefining names in built-ins. However, there are tools (e.g., pylint) that will tell you if you've accidentally (or not) created a clashing name.

LOCAL VARIABLES

If I define a variable inside a function, then it's considered to be a *local* variable. Local variables exist only as long as the function does; when the function goes away, so do the local variables it defined; for example

```
x = 100

def foo():
    x = 200
    print(x)

print(x)
foo()
print(x)
```

This code will print 100, 200, and then 100 again. In the code, we've defined two variables: x in the global scope is defined to be 100 and never changes, whereas x in the local scope, available only within the function foo, is 200 and never changes (figure 6.2). The fact that both are called x doesn't confuse Python, because from within the function, it'll see the local x and ignore the global one entirely.

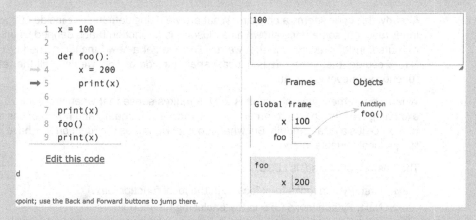

Figure 6.2   Inner vs. outer x

THE GLOBAL STATEMENT

What if, from within the function, I want to change the global variable? That requires the use of the `global` declaration, which tells Python that you're not interested in creating a local variable in this function. Rather, any retrievals or assignments should affect the global variable; for example

```
x = 100

def foo():
    global x
    x = 200
    print(x)

print(x)
foo()
print(x)
```

This code will print 100, 200, and then 200, because there's only one x, thanks to the `global` declaration.

Now, changing global variables from within a function is almost always a bad idea. And yet, there are rare times when it's necessary. For example, you might need to update a configuration parameter that's set as a global variable.

ENCLOSING

Finally, let's consider inner functions via the following code:

```
def foo(x):
    def bar(y):
        return x * y
    return bar

f = foo(10)
print(f(20))
```

Already, this code seems a bit weird. What are we doing defining `bar` inside of `foo`? This inner function, sometimes known as a *closure*, is a function that's defined when `foo` is executed. Indeed, every time that we run `foo`, we get a new function named `bar` back. But of course, the name `bar` is a local variable inside of `foo`; we can call the returned function whatever we want.

When we run the code, the result is 200. It makes sense that when we invoke f, we're executing `bar`, which was returned by `foo`. And we can understand how `bar` has access to y, since it's a local variable. But what about x? How does the function `bar` have access to x, a local variable in `foo`?

The answer, of course, is LEGB:

1 First, Python looks for x locally, in the local function `bar`.
2 Next, Python looks for x in the enclosing function `foo`.
3 If x were not in `foo`, then Python would continue looking at the global level.
4 And if x were not a global variable, then Python would look in the built-ins namespace.

(continued)

What if I want to change the value of x, a local variable in the enclosing function? It's not global, so the `global` declaration won't work. In Python 3, though, we have the `nonlocal` keyword. This keyword tells Python: "Any assignment we do to this variable should go to the outer function, not to a (new) local variable"; for example

```
def foo():
    call_counter = 0          Initializes call_counter
    def bar(y):               as a local variable in foo
        nonlocal call_counter          Tells bar that assignments to
        call_counter += 1              call_counter should affect the
        return f'y = {y}, call_counter = {call_counter}'    enclosing variable in foo
    return bar

b = foo()                                   Increments
for i in range(10, 100, 10):                call_counter,
    print(b(i))                             whose value
                                            sticks around
                                            across runs of bar
```

Initializes call_counter as a local variable in foo

Tells bar that assignments to call_counter should affect the enclosing variable in foo

Increments call_counter, whose value sticks around across runs of bar

Iterates over the numbers 10, 20, 30, ... 90

Calls b with each of the numbers in that range

The output from this code is

```
y = 10, call_counter = 1
y = 20, call_counter = 2
y = 30, call_counter = 3
y = 40, call_counter = 4
y = 50, call_counter = 5
y = 60, call_counter = 6
y = 70, call_counter = 7
y = 80, call_counter = 8
y = 90, call_counter = 9
```

So any time you see Python accessing or setting a variable—which is often!—consider the LEGB scoping rule and how it's always, without exception, used to find all identifiers, including data, functions, classes, and modules.

EXERCISE 26 ■ Prefix notation calculator

In Python, as in real life, we normally write mathematics using *infix* notation, as in 2+3. But there's also something known as *prefix* notation, in which the operator precedes the arguments. Using prefix notation, we would write + 2 3. There's also *postfix* notation, sometimes known as "reverse Polish notation" (or RPN), which is still in use on HP brand calculators. That would look like 2 3 +. And yes, the numbers must then be separated by spaces.

Prefix and postfix notation are both useful in that they allow us to do sophisticated operations without parentheses. For example, if you write 2 3 4 + * in RPN, you're telling the system to first add 3+4 and then multiply 2*7. This is why HP calculators have an Enter key but no "=" key, which confuses newcomers greatly. In the Lisp programming language, prefix notation allows you to apply an operator to many numbers (e.g., (+ 1 2 3 4 5)) rather than get caught up with lots of + signs.

For this exercise, I want you to write a function (calc) that expects a single argument—a string containing a simple math expression in prefix notation—with an operator and two numbers. Your program will parse the input and produce the appropriate output. For our purposes, it's enough to handle the six basic arithmetic operations in Python: addition, subtraction, multiplication, division (/), modulus (%), and exponentiation (**). The normal Python math rules should work, such that division always results in a floating-point number. We'll assume, for our purposes, that the argument will only contain one of our six operators and two valid numbers.

But wait, there's a catch—or a hint, if you prefer: you should implement each of the operations as a separate function, and you shouldn't use an if statement to decide which function should be run. Another hint: look at the operator module, whose functions implement many of Python's operators.

Working it out

The solution uses a technique known as a *dispatch table*, along with the operator module that comes with Python. It's my favorite solution to this problem, but it's not the only one—and it's likely not the one that you first thought of.

Let's start with the simplest solution and work our way up to the solution I wrote. We'll need a function for each of the operators. But then we'll somehow need to translate from the operator string (e.g., + or **) to the function we want to run. We could use if statements to make such a decision, but a more common way to do this in Python is with dicts. After all, it's pretty standard to have keys that are strings, and since we can store anything in the value, that includes functions.

> **NOTE** Many of my students ask me how to create a switch-case statement in Python. They're surprised to hear that they already know the answer, namely that Python doesn't have such a statement, and that we use if instead. This is part of Python's philosophy of having one, and only one, way to do something. It reduces programmers' choices but makes the code clearer and easier to maintain.

We can then retrieve the function from the dict and invoke it with parentheses:

```python
def add(a,b):
    return a + b

def sub(a,b):
    return a - b

def mul(a,b):
    return a * b

def div(a,b):
    return a / b

def pow(a,b):
    return a ** b
```

```
def mod(a,b):
    return a % b

def calc(to_solve):
    operations = {'+' : add,
                  '-' : sub,
                  '*' : mul,
                  '/' : div,
                  '**' : pow,
                  '%' : mod}

    op, first_s, second_s = to_solve.split()
    first = int(first_s)
    second = int(second_s)

    return operations[op](first, second)
```

The keys in the operations dict are the operator strings that a user might enter, while the values are our functions associated with those strings.

Breaks the user's input apart

Turns each of the user's inputs from strings into integers

Applies the user's chosen operator as a key in operations, returning a function—which we then invoke, passing it "first" and "second" as arguments

Perhaps my favorite part of the code is the final line. We have a dict in which the functions are the values. We can thus retrieve the function we want with `operations[operator]`, where `operator` is the first part of the string that we broke apart with `str.split`. Once we have a function, we can call it with parentheses, passing it our two operands, `first` and `second`.

But how do we get `first` and `second`? From the user's input string, in which we assume that there are three elements. We use `str.split` to break them apart, and immediately use unpacking to assign them to three variables.

Hedging your bets with maxsplit

If you're uncomfortable with the idea of invoking `str.split` and simply assuming that we'll get three results back, there's an easy way to deal with that. When you invoke `str.split`, pass a value to its optional `maxsplit` parameter. This parameter indicates how many splits will actually be performed. Another way to think about it is that it's the index of the final element in the returned list. For example, if I write

```
>>> s = 'a b c d e'
>>> s.split()
['a', 'b', 'c', 'd', 'e']
```

as you can see, I get (as always) a list of strings. Because I invoked `str.split` without any arguments, Python used any whitespace characters as separators.

But if I pass a value of 3 to `maxsplit`, I get the following:

```
>>> s = 'a b c d e'
>>> s.split(maxsplit=3)
['a', 'b', 'c', 'd e']
```

Notice that the returned list now has four elements. The Python documentation says that `maxsplit` tells `str.split` how many cuts to make. I prefer to think of that value as the largest index in the returned list—that is, because the returned list contains four elements, the final element will have an index of 3. Either way, `maxsplit` ensures that when we use unpacking on the result from it, we're not going to encounter an error.

All of this is fine, but this code doesn't seem very DRY. The fact that we have to define each of our functions, even when they're so similar to one another and are reimplementing existing functionality, is a bit frustrating and out of character for Python.

Fortunately, the `operator` module, which comes with Python, can help us. By importing `operator`, we get precisely the functions we need: add, sub, mul, truediv/floordiv, mod, and pow. We no longer need to define our own functions, because we can use the ones that the module provides. The add function in `operators` does what we would normally expect from the + operator: it looks to its left, determines the type of the first parameter, and uses that to know what to invoke. `operator.add`, as a function, doesn't need to look to its left; it checks the type of its first argument and uses that to determine which version of + to run.

In this particular exercise, we restricted the user's inputs to integers, so we didn't do any type checking. But you can imagine a version of this exercise in which we could handle a variety of different types, not just integers. In such a case, the various `operator` functions would know what to do with whatever types we'd hand them.

Solution

The operator module provides functions that implement all built-in operators.

```python
import operator

def calc(to_solve):
    operations = {'+': operator.add,
                  '-': operator.sub,
                  '*': operator.mul,
                  '/': operator.truediv,
                  '**': operator.pow,
                  '%': operator.mod}

    op, first_s, second_s = to_solve.split()
    first = int(first_s)
    second = int(second_s)

    return operations[op](first, second)

print(calc('+ 2 3'))
```

Yes, functions can be the values in a dict!

You can choose between truediv, which returns a float, as with the "/" operator, or floordiv, which returns an integer, as with the "//" operator.

Splits the line, assigning via unpacking

Calls the function retrieved via operator, passing "first" and "second" as arguments

You can work through a version of this code in the Python Tutor at http://mng.bz/YrGo.

Screencast solution

Watch this short video walkthrough of the solution: https://livebook.manning.com/video/python-workout.

Beyond the exercise

Treating functions as data, and storing them in data structures, is odd for many newcomers to Python. But it enables techniques that, although possible, are far more complex in other languages. Here are three more exercises that extend this idea even further:

- Expand the program you wrote, such that the user's input can contain any number of numbers, not just two. The program will thus handle + 3 5 7 or / 100 5 5, and will apply the operator from left to right—giving the answers 15 and 4, respectively.
- Write a function, `apply_to_each`, that takes two arguments: a function that takes a single argument, and an iterable. Return a list whose values are the result of applying the function to each element in the iterable. (If this sounds familiar, it might be—this is an implementation of the classic map function, still available in Python. You can find a description of map in chapter 7.)
- Write a function, `transform_lines`, that takes three arguments: a function that takes a single argument, the name of an input file, and the name of an output file. Calling the function will run the function on each line of the input file, with the results written to the output file. (Hint: the previous exercise and this one are closely related.)

EXERCISE 27 ▪ Password generator

Even today, many people use the same password on many different computers. This means that if someone figures out your password on system A, then they can log into systems B, C, and D where you used the same password. For this reason, many people (including me) use software that creates (and then remembers) long, randomly generated passwords. If you use such a system, then even if system A is compromised, your logins on systems B, C, and D are all safe.

In this exercise, we're going to create a password-generation function. Actually, we're going to create a factory for password-generation functions. That is, I might need to generate a large number of passwords, all of which use the same set of characters. (You know how it is. Some applications require a mix of capital letters, lowercase letters, numbers, and symbols; whereas others require that you only use letters; and still others allow both letters and digits.) You'll thus call the function create_password _generator with a string. That string will return a function, which itself takes an integer argument. Calling this function will return a password of the specified length, using the string from which it was created; for example

```
alpha_password = create_password_generator('abcdef')
symbol_password = create_password_generator('!@#$%')

print(alpha_password(5))     # efeaa
print(alpha_password(10))    # cacdacbada

print(symbol_password(5))    # %#@%@
print(symbol_password(10))   # @!%%$%$%%#
```

A useful function to know about in implementing this function is the random module
(http://mng.bz/Z2wj), and more specifically the random.choice function in that module. That function returns one (randomly chosen) element from a sequence.

The point of this exercise is to understand how to work with inner functions: defining them, returning them, and using them to create numerous similar functions.

Working it out

This is an example of where you might want to use an inner function, sometimes
known as a *closure*. The idea is that we're invoking a function (create_password
_generator) that returns a function (create_password). The returned, inner function knows what we did on our initial invocation but also has some functionality of its
own. As a result, it needs to be defined as an inner function so that it can access variables from the initial (outer) invocation.

The inner function is defined not when Python first executes the program, but
rather when the outer function (create_password_generator) is executed. Indeed,
we create a new inner function once for each time that create_password_generator
is invoked.

That new inner function is then returned to the caller. From Python's perspective,
there's nothing special here—we can return any Python object from a function: a list,
dict, or even a function. What is special here, though, is that the returned function
references a variable in the outer function, where it was originally defined.

After all, we want to end up with a function to which we can pass an integer, and
from which we can get a randomly generated password. But the password must contain
certain characters, and different programs have different restrictions on what characters
can be used for those passwords. Thus, we might want five alphanumeric characters, or
10 numbers, or 15 characters that are either alphanumeric or punctuation.

We thus define our outer function such that it takes a single argument, a string
containing the characters from which we want to create a new password. The result of
invoking this function is, as was indicated, a function—the dynamically defined create
_password. This inner function has access to the original characters variable in the
outer function because of Python's LEGB precedence rule for variable lookup. (See
sidebar, "Variable scoping in Python.") When, inside of create_password, we look for
the variable characters, it's found in the enclosing function's scope.

If we invoke create_password_generator twice, as shown in the visualization
via the Python Tutor (figure 6.3), each invocation will return a separate version of

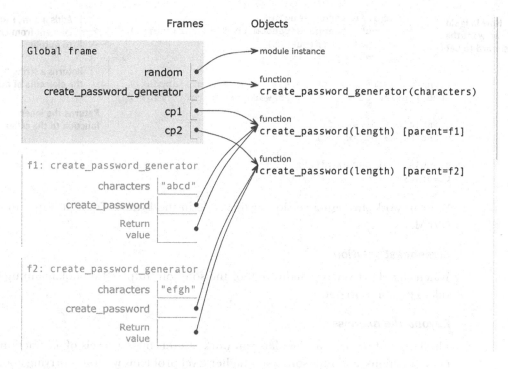

Figure 6.3 Python Tutor's depiction of two password-generating functions

create_password, with a separate value of characters. Each invocation of the outer function returns a new function, with its own local variables. At the same time, each of the returned inner functions has access to the local variables from its enclosing function. When we invoke one of the inner functions, we thus get a new password based on the combination of the inner function's local variables and the outer (enclosing) function's local variables.

NOTE Working with inner functions and closures can be quite surprising and confusing at first. That's particularly true because our instinct is to believe that when a function returns, its local variables and state all go away. Indeed, that's normally true—but remember that in Python, an object isn't released and garbage-collected if there's at least one reference to it. And if the inner function is still referring to the stack frame in which it was defined, then the outer function will stick around as long as the inner function exists.

Solution

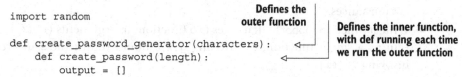

```
import random

def create_password_generator(characters):
    def create_password(length):
        output = []
```

Defines the
outer function

Defines the inner function,
with def running each time
we run the outer function

```
for i in range(length):
    output.append(random.choice(characters))
return ''.join(output)
return create_password

alpha_password = create_password_generator('abcdef')
symbol_password = create_password_generator('!@#$%')

print(alpha_password(5))
print(alpha_password(10))

print(symbol_password(5))
print(symbol_password(10))
```

How long do we want the password to be?

Adds a new, random element from characters to output

Returns a string based on the elements of output

Returns the inner function to the caller

You can work through a version of this code in the Python Tutor at http://mng.bz/ GVEM.

Screencast solution

Watch this short video walkthrough of the solution: https://livebook.manning.com/ video/python-workout.

Beyond the exercise

Thinking of functions as data lets you work at even higher levels of abstraction than usual functions, and thus solve even higher level problems without worrying about the low-level details. However, it can take some time to internalize and understand how to pass functions as arguments to other functions, or to return functions from inside other functions. Here are some additional exercises you can try to better understand and work with them:

- Now that you've written a function to create passwords, write create_password_checker, which checks that a given password meets the IT staff's acceptability criteria. In other words, create a function with four parameters: min_uppercase, min_lowercase, min_punctuation, and min_digits. These represent the minimum number of uppercase letters, lowercase letters, punctuations, and digits for an acceptable password. The output from create_password_checker is a function that takes a potential password (string) as its input and returns a Boolean value indicating whether the string is an acceptable password.
- Write a function, getitem, that takes a single argument and returns a function f. The returned f can then be invoked on any data structure whose elements can be selected via square brackets, and then returns that item. So if I invoke f = getitem('a'), and if I have a dict d = {'a':1, 'b':2}, then f(d) will return 1. (This is very similar to operator.itemgetter, a very useful function in many circumstances.)
- Write a function, doboth, that takes two functions as arguments (f1 and f2) and returns a single function, g. Invoking g(x) should return the same result as invoking f2(f1(x)).

Summary

Writing simple Python functions isn't hard. But where Python's functions really shine is in their flexibility—especially when it comes to parameter interpretation—and in the fact that functions are data too. In this chapter, we explored all of these ideas, which should give you some thoughts about how to take advantage of functions in your own programs.

If you ever find yourself writing similar code multiple times, you should seriously consider generalizing it into a function that you can call from those locations. Moreover, if you find yourself implementing something that you might want to use in the future, implement it as a function. Besides, it's often easier to understand, maintain, and test code that has been broken into functions, so even if you aren't worried about reuse or higher levels of abstraction, it might still be beneficial to write your code as functions.

Functional programming with comprehensions

Programmers are always trying to do more with less code, while simultaneously making that code more reliable and easier to debug. And indeed, computer scientists have developed a number of techniques, each meant to bring us closer to that goal of short, reliable, maintainable, powerful code.

One set of techniques is known as *functional programming*. It aims to make programs more reliable by keeping functions short and data immutable. I think most developers would agree that short functions are a good idea, in no small part because they're easier to understand, test, and maintain.

But how can you enforce the writing of short functions? Immutable data. If you can't modify data from within a function, then the function will (in my experience) end up being shorter, with fewer potential paths to be tested. Functional programs thus end up having many short functions—in contrast with nonfunctional programs, which often have a smaller number of very long functions. Functional programming also assumes that functions can be passed as arguments to other functions, something that we've already seen to be the case in Python.

The good news is that functional techniques have the potential to make code short and elegant. The bad news is that for many developers, functional techniques aren't natural. Not modifying any values, and not keeping track of state, might be great ways to make your software more reliable, but they're almost guaranteed to confuse and frustrate many developers.

Consider, for example, that you have a `Person` object in a purely functional language. If the person wants to change their name, you're out of luck, because all data is immutable. Instead, you'll have to create a new person object based on the old one, but with the name changed. This isn't terrible in and of itself, but given that the real world changes, and that we want our programs to model the real world, keeping everything immutable can be frustrating.

Then again, because functional languages can't modify data, they generally provide mechanisms for taking a sequence of inputs, transforming them in some way, and producing a sequence of outputs. We might not be able to modify one `Person` object, but we can write a function that takes a list of `Person` objects, applies a Python expression to each one, and then gets a new list of `Person` objects back. In such a scenario, we perhaps haven't modified our original data, but we've accomplished the task. And the code needed to do this is generally quite short.

Now, Python isn't a functional language; we have mutable data types and assignment. But some functional techniques have made their way into the language and are considered standard Pythonic ways to solve some problems.

Specifically, Python offers *comprehensions,* a modern take on classic functions that originated in Lisp, one of the first high-level languages to be invented. Comprehensions make it relatively easy to create lists, sets, and dicts based on other data structures. The fact that Python's functions are objects, and can thus be passed as arguments or stored in data structures, also comes from the functional world.

Some exercise solutions have already used, or hinted at, comprehensions. In this chapter, we're going to concentrate on how and when to use these techniques, and expand on the ways we can use them.

In my experience, it's common to be indifferent to functional techniques, and particularly to comprehensions, when first learning about them. But over time—and yes, it can take years!—developers increasingly understand how, when, and why to apply them. So even if you can solve the problems in this chapter without using functional techniques, the point here is to get your hands dirty, try them, and start to see the logic and elegance behind this way of doing things. The benefits might not be immediately obvious, but they'll pay off over time.

If this all sounds very theoretical and you'd like to see some concrete examples of comprehensions versus traditional, procedural programming, then check out the "Writing comprehensions" sidebar coming up in this chapter, where I go through the differences more thoroughly.

Table 7.1 What you need to know

Concept	What is it?	Example	To learn more
List comprehension	Produces a list based on the elements of an iterable	`[x*x for x in range(5)]`	http://mng.bz/lGpy
Dict comprehension	Produces a dict based on the elements of an iterable	`{x : 2*x for x in range(5)}`	http://mng.bz/Vggy
Set comprehension	Produces a set based on the elements of an iterable	`{x*x for x in range(5)}`	http://mng.bz/GVxO

Table 7.1   What you need to know *(continued)*

Concept	What is it?	Example	To learn more
input	Prompts the user to enter a string, and returns a string	`input('Name: ')`	http://mng.bz/wB27
str.isdigit	Returns True or False, if the string is nonempty and contains only 0–9	`# returns True` `'5'.isdigit()`	http://mng.bz/oPVN
str.split	Breaks strings apart, returning a list	`# Returns ['ab', 'cd', 'ef']` `'ab cd ef'.split()`	http://mng.bz/aR4z

str.join	Combines strings to create a new one	`# Returns 'ab*cd*ef'`
		`'*'.join(['ab', 'cd',`
		`   'ef'])`
			http://mng.bz/gyYl

string.ascii _lowercase	All English lowercase letters	`string.ascii_lowercase`	http://mng.bz/zjxQ
enumerate	Returns an iterator of two-element tuples, with an index	`enumerate('abcd')`	http://mng.bz/qM1K

EXERCISE 28 ▪ Join numbers

People often ask me, "When should I use a comprehension, as opposed to a traditional for loop?"

My answer is basically as follows: when you want to transform an iterable into a list, you should use a comprehension. But if you just want to execute something for each element of an iterable, then a traditional for loop is better.

Put another way, is the point of your for loop the creation of a new list? If so, then use a comprehension. But if your goal is to execute something once for each element in an iterable, throwing away or ignoring any return value, then a for loop is preferable.

For example, I want to get the lengths of words in the string s. I can say

```
[len(one_word)
 for one_word in s.split()]
```

In this example, I care about the list we're creating, so I use a comprehension.

But if my string s contains a list of filenames, and I want to create a new file for each of these filenames, then I'm not interested in the return value. Rather, I want to iterate over the filenames and create a file, as follows:

```
for one_filename in s.split():
    with open(one_filename, 'w') as f:
        f.write(f'{one_filename}\n')
```

In this example, I open (and thus create) each file, and write to it the name of the file. Using a comprehension in this case would be inappropriate, because I'm not interested in the return value.

Transformations—taking values in a list, string, dict, or other iterable and producing a new list based on it—are common in programming. You might need to transform filenames into file objects, or words into their lengths, or usernames into user IDs. In all of these cases, a comprehension is the most Pythonic solution.

This exercise is meant to get your feet wet with comprehensions, and with implementing this idea. It might seem simple, but the underlying idea is deep and powerful and will help you to see additional opportunities to use comprehensions.

For this exercise, write a function (`join_numbers`) that takes a range of integers. The function should return those numbers as a string, with commas between the numbers. That is, given `range(15)` as input, the function should return this string:

```
0,1,2,3,4,5,6,7,8,9,10,11,12,13,14
```

Hint: if you're thinking that `str.join` (http://mng.bz/gyYl) is a good idea here, then you're mostly right—but remember that `str.join` won't work on a list of integers.

Working it out

In this exercise, we want to use `str.join` on a range, which is similar to a list of integers. If we try to invoke `str.join` right away, we'll get an error:

```
>>> numbers = range(15)
>>> ','.join(numbers)
Traceback (most recent call last):
  File "<stdin>", line 1, in <module>
TypeError: sequence item 0: expected str instance, int found
```

That's because `str.join` only works on a sequence of strings. We'll thus need to convert each of the integers in our range (`numbers`) into a string. Then, when we have a list of strings based on our range of integers, we can run `str.join`.

The solution is to use a list comprehension to invoke `str` on each of the numbers in the range. That will produce a list of strings, which is what `str.join` expects. How?

Consider this: a list comprehension says that we're going to create a new list. The elements of the new list are all based on the elements in the source iterator, after an expression is run on them. What we're doing is describing the new list in terms of the old one.

Here are some examples that can help you to see where and how to use list comprehensions:

■ I want to know the age of each student in a class. So we're starting with a list of student objects and ending up with a list of integers. You can imagine a `student_age` function being applied to each student to get their age:

```
[student_age(one_student)
 for one_student in all_students]
```

- I want to know how many mm of rain fell on each day of the previous month. So we're starting with a list of days and ending with a list of floats. You can imagine a `daily_rain` function being applied to each day:

```
[daily_rain(one_day)
 for one_day in most_recent_month]
```

- I want to know how many vowels were used in a book. So we would apply a `number_of_vowels` function to each word in the book, and then run the `sum` function on the resulting list:

```
[number_of_vowels(one_word)
 for one_word in open(filename).read().split()]
```

If these three examples look quite similar, that's because they are; part of the power of list comprehensions is the simple formula that we repeat. Each list comprehension contains two parts:

1 The source iterable
2 The expression we'll invoke once for each element

In the case of our exercise here, we had a list of integers. By applying the `str` function on each int in the list, we got back a list of strings. `str.join` works fine on lists of strings.

> **NOTE** We'll get into the specifics of the iterator protocol in chapter 10, which is dedicated to that subject. You don't need to understand those details to use comprehensions. However, if you're particularly interested in what counts as an "iterable," go ahead and read the first part of that chapter before continuing here.

Writing comprehensions

Comprehensions are traditionally written on a single line:

```
[x*x for x in range(5)]
```

I find that especially for new Python developers, but even for experienced ones, it's hard to figure out what's going on. Things get even worse if you add a condition:

```
[x*x for x in range(5) if x%2]
```

For this reason, I strongly suggest that Python developers break up their list comprehensions. Python is forgiving about whitespace if we're inside of parentheses, which is always (by definition) the case when we're in a comprehension. We can break up this comprehension as follows:

```
[x*x                          ⟵┐ Expression
 for x in range(5)            ⟵──┐ Iteration
 if x%2]                      ⟵┐
                                 Condition
```

By separating the expression, iteration, and condition on different lines, the comprehension becomes more ... comprehensible. It's also easier to experiment with the comprehension in this way. I'll be writing most of my comprehensions in this book using this two- or three-line format, and I encourage you to do the same.

Note that using this technique, nested list comprehensions also become easier to understand:

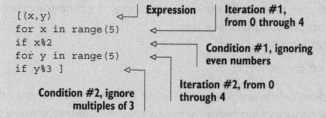

In other words, this list comprehension produces pairs of integers in which the first number must be odd, and the second number can't be divisible by 3. Nested comprehensions can be hard for anyone to understand, but when each of these sections appears on a line by itself, it's easier to understand what's happening.

Nested list comprehensions are great for working through complex data structures, such as lists of lists or lists of tuples. For example, let's assume that I have a dict describing the countries and cities I've visited in the last year:

```
all_places = {'USA': ['Philadelphia', 'New York', 'Cleveland', 'San Jose',
              'San Francisco'],
    'China': ['Beijing', 'Shanghai', 'Guangzhou'],
    'UK': ['London'],
    'India': ['Hyderabad']}
```

If I want a list of cities I've visited, ignoring the countries, I can use a nested list comprehension:

```
[one_city
 for one_country, all_cities in all_places.items()
 for one_city in all_cities]
```

I can also create a list of (city, country) tuples:

```
[(one_city, one_country)
 for one_country, all_cities in all_places.items()
 for one_city in all_cities]
```

And of course, I can always sort them using sorted:

```
[(one_city, one_country)
 for one_country, all_cities in sorted(all_places.items())
 for one_city in sorted(all_cities)]
```

Now, a list comprehension immediately produces a list—which, if you're dealing with large quantities of data, can result in the use of a great deal of memory. For this reason, many Python developers would argue that we'd be better off using a generator expression (http://mng.bz/K2M0).

Generator expressions look just like list comprehensions, except that instead of using square brackets, they use regular, round parentheses. However, this turns out to make a big difference: a list comprehension has to create and return its output list in one fell swoop, which can potentially use lots of memory. A generator expression, by contrast, returns its output one piece at a time.

For example, consider

```
sum([x*x for x in range(100000)])
```

In this code, sum is given one input, a list of integers. It iterates over the list of integers and sums them. But consider that before sum can run, the comprehension needs to finish creating the entire list of integers. This list can potentially be quite large and consume a great deal of memory.

By contrast, consider this code:

```
sum((x*x for x in range(100000)))
```

Here, the input to sum isn't a list; it's a generator, one that we created via our generator expression. sum will return precisely the same result as it did previously. However, whereas our first example created a list containing 100,000 elements, the latter uses much less memory. The generator returns one element at a time, waiting for sum to request the next item in line. In this way, we're only consuming one integer's worth of memory at a time, rather than a huge list of integers' memory. The bottom line, then, is that you can use generator expressions almost anywhere you can use comprehensions, but you'll use much less memory.

It turns out that when we put a generator expression in a function call, we can remove the inner parentheses:

```
sum(x*x for x in range(100000))
```

And thus, here's the syntax that you saw in the solution to this exercise, but using a generator expression:

```
numbers = range(15)

print(','.join(str(number)
               for number in numbers))
```

Solution

```
def join_numbers(numbers):
    return ','.join(str(number)      ◁── 
                    for number in numbers)   ◁──


print(join_numbers(range(15)))
```

Applies str to each number and puts the new string in the output list

Iterates over the elements of numbers

You can work through a version of this code in the Python Tutor at http://mng.bz/zj4w.

Screencast solution

Watch this short video walkthrough of the solution: https://livebook.manning.com/video/python-workout.

Beyond the exercise

Here are a few ways you might want to go beyond this exercise, and push yourself to use list comprehensions in new ways:

- As in the exercise, take a list of integers and turn them into strings. However, you'll only want to produce strings for integers between 0 and 10. Doing this will require understanding the if statement in list comprehensions as well.
- Given a list of strings containing hexadecimal numbers, sum the numbers together.
- Use a list comprehension to reverse the word order of lines in a text file. That is, if the first line is abc def and the second line is ghi jkl, then you should return the list ['def abc', 'jkl ghi'].

---

map, filter, and comprehensions

Comprehensions, at their heart, do two different things. First, they transform one sequence into another, applying an expression on each element of the input sequence. Second, they filter out elements from the output. Here's an example:

```
[x*x                      ◁———| x squared
  for x in range(10)      ◁——— For each number from 0–9
  if x%2 == 0]            ◁———| But only if x is even
```

The first line is where the transformation takes place, and the third line is where the filtering takes place. Before Python's comprehensions, these features were traditionally implemented using two functions: map and filter. Indeed, these functions continue to exist in Python, even if they're not used all that often.

map takes two arguments: a function and an iterable. It applies the function to each element of the iterable, returning a new iterable; for example

```
words = 'this is a bunch of words'.split()   ◁——| Creates a list of strings, and assigns it to "words"
x = map(len, words)                           ◁——| Applies the len function to each word, resulting in an iterable of integers
print(sum(x))         ◁——| Uses the sum function on x
```

(continued)

Notice that map always returns an iterable that has the same length as its input. That's because it doesn't have a way to remove elements. It applies its input function once per input element. We can thus say that map transforms but doesn't filter.

The function passed to map can be any function or method that takes a single argument. You can use built-in functions or write your own. The key thing to remember is that it's the output from the function that's placed in the output iterable.

filter also takes two arguments, a function and an iterable, and it applies the function to each element. But here, the output of the function determines whether the element will appear in the output—it doesn't transform the element at all; for example

```
words = 'this is a bunch of words'.split()
```
Creates a list of strings, and assigns it to "words"

```
def is_a_long_word(one_word):
    return len(one_word) > 4
```
Defines a function that returns a True or False value, based on the word passed to it

```
x = filter(is_a_long_word, words)
print(' '.join(x))
```
Applies our function to each word in "words"

Shows the words that passed through the filter

While the function passed to filter doesn't have to return a True or False value, its result will be interpreted as a Boolean and used to determine if the element is put into the output sequence. So it's usually a good idea to pass a function that returns a True or False.

The combination of map and filter means that you can take an iterable, filter its elements, then apply a function to each of its elements. This turns out to be extremely useful and explains why map and filter have been around for so long—about 50 years, in fact.

The fact that functions can be passed as arguments is central to the ability of both map and filter to even execute. That's one reason why these techniques are a core part of functional programming, because they require that functions can be treated as data.

That said, comprehensions are considered to be the modern way to do this kind of thing in Python. Whereas we pass functions to map and filter, we pass expressions to comprehensions.

Why, then, do map and filter continue to exist in the language, if comprehensions are considered to be better? Partly for nostalgic and historical reasons, but also because they can sometimes do things you can't easily do with comprehensions. For example, map can take multiple iterables in its input and then apply functions that will work with each of them:

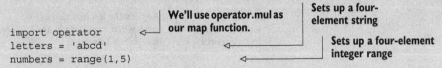

We'll use operator.mul as our map function.
Sets up a four-element string
Sets up a four-element integer range

```
import operator
letters = 'abcd'
numbers = range(1,5)
```

```
x = map(operator.mul, letters, numbers)          ◁──── Applies operator.mul (multiply)
print(' '.join(x))    ◁──                                to the corresponding elements
                        │                                of letters and numbers
                        │   Joins the strings
                        │   together with spaces
                        │   and prints the result
```

This code prints the following:

```
a bb ccc dddd
```

Using a comprehension, we could rewrite the code as

```
import operator
letters = 'abcd'
numbers = range(1,5)

print(' '.join(operator.mul(one_letter, one_number)
            for one_letter, one_number in zip(letters, numbers)))
```

Notice that to iterate over both `letters` and `numbers` at the same time, I had to use `zip` here. By contrast, `map` can simply take additional iterable arguments.

What is an expression?

An *expression* is anything in Python that returns a value. If that seems a bit abstract to you, then you can just think of an expression as anything you can assign to a variable, or return from a function. So `5` is an expression, as is `5+3`, as is `len('abcd')`.

When I say that comprehensions use expressions, rather than functions, I mean that we don't pass a function. Rather, we just pass the thing that we want Python to evaluate, akin to passing the body of the function without passing the formal function definition.

EXERCISE 29 ▪ Add numbers

In the previous exercise, we took a sequence of numbers and turned it into a sequence of strings. This time, we'll do the opposite—take a sequence of strings, turn them into numbers, and then sum them. But we're going to make it a bit more complicated, because we're going to filter out those strings that can't be turned into integers.

Our function (`sum_numbers`) will take a string as an argument; for example

```
10 abc 20 de44 30 55fg 40
```

Given that input, our function should return `100`. That's because the function will ignore any word that contains nondigits.

Ask the user to enter integers, all at once, using `input` (http://mng.bz/wB27).

Working it out

In this exercise, we're given a string, which we assume contains integers separated by spaces. We want to grab the individual integers from the string and then sum them together. The easiest way to do this is to invoke str.split on the string, which returns a list of strings. By invoking str.split without any parameters, we tell Python that any combination of whitespace should be used as a delimiter.

Now we have a list of strings, rather than a list of integers. What we need to do is iterate over the strings, turning each one into an integer by invoking int on it. The easiest way to turn a list of strings into a list of integers is to use a list comprehension, as in the solution code. In theory, we could then invoke the built-in sum function on the list of integers, and we would be done.

But there's a catch. It's possible that the user's input includes elements that can't be turned into integers. We need to get rid of those; if we try to run int on the string abcd, the program will exit with an error.

Fortunately, list comprehensions can help us here too. We can use the third (filtering) line of the comprehension to indicate that only those strings that can be turned into numbers will pass through to the first line. We do this with an if statement, applying the str.isdigit method to find out whether we can successfully turn the word into an integer.

We then invoke sum on the generator expression, returning an integer. Finally, we print the sum using an f-string.

Solution

```
def sum_numbers(numbers):                 Creates an
    return sum(int(number)                integer based      Iterates through
                                          on number          each of the words
            for number in numbers.split()                    in numbers
            if number.isdigit())

print(sum_numbers('1 2 3 a b c 4'))       Ignores words that can't
                                          be turned into integers
```

You can work through a version of this code in the Python Tutor at http://mng.bz/046p.

Screencast solution

Watch this short video walkthrough of the solution: https://livebook.manning.com/video/python-workout.

Beyond the exercise

One of the most common uses for list comprehensions, at least in my experience, is for doing this combination of transformation and filtering. Here are a few additional exercises you could do to ensure that you understand not just the syntax, but also their potential:

- Show the lines of a text file that contain at least one vowel and contain more than 20 characters.

- In the United States, phone numbers have 10 digits—a three-digit area code, followed by a seven-digit number. Several times during my childhood, area codes would run out of phone numbers, forcing half of the population to get a new area code. After such a split, XXX-YYY-ZZZZ might remain XXX-YYY-ZZZZ, or it might become NNN-YYY-ZZZZ, with NNN being the new area code. The decision regarding which numbers remained and which changed was often made based on the phone numbers' final seven digits. Use a list comprehension to return a new list of strings, in which any phone number whose YYY begins with the digits 0–5 will have its area code changed to XXX+1. For example, given the list of strings `['123-456-7890', '123-333-4444', '123-777-8888']`, we want to convert them to `['124-456-7890', '124-333-4444', '124-777-8888']`.

- Define a list of five dicts. Each dict will have two key-value pairs, name and age, containing a person's name and age (in years). Use a list comprehension to produce a list of dicts in which each dict contains three key-value pairs: the original name, the original age, and a third `age_in_months` key, containing the person's age in months. However, the output should exclude any of the input dicts representing people over 20 years of age.

EXERCISE 30 ▪ Flatten a list

It's pretty common to use complex data structures to store information in Python. Sure, we could create a new class, but why do that when we can just use combinations of lists, tuples, and dicts? This means, though, that you'll sometimes need to unravel those complex data structures, turning them into simpler ones.

In this exercise, we'll practice doing such unraveling. Write a function that takes a list of lists (just one element deep) and returns a flat, one-dimensional version of the list. Thus, invoking

```
flatten([[1,2], [3,4]])
```

will return

```
[1,2,3,4]
```

Note that there are several possible solutions to this problem; I'm asking you to solve it with list comprehensions. Also note that we only need to worry about flattening a two-level list.

Working it out

As we've seen, list comprehensions allow us to evaluate an expression on each element of an iterable. But in a normal list comprehension, you can't return more elements than were in the input iterable. If the input iterable has 10 elements, for example, you can only return 10, or fewer than 10 if you use an `if` clause.

Nested list comprehensions change this a bit, in that the result may contain as many elements as there are sub-elements of the input iterable. Given a list of lists, the first `for` loop will iterate over every element in `mylist`. But the second `for` loop will iterate over the elements of the inner list. We can produce one output element for each inner input element, and that's what we do:

```
def flatten(mylist):
    return [one_element
            for one_sublist in mylist
            for one_element in one_sublist]
```

Solution

```
def flatten(mylist):
    return [one_element
            for one_sublist in mylist          Iterates through each
                                               element of mylist
            for one_element in one_sublist]
                                               Iterates through each
print(flatten([[1,2], [3,4]]))                 element of one_sublist
```

You can work through a version of this code in the Python Tutor at http://mng.bz/jg4P.

Screencast solution

Watch this short video walkthrough of the solution: https://livebook.manning.com/video/python-workout.

Beyond the exercise

Nested list comprehensions can be a bit daunting at first, but they can be quite helpful in many circumstances. Here are some exercises you can try to improve your understanding of how to use them:

- Write a version of the `flatten` function mentioned earlier called `flatten_odd_ints`. It'll do the same thing as `flatten`, but the output will only contain odd integers. Inputs that are neither odd nor integers should be excluded. Inputs containing strings that could be converted to integers should be converted; other strings should be excluded.
- Define a dict that represents the children and grandchildren in a family. (See figure 7.1 for a graphic representation.) Each key will be a child's name, and each value will be a list of strings representing their children (i.e., the family's grandchildren). Thus the dict `{'A':['B', 'C', 'D'], 'E':['F', 'G']}` means

that A and E are siblings; A's children are B, C, and D; and E's children are F and G. Use a list comprehension to create a list of the grandchildren's names.

■ Redo this exercise, but replace each grandchild's name (currently a string) with a dict. Each dict will contain two name-value pairs, name and age. Produce a list of the grandchildren's names, sorted by age, from eldest to youngest.

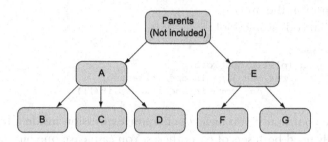

Figure 7.1 Graph of the family for nested list comprehensions

EXERCISE 31 ■ Pig Latin translation of a file

List comprehensions are great when you want to transform a list. But they can actually work on any iterable—that is, any Python object on which you can run a for loop. This means that the source data for a list comprehension can be a string, list, tuple, dict, set, or even a file.

In this exercise, I want you to write a function that takes a filename as an argument. It returns a string with the file's contents, but with each word translated into Pig Latin, as per our `plword` function in chapter 2 on "strings." The returned translation can ignore newlines and isn't required to handle capitalization and punctuation in any specific way.

Working it out

We've seen that nested list comprehensions can be used to iterate over complex data structures. In this case, we're iterating over a file. And indeed, we could iterate over each line of the file.

But we can break the problem down further, using a nested list comprehension to first iterate over each line of the file, and then over each word within the current line. Our `plword` function can then operate on a single word at a time.

I realize that nested list comprehensions can be hard, at least at first, to read and understand. But as you use them, you'll likely find that they allow you to elegantly break down a problem into its components.

There is a bit of a problem with what we've done here, but it might not seem obvious at first. List comprehensions, by their very nature, produce lists. This means that if we translate a large file into Pig Latin, we might find ourselves with a very long list. It would be better to return an iterator object that would save memory, only calculating the minimum necessary for each iteration.

It turns out that doing so is quite easy. We can use a generator expression (as suggested in this chapter's first exercise), which looks almost precisely like a list comprehension, but using round parentheses rather than square brackets. We can put a generator expression in a call to `str.join`, just as we could put in a list comprehension, saving memory in the process.

Here's how that code would look:

```python
def plfile(filename):
    return ' '.join((plword(one_word)
                     for one_line in open(filename)
                     for one_word in one_line.split())))
```

But wait—it turns out that if you have a generator expression inside a function call, you don't actually need both sets of parentheses. You can leave one out, which means the code will look like this:

```python
def plfile(filename):
    return ' '.join(plword(one_word)
                    for one_line in open(filename)
                    for one_word in one_line.split())
```

We've now not only accomplished our original task, we've done so using less memory than a list comprehension requires. There might be a slight trade-off in terms of speed, but this is usually considered worthwhile, given the potential problems you'll encounter reading a huge file into memory all at once.

Solution

```python
def plword(word):
    if word[0] in 'aeiou':
        return word + 'way'

    return word[1:] + word[0] + 'ay'
```

```python
def plfile(filename):
    return ' '.join(plword(one_word)
                    for one_line in open(filename)   ⬅  Iterates through each
                    for one_word in one_line.split())  ⬅  line of filename

                                                          Iterates through
                                                          each word in the
                                                          current line
```

You can work through a version of this code in the Python Tutor at http://mng.bz/ K2xP.

Note that because the Python Tutor doesn't support working with external files, I used an instance of `StringIO` to simulate a file.

Screencast solution

Watch this short video walkthrough of the solution: https://livebook.manning.com/video/python-workout.

Beyond the exercise

Whenever you're transforming and/or filtering complex or nested data structures, or (as in the case of a file) something that can be treated as a nested data structure, it's often useful to use a nested list comprehension:

- In this exercise, `plfile` applied the `plword` function to every word in a file. Write a new function, `funcfile`, that will take two arguments—a filename and a function. The output from the function should be a string, the result of invoking the function on each word in the text file. You can think of this as a generic version of `plfile`, one that can return any string value.

- Use a nested list comprehension to transform a list of dicts into a list of two-element (name-value) tuples, each of which represents one of the name-value pairs in one of the dicts. If more than one dict has the same name-value pair, then the tuple should appear twice.

- Assume that you have a list of dicts, in which each dict contains two name-value pairs: `name` and `hobbies`, where `name` is the person's name and `hobbies` is a set of strings representing the person's hobbies. What are the three most popular hobbies among the people listed in the dicts?

EXERCISE 32 ▪ Flip a dict

The combination of comprehensions and dicts can be quite powerful. You might want to modify an existing dict, removing or modifying certain elements. For example, you might want to remove all users whose ID number is lower than 500. Or you might want to find the user IDs of all users whose names begin with the letter "A".

It's also not uncommon to want to flip a dict—that is, to exchange its keys and values. Imagine a dict in which the keys are usernames and the values are user ID numbers; it might be useful to flip that so that you can search by ID number.

For this exercise, first create a dict of any size, in which the keys are unique and the values are also unique. (A key may appear as a value, or vice versa.) Here's an example:

```
d = {'a':1, 'b':2, 'c':3}
```

Turn the dict inside out, such that the keys and the values are reversed.

Working it out

Just as list comprehensions provide an easy way to create lists based on another iterable, dict comprehensions provide an easy way to create a dict based on an iterable. The syntax is as follows:

```
{ KEY : VALUE
    for ITEM in ITERABLE }
```

In other words

- The source for our dict comprehension is an iterable—typically a string, list, tuple, dict, set, or file.
- We iterate over each such item in a `for` loop.
- For each item, we then output a key-value pair.

Notice that a colon (`:`) separates the key from the value. That colon is part of the syntax, which means that the expressions on either side of the colon are evaluated separately and can't share data.

In this particular case, we're looping over the elements of a dict named d. We use the `dict.items` method to do so, which returns two values—the key and value—with each iteration. These two values are passed by parallel assignment to the variables `key` and `value`.

Another way of solving this exercise is to iterate over d, rather than over the output of `d.items()`. That would provide us with the keys, requiring that we retrieve each value:

```
{ d[key]:key for key in d }
```

In a comprehension, I'm trying to create a new object based on an old one. It's all about the values that are returned by the expression at the start of the comprehension. By contrast, `for` loops are about commands, and executing those commands.

Consider what your goal is, and whether you're better served with a comprehension or a `for` loop; for example

- Given a string, you want a list of the `ord` values for each character. This should be a list comprehension, because you're creating a list based on a string, which is iterable.
- You have a list of dicts, in which each dict contains your friends' first and last names, and you want to insert this data into a database. In this case, you'll use a regular `for` loop, because you're interested in the side effects, not the return value.

Solution

```
def flipped_dict(a_dict):
    return {value: key
            for key, value in a_dict.items()}

print(flipped_dict({'a':1, 'b':2, 'c':3}))
```

All iterables are acceptable in a comprehension, even those that return two-element tuples, such as dict.items.

You can work through this code in the Python Tutor at http://mng.bz/905x.

Screencast solution

Watch this short video walkthrough of the solution: https://livebook.manning.com/video/python-workout.

Beyond the exercise

Dict comprehensions provide us with a useful way to create new dicts. They're typically used when you want to create a dict based on an iterable, such as a list or file. I'm especially partial to using them when I want to read from a file and turn the file's contents into a dict. Here are some additional ideas for ways to practice the use of dict comprehensions:

- Given a string containing several (space-separated) words, create a dict in which the keys are the words, and the values are the number of vowels in each word. If the string is "this is an easy test," then the resulting dict would be `{'this':1, 'is':1, 'an':1, 'easy':2, 'test':1}`.
- Create a dict whose keys are filenames and whose values are the lengths of the files. The input can be a list of files from `os.listdir` (http://mng.bz/YreB) or `glob.glob` (http://mng.bz/044N).
- Find a configuration file in which the lines look like "name=value." Use a dict comprehension to read from the file, turning each line into a key-value pair.

EXERCISE 33 ■ Transform values

This exercise combines showing how you can receive a function as a function argument, and how comprehensions can help us to elegantly solve a wide variety of problems.

The built-in map (http://mng.bz/Ed2O) takes two arguments: (a) a function and (b) an iterable. It returns a new sequence, which is the result of applying the function to each element of the input iterable. A full discussion of map is in the earlier sidebar, "map, filter, and comprehensions."

In this exercise, we're going to create a slight variation on map, one that applies a function to each of the values of a dict. The result of invoking this function, transform_values, is a new dict whose keys are the same as the input dict, but whose values have been transformed by the function. (The name of the function comes from Ruby on Rails, which provides a function of the same name.) The function passed to transform_values should take a single argument, the dict's value.

When your transform_values function works, you should be able to invoke it as follows:

```
d = {'a':1, 'b':2, 'c':3}
transform_values(lambda x: x*x, d)
```

The result of this call will be the following dict:

```
{'a': 1, 'b': 4, 'c': 9}
```

Working it out

The idea of `transform_values` is a simple one: you want to invoke a function repeatedly on the values of a dict. This means that you must iterate over the dict's key-value pairs. For each pair, you want to invoke a user-supplied function on the value.

We know that functions can be passed as arguments, just like any other data types. In this case, we're getting a function from the user so we can apply it. We apply functions with parentheses, so if we want to invoke the function `func` that the user passed to us, we simply say `func()`. Or in this case, since the function should take a single argument, we say `func(value)`.

We can iterate over a dict's key-value pairs with `dict.items` (http://mng.bz/4AeV), which returns an iterator that provides, one by one, the dict's key-value pairs. But that doesn't solve the problem of how to take these key-value pairs and turn them back into a dict.

The easiest, fastest, and most Pythonic way to create a dict based on an existing iterable is a dict comprehension. The dict we return from `transform_values` will have the same keys as our input dict. But as we iterate over the key-value pairs, we invoke `func(value)`, applying the user-supplied function to each value we get and using the output from that expression as our value. We don't even need to worry about what type of value the user-supplied function will return, because dict values can be of any type.

Solution

```
def transform_values(func, a_dict):
    return {key: func(value)            ← Applies the user-supplied function
                                              to each value in the dict
            for key, value in a_dict.items()}   ← Iterates through each
                                                    key-value pair in the dict
d = {'a':1, 'b':2, 'c':3}
print(transform_values(lambda x: x*x, d))
```

You can work through a version of this code in the Python Tutor at http://mng.bz/jg2z.

Screencast solution

Watch this short video walkthrough of the solution: https://livebook.manning.com/video/python-workout.

Beyond the exercise

Dict comprehensions are a powerful tool in any Python developer's arsenal. They allow us to create new dicts based on existing iterables. However, they can take some time to get used to, and to integrate into your development. Here are some additional exercises you can try to improve your understanding and use of dict comprehensions:

- Expand the `transform_values` exercise, taking two function arguments, rather than just one. The first function argument will work as before, being applied to the value and producing output. The second function argument takes two arguments, a key and a value, and determines whether there will be any output at all. That is, the second function will return `True` or `False` and will allow us to selectively create a key-value pair in the output dict.

- Use a dict comprehension to create a dict in which the keys are usernames and the values are (integer) user IDs, based on a Unix-style /etc/passwd file. Hint: in a typical /etc/passwd file, the usernames are the first field in a row (i.e., index 0), and the user IDs are the third field in a row (i.e., index 2). If you need to download a sample /etc/passwd file, you can get it from http://mng.bz/ 2XXg. Note that this sample file contains comment lines, meaning that you'll need to remove them when creating your dict.

- Write a function that takes a directory name (i.e., a string) as an argument. The function should return a dict in which the keys are the names of files in that directory, and the values are the file sizes. You can use `os.listdir` or `glob .glob` to get the files, but because only regular files have sizes, you'll want to filter the results using methods from `os.path`. To determine the file size, you can use `os.stat` or (if you prefer) just check the length of the string resulting from reading the file.

EXERCISE 34 ■ (Almost) supervocalic words

Part of the beauty of Python's basic data structures is that they can be used to solve a wide variety of problems. But it can sometimes be a challenge, especially at first, to decide which of the data structures is appropriate, and which of their methods will help you to solve problems most easily. Often, it's a combination of techniques that will provide the greatest help.

In this exercise, I want you to write a `get_sv` function that returns a set of all "supervocalic" words in the dict. If you've never heard the term *supervocalic* before, you're not alone: I only learned about such words several years ago. Simply put, such words contain all five vowels in English (a, e, i, o, and u), each of them appearing once and in alphabetical order.

For the purposes of this exercise, I'll loosen the definition, accepting any word that has all five vowels, in any order and any number of times. Your function should find all of the words that match this definition (i.e., contain a, e, i, o, and u) and return a set containing them.

Your function should take a single argument: the name of a text file containing one word per line, as in a Unix/Linux dict. If you don't have such a "words" file, you can download one from here: http://mng.bz/D2Rw.

Working it out

Before we can create a set of supervocalic words, or read from a file, we need to find a way to determine if a word is supervocalic. (Again, this isn't the precise, official definition.) One way would be to use in five times, once for each vowel. But this seems a bit extreme and inefficient.

What we can instead do is create a set from our word. After all, a string is a sequence, and we can always create a set from any sequence with the set built in.

Fine, but how does that help us? If we already have a set of vowels, we can check to see if they're all in the word with the < operator. Normally, < checks to see if one data point is less than another. But in the case of sets, it returns True if the item on the left is a subset of the item on the right.

This means that, given the word "superlogical," I can do the following:

```
vowels = {'a', 'e', 'i', 'o', 'u'}
word = 'superlogical'

if vowels < set(word):
    print('Yes, it is supervocalic!')
else:
    print('Nope, just a regular word')
```

This is good for one word. But how can we do it for many words in a file? The answer could be a list comprehension. After all, we can think of our file as an iterator, one that returns strings. If the words file contains one word per line, then iterating over the lines of the file really means iterating over the different lines. If a set of the vowels is a set based on the current word, then we'll consider it to be supervocalic and will include the current word in the output list.

But we don't want a list, we want a set! Fortunately, the difference between creating a list comprehension and a set comprehension is a pair of brackets. We use square brackets ([]) for a list comprehension and curly braces ({}) for a set comprehension. A comprehension with curly braces and a colon is a dict comprehension; without the colon, it's a set comprehension.

To summarize

- We iterate over the lines of the file.
- We turn each word into a set and check that the vowels are a subset of our word's letters.
- If the word passes this test, we include it (the word) in the output.
- The output is all put into a set, thanks to a set comprehension.

Using sets as the basis for textual comparisons might not seem obvious, at least at first. But it's good to learn to think in these ways, taking advantage of Python's data structures in ways you never considered before.

Solution

```
def get_sv(filename):
    vowels = {'a', 'e', 'i', 'o', 'u'}

    return {word.strip()
            for word in open(filename)
            if vowels < set(word.lower())}
```

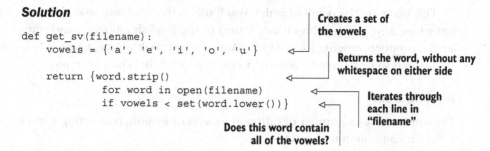

Creates a set of the vowels

Returns the word, without any whitespace on either side

Iterates through each line in "filename"

Does this word contain all of the vowels?

You can work through a version of this code in the Python Tutor at http://mng.bz/lG18. Note that because the Python Tutor doesn't support working with external files, I used an instance of `StringIO` to simulate a file.

Screencast solution

Watch this short video walkthrough of the solution: https://livebook.manning.com/video/python-workout.

Beyond the exercise

Set comprehensions are great in a variety of circumstances, including when you have inputs and you want to crunch them down to only have the distinct (unique) elements. Here are some additional ways for you to use and practice your set-comprehension chops:

- In the /etc/passwd file you used earlier, what different shells (i.e., command interpreters, named in the final field on each line) are assigned to users? Use a set comprehension to gather them.
- Given a text file, what are the lengths of the different words? Return a set of different word lengths in the file.
- Create a list whose elements are strings—the names of people in your family. Now use a set comprehension (and, better yet, a nested set comprehension) to find which letters are used in your family members' names.

EXERCISE 35A ▪ Gematria, part 1

In this exercise, we're going to again try something that sits at the intersection of strings and comprehensions. This time, it's dict comprehensions.

When you were little, you might have created or used a "secret" code in which a was 1, b was 2, c was 3, and so forth, until z (which was 26). This type of code happens to be quite ancient and was used by a number of different groups more than 2,000 years ago. "Gematria," (http://mng.bz/B2R8) as it is known in Hebrew, is the way in which biblical verses have long been numbered. And of course, it's not even worth describing it as a secret code, despite what you might have thought while little.

This exercise, the result of which you'll use in the next one, asks that you create a dict whose keys are the (lowercase) letters of the English alphabet, and whose values are the numbers ranging from 1 to 26. And yes, you could simply type {'a':1, 'b':2, 'c':3} and so forth, but I'd like you to do this with a dict comprehension.

Working it out

The solution uses a number of different aspects of Python, combining them to create a dict with a minimum of code.

First, we want to create a dict, and thus turn to a dict comprehension. Our keys are going to be the lowercase letters of the English alphabet, and the values are going to be the numbers from 1 to 26.

We could create the string of lowercase letters. But, rather than doing that ourselves, we can rely on the string module, and its string.ascii_lowercase attribute, which comes in handy in such situations.

But how can we number the letters? We can use the enumerate built-in iterator, which will number our characters one at a time. We can then catch the iterated tuples via unpacking, grabbing the index and character separately:

```
{char:index
 for index, char in enumerate(string.ascii_lowercase)}
```

The only problem with doing this is that enumerate starts counting at 0, and we want to start counting at 1. We could, of course, just add 1 to the value of index. However, we can do even better than that by asking enumerate to start counting at 1, and we do so by passing 1 to it as the second argument:

```
{char:index
 for index, char in enumerate(string.ascii_lowercase, 1)}
```

And, sure enough, this produces the dict that we want. We'll use it in the next exercise.

Solution

```
import string

def gematria_dict():
    return {char: index              ◄──  Returns the key-value pair,
            for index, char                with the character and an
                in enumerate(string.ascii_lowercase,   integer
                    1)}              ◄──
                                          Iterates over lowercase
print(gematria_dict())                    letters with enumerate
```

You can work through a version of this code in the Python Tutor at http://mng.bz/WPx4.

Screencast solution

Watch this short video walkthrough of the solution: https://livebook.manning.com/video/python-workout.

Beyond the exercise

Dicts are also known as key-value pairs, for the simple reason that they contain keys and values—and because associations between two different types of data are extremely common in programming contexts. Often, if you can get your data into a dict, it becomes easier to work with and manipulate. For that reason, it's important to know how to get information into a dict from a variety of different formats and sources. Here are some additional exercises to practice doing so:

- Many programs' functionality is modified via configuration files, which are often set using name-value pairs. That is, each line of the file contains text in the form of name=value, where the = sign separates the name from the value. I've prepared one such sample config file at http://mng.bz/rryD. Download this file, and then use a dict comprehension to read its contents from disk, turning it into a dict describing a user's preferences. Note that all of the values will be strings.
- Create a dict based on the config file, as in the previous exercise, but this time, all of the values should be integers. This means that you'll need to filter out (and ignore) those values that can't be turned into integers.
- It's sometimes useful to transform data from one format into another. Download a JSON-formatted list of the 1,000 largest cities in the United States from http://mng.bz/Vgd0. Using a dict comprehension, turn it into a dict in which the keys are the city names, and the values are the populations of those cities. Why are there only 925 key-value pairs in this dict? Now create a new dict, but set each key to be a tuple containing the state and city. Does that ensure there will be 1,000 key-value pairs?

EXERCISE 35B ▪ Gematria, part 2

In the previous exercise, you created a dict that allows you to get the numeric value from any lowercase letter. As you can imagine, we can use this dict not only to find the numeric value for a single letter, but to sum the values from the letters in a word, thus getting the word's "value." One of the games that Jewish mystics enjoy playing (although they would probably be horrified to hear me describe it as a game) is to find words with the same gematria value. If two words have the same gematria value, then they're linked in some way.

In this exercise, you'll write two functions:

- gematria_for, which takes a single word (string) as an argument and returns the gematria score for that word

- gematria_equal_words, which takes a single word and returns a list of those dict words whose gematria scores match the current word's score.

For example, if the function is called with the word cat, with a gematria value of 24 (3 + 1 + 20), then the function will return a list of strings, all of whose gematria values are also 24. (This will be a long list!) Any nonlowercase characters in the user's input should count 0 toward our final score for the word. Your source for the dict words will be the Unix file you used earlier in this chapter, which you can load into a list comprehension.

Working it out

This solution combines a large number of techniques that we've discussed so far in this book, and that you're likely to use in your Python programming work. (However, I do hope that you're not doing too many gematria calculations.)

First, how do we calculate the gematria score for a word, given our gematria dict? We want to iterate through each letter in a word, grabbing the score from the dict. And if the letter isn't in the dict, we'll give it a value of 0.

The standard way to do this would be with a for loop, using dict.get:

```
total = 0
for one_letter in word:
    total += gematria.get(one_letter, 0)
```

And there's nothing wrong with this, per se. But comprehensions are usually your best bet when you're starting with one iterable and trying to produce another iterable. And in this case, we can iterate over the letters in our word in a list comprehension, invoking sum on the list of integers that will result:

```
def gematria_for(word):
    return sum(gematria.get(one_char,0)
               for one_char in word)
```

Once we can calculate the gematria for one word, we need to find all of the dict words that are equivalent to it. We can do that, once again, with a list comprehension—this time, using the if clause to filter out those words whose gematria isn't equal:

```
def gematria_equal_words(word):
    our_score = gematria_for(input_word.lower())
    return [one_word.strip()
            for one_word in open('/usr/share/dict/words')
            if gematria_for(one_word.lower()) == our_score]
```

As you can see, we're forcing the words to be in lowercase. But we're not modifying or otherwise transforming the word on the first line of our comprehension. Rather, we're just filtering.

Meanwhile, we're iterating over each of the words in the dict file. Each word in that file ends with a newline, which doesn't affect our gematria score but isn't something we want to return to the user in our list comprehension.

Finally, this exercise demonstrates that when you're using a comprehension, and your output expression is a complex one, it's often a good idea to create a separate function that you can repeatedly call.

Solution

```
import string

def gematria_dict():
    return {char: index
            for index, char
            in enumerate(string.ascii_lowercase,
                         1)}

GEMATRIA = gematria_dict()

def gematria_for(word):
    return sum(GEMATRIA.get(one_char, 0)
               for one_char in word)


def gematria_equal_words(input_word):
    our_score = gematria_for(input_word.lower())
    return [one_word.strip()
            for one_word in
                open('/usr/share/dict/words')
            if gematria_for(one_word.lower()) ==
                our_score]
```

Gets the value for the current character, or 0 if the character isn't in the "GEMATRIA" dict

Iterates over the characters in "word"

Gets the total score for the input word

Removes leading and trailing whitespace from "one_word"

Iterates over each word in the English-language dict

Only adds the current word to our returned list if its gematria score matches ours

Note: there is no Python Tutor link for this exercise, because it uses an external file.

Screencast solution

Watch this short video walkthrough of the solution: https://livebook.manning.com/video/python-workout.

Beyond the exercise

Once you have data in a dict, you can often use a comprehension to transform it in various ways. Here are some additional exercises you can use to sharpen your skills with dicts and dict comprehensions:

■ Create a dict whose keys are city names, and whose values are temperatures in Fahrenheit. Now use a dict comprehension to transform this dict into a new one, keeping the old keys but turning the values into the temperature in degrees Celsius.

■ Create a list of tuples in which each tuple contains three elements: (1) the author's first and last names, (2) the book's title, and (3) the book's price in U.S. dollars. Use a dict comprehension to turn this into a dict whose keys are the book's titles, with the values being another (sub-) dict, with keys for (a) the author's first name, (b) the author's last name, and (c) the book's price in U.S. dollars.

- Create a dict whose keys are currency names and whose values are the price of that currency in U.S. dollars. Write a function that asks the user what currency they use, then returns the dict from the previous exercise as before, but with its prices converted into the requested currency.

Summary

Comprehensions are, without a doubt, one of the most difficult topics for people to learn when they start using Python. The syntax is a bit weird, and it's not even obvious where and when to use comprehensions. In this chapter, you saw many examples of how and when to use comprehensions, which will hopefully help you not only to use them, but also to see opportunities to do so.

Modules and packages

8

Functional programming, which we explored in the previous chapter, is one of the knottiest topics you'll encounter in the programming world. I'm happy to tell you that this chapter, about Python's modules, will provide a stark contrast, and will be one of the easiest in this book. Modules are important, but they're also very straightforward to create and use. So if you find yourself reading this chapter and thinking, "Hey, that's pretty obvious," well, that's just fine.

What are modules in Python, and how do they help us? I've already mentioned the acronym DRY, short for "Don't repeat yourself," several times in this book. As programmers, we aim to "DRY up" our code by taking identical sections of code and using them multiple times. Doing so makes it easier to understand, manage, and maintain our code. We can also more easily test such code.

When we have repeated code in a single program, we can DRY it up by writing a function and then calling that function repeatedly. But what if we have repeated code that's used across multiple programs? We can then create a library—or, as it's known in the world of Python, a *module*.

Modules actually accomplish two things in Python. First, they make it possible for us to reuse code across programs, helping us to improve the reusability and maintainability of our code. In this way, we can define functions and classes once, stick them into a module, and reuse them any number of times. This not only reduces the amount of work we need to do when implementing a new system, but also reduces our cognitive load, since we don't have to worry about the implementation details.

For example, let's say that your company has come up with a special pricing formula that combines the weather with stock-market indexes. You'll want to use that pricing formula in many parts of your code. Rather than repeating the code, you could define the function once, put it into a module, and then use that module everywhere in your program that you want to calculate and display prices.

You can define any Python object—from simple data structures to functions to classes—in a module. The main question is whether you want it to be shared across multiple programs, now or in the future.

Second, modules are Python's way of creating namespaces. If two people are collaborating on a software project, you don't want to have to worry about collisions between their chosen variable and function names, right? Each file—that is, module—has its own namespace, ensuring that there can't be conflicts between them.

Python comes with a large number of modules, and even the smallest nontrivial Python program will use import (http://mng.bz/xWme), to use one or more of them. In addition to the *standard library*, as it's known, Python programmers can take advantage of a large number of modules available on the Python Package Index (https://pypi.org). In this chapter, we'll explore the use and creation of modules, including packages.

> **HINT** If you visit PyPI at https://pypi.org, you'll discover that the number of community-contributed, third-party packages is astonishingly large. Just as of this writing, there are more than 200,000 packages on PyPI, many of which are buggy or unmaintained. How can you know which of these packages is worthwhile and which isn't? The site "Awesome Python," at http://mng.bz/AA0K, is an attempt to remedy this situation, with edited lists of known stable, maintained packages on a variety of topics. This is a good first place to check for packages before going to PyPI. Although it doesn't guarantee that the package you use will be excellent, it certainly improves the chances of this being the case.

Table 8.1 What you need to know

Concept	What is it?	Example	To learn more
`import`	Statement for importing modules	`import os`	http://mng.bz/xWme
`from X import Y`	Imports module X, but only defines Y as a global variable	`from os import sep`	http://mng.bz/xWme
`importlib.reload`	Re-imports an already loaded module, typically to update definitions during development	`importlib.reload (mymod)`	http://mng.bz/Z2P0
`pip`	Command-line program for installing packages from PyPI	`pip install packagename`	https://pypi.org/
`Decimal`	Class that accurately handles floating-point numbers	`from decimal import Decimal`	http://mng.bz/RAX0

Importing modules

One of the catchphrases in the Python world is "batteries included." This refers to the many TV commercials I saw as a child that would spend their first 29.5 seconds enticing us to buy their exciting, fun-looking, beautiful toys ... only to spend the final half second saying, "batteries not included"—meaning that it wasn't enough to buy the product to enjoy it, we had to buy batteries as well.

"Batteries included" refers to the fact that when you download and install Python, you have everything you're going to need to get your work done. This isn't quite as true as used to be the case, and PyPI (the Python Package Index, described separately in this chapter) provides us with a huge collection of third-party Python modules that we can use to improve our products. But the fact remains that the *standard library*, meaning the stuff that comes with Python when we install it, includes a huge number of modules that we can use in our programs.

The most commonly used things in the standard library, such as lists and dicts, are built into the language, thanks to a namespace known as `builtins`. You don't need to worry about importing things in the `builtins` module, thanks to the LEGB rule that I discussed back in chapter 6. But anything else in the standard library must be loaded into memory before it can be used.

We load such a module using the `import` statement. The simplest version of `import` looks like

```
import MODULENAME
```

For example, if I want to use the `os` module, then I'll write

```
import os
```

Notice a couple of things about this statement:

First, it's not a function; you don't say `import(os)`, but rather `import os`.

Second, we don't import a filename. Rather, we indicate the variable that we want to define, rather than the file that should be loaded from the disk. So don't try to `import "os"` or even `import "os.py"`. Just as `def` defines a new variable that references a function, so too `import` defines a new variable that references a module.

When you `import os`, Python tries to find a file that matches the variable name you're defining. It'll typically look for `os.py` and `os.pyc`, where the former is the original source code and the latter is the byte-compiled version. (Python uses the filesystem's time-stamp to figure out which one is newer and creates a new byte-compiled version as necessary. So don't worry about compiling!)

Python looks for matching files in a number of directories, visible to you in `sys.path`. This is a list of strings representing directories; Python will iterate over each directory name until it finds a matching module name. If more than one directory contains a module with the same name, then the first one Python encounters is loaded, and any subsequent modules will be completely ignored. This can often lead to confusion and conflicts, in my experience, so try to choose unusual and distinct names for your modules.

(continued)

Now, `import` has a number of variations that are useful to know, and that you'll probably see in existing code—as well as use in your own code. That said, the ultimate goal is the same: load a module, and define one or more module-related names in your name-space.

If you're happy loading a module and using its name as a variable, then `import MODULENAME` is a great way to go. But sometimes, that name is too long. For that reason, you'll want to give the module name an alias. You can do that with

```
import mymod as mm
```

When you use `as`, the name `mymod` will not be defined. However, the name `mm` will be defined. This is silly and unnecessary if your module name is going to be short. But if the name is long, or you're going to be referring to it a lot, then you might well want to give it a shorter alias. A classic example is NumPy (https://numpy.org/), which sits at the core of all of Python's scientific and numeric computing systems, including data science and machine learning. That module is typically imported with an alias of `np`:

```
import numpy as np
```

Once you've imported a module, all of the names that were defined in the file's global scope are available as attributes, via the module object. For example, the `os` module defines `sep`, which indicates what string separates elements of a directory path. You can access that value as `os.sep`. But if you're going to use it a lot, then it's a bit of a pain to constantly say `os.sep`. Wouldn't it be nice to just call it `sep`? You can't do that, of course, because the name `sep` would be a variable, whereas `os.sep` is an attribute.

However, you can bridge the gap and get the attribute loaded by using the following syntax:

```
from os import sep
```

Note that this won't define the `os` variable, but it will define the `sep` variable. You can use `from .. import` on more than one variable too:

```
from os import sep, path
```

Now, both `sep` and `path` will be defined as variables in your global scope.

Worried about one of these imported attributes clashing with an existing variable, method, or module name? Then you can use `from .. import .. as`:

```
from os import sep as s
```

There's a final version that I often see, and that I generally advise people not to use. It looks like this:

```
from os import *
```

This will load the os module into memory, but (more importantly) will take all of the attributes from os and define them as global variables in the current namespace. Given that we generally want to avoid global variables unless necessary, I see it as a problem when we allow the module to decide what variables should be defined.

> **NOTE** Not *all* names from a module will be imported with import *. Names starting with _ (underscore) will be ignored. Moreover, if the module defines a list of strings named __all__, only names specified in the module will be loaded with import *. However, from X import Y will always work, regardless of whether __all__ is defined.

At the end of the day, import makes functions, classes, and data available to you in your current namespace. Given the huge number of modules available, both in Python's standard library and on PyPI, that puts a lot of potential power at your fingertips—and explains why so many Python programs start with several lines of import statements.

EXERCISE 36 ■ Sales tax

Modules allow us to concentrate on higher-level thinking and avoid digging into the implementation details of complex functionality. We can thus implement a function once, stick it into a module, and use it many times to implement algorithms that we don't want to think about on a day-to-day basis. If you had to actually understand and wade through the calculations involved in internet security, for example, just to create a web application, you would never finish.

In this exercise, you'll implement a somewhat complex (and whimsical) function, in a module, to implement tax policy in the Republic of Freedonia. The idea is that the tax system is so complex that the government will supply businesses with a Python module implementing the calculations for them.

Sales tax on purchases in Freedonia depends on where the purchase was made, as well as the time of the purchase. Freedonia has four provinces, each of which charges its own percentage of tax:

- Chico: 50%
- Groucho: 70%
- Harpo: 50%
- Zeppo: 40%

Yes, the taxes are quite high in Freedonia (so high, in fact, that they're said to have a Marxist government). However, these taxes rarely apply in full. That's because the amount of tax applied depends on the hour at which the purchase takes place. The tax percentage is always multiplied by the hour at which the purchase was made. At midnight (i.e., when the 24-hour clock is 0), there's no sales tax. From 12 noon until 1 p.m., only 50% (12/24) of the tax applies. And from 11 p.m. until midnight, 95.8% (i.e., 23/24) of the tax applies.

Your job is to implement that Python module, freedonia.py. It should provide a function, calculate_tax, that takes three arguments: the amount of the purchase, the province in which the purchase took place, and the hour (an integer, from 0–24) at which it happened. The calculate_tax function should return the final price, as a float.

Thus, if I were to invoke

```
calculate_tax(500, 'Harpo', 12)
```

a $500 purchase in Harpo province (with 50%) tax would normally be $750. However, because the purchase was done at 12 noon, the tax is only half of its maximum, or $125, for a total of $625. If the purchase were made at 9 p.m. (i.e, 21:00 on a 24-hour clock), then the tax would be 87.5% of its full rate, or 43.75%, for a total price of $718.75.

Moreover, I want you to write this solution using two separate files. The calculate_tax function, as well as any supporting data and functions, should reside in the file freedonia.py, a Python module. The program that calls calculate_tax should be in a file called use_freedonia.py, which then uses import to load the function.

Working it out

The freedonia module does precisely what a Python module should do. Namely, it defines data structures and functions that provide functionality to one or more other programs. By providing this layer of abstraction, it allows a programmer to focus on what's important to them, such as the implementation of an online store, without having to worry about the nitty-gritty of particular details.

While some countries have extremely simple systems for calculating sales tax, others—such as the United States—have many overlapping jurisdictions, each of which applies its own sales tax, often at different rates and on different types of goods. Thus, while the Freedonia example is somewhat contrived, it's not unusual to purchase or use libraries to calculate taxes.

Our module defines a dict (RATES), in which the keys are the provinces of Freedonia, and the values are the taxation rates that should be applied there. Thus, we can find out the rate of taxation in Groucho province with RATES['Groucho']. Or we can ask the user to enter a province name in the province variable, and then get RATES[province]. Either way, that will give us a floating-point number that we can use to calculate the tax.

A wrinkle in the calculation of Freedonian taxation is the fact that taxes get progressively higher as the day goes on. To make this calculation easier, I wrote a time_percentage function, which simply takes the hour and returns it as a percentage of 24 hours.

NOTE In Python 2, integer division always returns an integer, even when that means throwing away the remainder. If you're using Python 2, be sure to divide the current hour not by 24 (an int) but by 24.0 (a float).

Finally, the `calculate_tax` function takes three parameters—the amount of the sale, the name of the province in which the sale took place, and the hour at which the sale happened—and returns a floating-point number indicating the actual, current tax rate.

The Decimal version

If you're actually doing calculations involving serious money, you should almost certainly *not* be using floats. Rather, you should use integers or the `Decimal` class, both of which are more accurate. (See chapter 1 for some more information on the inaccuracy of floats.) I wanted this exercise to concentrate on the creation of a module, and not the use of the `Decimal` class, so I didn't require it.

Here's how my solution would look using `Decimal`:

```
from decimal import Decimal

rates = {
    'Chico': Decimal('0.5'),
    'Groucho': Decimal('0.7'),
    'Harpo': Decimal('0.5'),
    'Zeppo': Decimal('0.4')
}

def time_percentage(hour):
    return hour / Decimal('24.0')

def calculate_tax(amount, state, hour):
    return float(amount + (amount * rates[state] * time_percentage(hour)))
```

Notice that this code uses `Decimal` on strings, rather than floats, to ensure maximum accuracy. We then return a floating-point number at the last possible moment. Also note that any `Decimal` value multiplied or divided by a number remains a `Decimal`, so we only need to make a conversion at the end.

Here's a program that uses our freedonia module:

```
from freedonia import calculate_tax

tax_at_12noon = calculate_tax(100, 'Harpo', 12)
tax_at_9pm = calculate_tax(100, 'Harpo', 21)

print(f'You owe a total of: {tax_at_12noon}')
print(f'You owe a total of: {tax_at_9pm}')
```

Error checking the Pythonic way

Since a module will be used by many other programs, it's important for it to not only be accurate, but also have decent error checking. In our particular case, for example, we would want to check that the hour is between 0 and 24.

(continued)

Right now, someone who passes an invalid hour to our function will still get an answer, albeit a nonsensical one. A better solution would be to have the function raise an exception if the input is invalid. And while we could raise a built-in Python exception (e.g., ValueError), it's generally a better idea to create your own exception class and raise it; for example

```python
class HourTooLowError(Exception): pass
class HourTooHighError(Exception): pass

def calculate_tax(amount, state, hour):
    if hour < 0:
        raise HourTooLowError(f'Hour of {hour} is < 0')

    if hour >= 24:
        raise HourTooHighError(f'Hour of {hour} is >= 24')

    return amount + (amount * rates[state] * time_percentage(hour))
```

Adding such exceptions to your code is considered very Pythonic and helps to ensure that anyone using your module will not accidentally get a bad result.

Solution

```python
RATES = {
    'Chico': 0.5,
    'Groucho': 0.7,
    'Harpo': 0.5,
    'Zeppo': 0.4
}

def time_percentage(hour):
    return hour / 24
```

This means we'll get 0% at midnight and just under 100% at 23:59.

```python
def calculate_tax(amount, state, hour):
    return amount + (amount * RATES[state] * time_percentage(hour))


print(calculate_tax(500, 'Harpo', 12))
```

You can work through a version of this code in the Python Tutor at http://mng.bz/oP1j.

Note that the Python Tutor site doesn't support modules, so this solution was placed in a single file, without the use of import.

Screencast solution

Watch this short video walkthrough of the solution: https://livebook.manning.com/video/python-workout.

Beyond the exercise

Now that you've written a simple function that masks more complex functionality, here are some other functions you can write as modules:

- Income tax in many countries is not a flat percentage, but rather the combination of different "brackets." So a country might not tax you on your first $1,000 of income, and then 10% on the next $10,000, and then 20% on the next $10,000, and then 50% on anything above that. Write a function that takes someone's income and returns the amount of tax they will have to pay, totaling the percentages from various brackets.

- Write a module providing a function that, given a string, returns a dict indicating how many characters provide a `True` result to each of the following functions: `str.isdigit`, `str.isalpha`, and `str.isspace`. The keys should be `isdigit`, `isalpha`, and `isspace`.

- The `dict.fromkeys` method (http://mng.bz/1zrV) makes it easy to create a new dict. For example, `dict.fromkeys('abc')` will create the dict `{'a':None, 'b':None, 'c':None}`. You can also pass a value that will be assigned to each key, as in `dict.fromkeys('abc', 5)`, resulting in the dict `{'a':5, 'b':5, 'c':5}`. Implement a function that does the same thing as `dict.keys` but whose second argument is a function. The value associated with the key will be the result of invoking `f(key)`.

Loading and reloading modules

When you use `import` to load a module, what happens? For example, if you say

```
import mymod
```

then Python looks for `mymod.py` in a number of directories, defined in a list of strings called `sys.path`. If Python encounters a file in one of those directories, it loads the file and stops searching in any other directories.

> **NOTE** There are a number of ways to modify `sys.path`, including by setting the environment variable `PYTHONPATH` and creating files with a `.pth` suffix in your Python installation's `site-packages` directory. For more information on setting `sys.path`, see the Python documentation, or read this helpful article: http://mng.bz/PAP9.

This means `import` normally does two distinct things: it loads the module and defines a new variable. But what happens if your program loads two modules, each of which in turn loads modules? For example, let's say that your program imports both `pandas` and `scipy`, both of which load the `numpy` module. In such a case, Python will load the module the first time, but only define the variable the second time. `import` only loads a module once, but it will always define the variable that you've asked it to create.

(continued)

This is done via a dict defined in sys called sys.modules. Its keys are the names of modules that have been loaded, and its values are the actual module objects. Thus, when we say import mymod, Python first checks to see if mymod is in sys.modules. If so, then it doesn't search for or load the module. Rather, it just defines the name.

This is normally a great thing, in that there's no reason to reload a module once the program has started running. But when you're debugging a module within an interactive Python session, you want to be able to reload it repeatedly, preferably without exiting from the current Python session.

In such cases, you can use the reload function defined in the importlib module. It takes a module object as an argument, so the module must already have been defined and imported. And it's the sort of thing that you'll likely use all the time in development, and almost never in actual production.

NOTE   In previous versions of Python, reload was a built-in function. As of Python 3, it's in the importlib module, which you must import to use it.

EXERCISE 37 ▪ Menu

If you find yourself writing the same function multiple times across different programs or projects, you almost certainly want to turn that function into a module. In this exercise, you're going to write a function that's generic enough to be used in a wide variety of programs.

Specifically, write a new module called "menu" (in the file menu.py). The module should define a function, also called menu. The function takes any number of key-value pairs as arguments. Each value should be a *callable,* a fancy name for a function or class in Python.

When the function is invoked, the user is asked to enter some input. If the user enters a string that matches one of the keyword arguments, the function associated with that keyword will be invoked, and its return value will be returned to menu's caller. If the user enters a string that's *not* one of the keyword arguments, they'll be given an error message and asked to try again.

The idea is that you'll be able to define several functions, and then indicate what user input will trigger each function:

```
from menu import menu

def func_a():
    return "A"

def func_b():
    return "B"

return_value = menu(a=func_a, b=func_b)
print(f'Result is {return_value}')
```

In this example, `return_value` will contain A if the user chooses a, or B if the user chooses b. If the user enters any other string, they're told to try again. And then we'll print the user's choice, just to confirm things.

Working it out

The solution presented here is another example of a *dispatch table*, which we saw earlier in the book, in the "prefix calculator" exercise. This time, we're using the `**kwargs` parameter to create that dispatch table dynamically, rather than with a hard-coded dict.

In this case, whoever invokes the `menu` function will provide the keywords—which function as menu options—and the functions that will be invoked. Note that these functions all take zero arguments, although you can imagine a scenario in which the user could provide more inputs.

We use `**` here, which we previously saw in the XML-creation exercise. We could have instead received a dict as a single argument, but this seems like an easier way for us to create the dict, using Python's built-in API for turning `**kwargs` into a dict.

While I didn't ask you to do so, my solution presents the user with a list of the valid menu items. I do this by invoking `str.join` on the dict, which has the effect of creating a string from the keys, with / characters between them. I also decided to use `sorted` to present them in alphabetical order.

With this in place, we can now ask the user for input from any zero-argument function.

Why do we check `__name__`?

One of the most famous lines in all of Python reads as follows:

```
if __name__ == '__main__':
```

What does this line do? How does it help? This line is the result of a couple different things happening when we load a module:

- First, when a module is loaded, its code is executed from the start of the file until the end. You're not just defining things; any code in the file is actually executed. That means you can (in theory) invoke `print` or have `for` loops. In this case, we're using `if` to make some code execute conditionally when it's loaded.
- Second, the `__name__` variable is either defined to be `__main__`, meaning that things are currently running in the initial, default, and top-level namespace provided by Python, *or* it's defined to be the name of the current module. The `if` statement here is thus checking to see if the module was run directly, or if it was imported by another piece of Python code.

In other words, the line of code says, "Only execute the below code (i.e., inside of the `if` statement) if this is the top-level program being executed. Ignore the stuff in the `if` when we `import` this module."

(continued)

You can use this code in a few different ways:

- Many modules run their own tests when invoked directly, rather than imported.
- Some modules can be run interactively, providing user-facing functionality and an interface. This code allows that to happen, without interfering with any function definitions.
- In some odd cases, such as the `multiprocessing` module in Windows, the code allows you to differentiate between versions of the program that are being loaded and executed in separate processes.

While you can theoretically have as many `if __name__ == '__main__'` lines in your code as you want, it's typical for this line to appear only once, at the end of your module file.

You'll undoubtedly encounter this code, and might even have written it yourself in the past. And now you know how it works!

Solution

```
def menu(**options):
    while True:
        option_string = '/'.join(sorted(options))
        choice = input(
            f'Enter an option ({option_string}): ')
        if choice in options:
            return options[choice]()

        print('Not a valid option')

def func_a():
    return "A"

def func_b():
    return "B"
return_value = menu(a=func_a, b=func_b)
print(f'Result is {return_value}')
```

"options" is a dict populated by the keyword arguments.

An infinite loop, which we'll break out of when the user gives valid input

Creates a string of sorted options, separated by "/"

Asks the user to enter an option

Has the user entered a key from "**options"?

If so, then return the result of executing the function.

Otherwise, scold the user and have them try again.

You can work through a version of this code in the Python Tutor at http://mng.bz/nPW8.

Note that the Python Tutor site doesn't support modules, so this solution was placed in a single file, without the use of `import`.

Screencast solution

Watch this short video walkthrough of the solution: https://livebook.manning.com/video/python-workout.

Beyond the exercise

Now that you've written and used two different Python modules, let's go beyond that and experiment with some more advanced techniques and problems:

- Write a version of menu.py that can be imported (as in the exercise), but that when you invoke the file as a stand-alone program from the command line, tests the function. If you aren't familiar with testing software such as pytest, you can just run the program and check the output.
- Turn menu.py into a Python package and upload it to PyPI. (I suggest using your name or initials, followed by "menu," to avoid name collisions.) See the sidebar on the difference between modules and packages, and how you can participate in the PyPI ecosystem with your own open-source projects.
- Define a module stuff with three variables—a, b, and c—and two functions—foo and bar. Define __all__ such that from stuff import * will cause a, c, and bar to be imported, but not b and foo.

Modules vs. packages

This chapter is all about modules—how to create, import, and use them. But you might have noticed that we often use another term, *package*, to discuss Python code. What's the difference between a module and a package?

A module is a single file, with a ".py" suffix. We can load the module using import, as we've seen. But what if your project is large enough that it would make more sense to have several separate files? How can you distribute those files together?

The answer is a package, which basically means a directory containing one or more Python modules. For example, assume you have the modules first.py, second.py, and third.py, and want to keep them together. You can put them all into a directory, mypackage. Assuming that directory is in sys.path, you can then say

```
from mypackage import first
```

Python will go into the mypackage directory, look for first.py, and import it. You can then access all of its attributes via first.x, first.y, and so forth.

Alternatively, you could say

```
import mypackage.first
```

In this case, Python will still load the module first, but it'll be available in your program via the long name, mypackage.first. You can then use mypackage.first.x and mypackage.first.y.

Alternatively, you could say

```
import mypackage
```

(continued)

But this will only be useful if, in the mypackage directory, you have a file named
__init__.py. In such a case, importing mypackage effectively means that __init__.py
is loaded, and thus executed. You can, inside of that file, import one or more of the modules within the package.

What about if you want to distribute your package to others? Then you'll have to create
a package. If this sounds strange, that you need a package to distribute your package,
that's because the same term, *package*, is used for two different concepts. A *PyPI package*, or *distribution package*, is a wrapper around a Python package containing information about the author, compatible versions, and licensing, as well as automated tests,
dependencies, and installation instructions.

Even more confusing than the use of "package" to describe two different things is the
fact that both the distribution package and the Python package are directories, and that
they should have the same name. If your distribution package is called mypackage, you'll
have a directory called mypackage. Inside that directory, among other things, will be a
subdirectory called mypackage, which is where the Python package goes.

Creating a distribution package means creating a file called setup.py (documented
here: http://mng.bz/wB9q), and I must admit that for many years, I found this to be a
real chore. It turns out that I wasn't alone, and a number of Python developers have
come up with ways to create distribution packages with relative ease. One that I've been
using for a while is called "Poetry" (http://mng.bz/2Xzd), and makes the entire process
easy and straightforward.

If you want to distribute packages via PyPI, you'll need to register for a username and
password at https://pypi.org/. Once you have that, here are the minimal steps you'll
need to take an existing package and upload it to PyPI with Poetry, using Unix shell
commands:

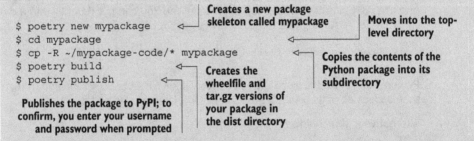

```
$ poetry new mypackage
$ cd mypackage
$ cp -R ~/mypackage-code/* mypackage
$ poetry build
$ poetry publish
```

Creates a new package
skeleton called mypackage

Moves into the top-
level directory

Copies the contents of the
Python package into its
subdirectory

Creates the
wheelfile and
tar.gz versions of
your package in
the dist directory

Publishes the package to PyPI; to
confirm, you enter your username
and password when prompted

Note that you can't upload the specific name mypackage to PyPI. I suggest prefacing
your package name with your username or initials, unless you intend to publish it for public consumption.

You could add plenty of other steps to the ones I've listed—for example, you can (and
should) edit the pyproject.toml configuration file, in which you describe your package's
version, license, and dependencies. But creating a distribution package is no longer
difficult. Rather, the hard part will be deciding what code you want to share with the
community.

Summary

Modules and packages are easy to write and use, and help us to DRY up our code—making it shorter and more easily maintainable. This benefit is even greater when you take advantage of the many modules and packages in the Python standard library, and on PyPI. It's thus no wonder that so many Python programs begin with several lines of import statements. As you become more fluent in Python, your familiarity with third-party modules will grow, allowing you to take even greater advantage of them in your code.

Objects

9

Object-oriented programming has become a mainstream, or even *the* mainstream, way of approaching programming. The idea is a simple one: instead of defining our functions in one part of the code, and the data on which those functions operate in a separate part of the code, we define them together.

Or, to put it in terms of language, in traditional, *procedural* programming, we write a list of nouns (data) and a separate list of verbs (functions), leaving it up to the programmer to figure out which goes with which. In object-oriented programming, the verbs (functions) are defined along with the nouns (data), helping us to know what goes with what.

In the world of object-oriented programming, each noun is an *object*. We say that each object has a *type*, or a *class*, to which it belongs. And the verbs (functions) we can invoke on each object are known as *methods*.

For an example of traditional, procedural programming versus object-oriented programming, consider how we could calculate a student's final grade, based on the average of their test scores. In procedural programming, we'd make sure the grades were in a list of integers and then write an average function that returned the arithmetic mean:

```
def average(numbers):
    return sum(numbers) / len(numbers)

scores = [85, 95, 98, 87, 80, 92]
print(f'The final score is {average(scores)}.')
```

This code works, and works reliably. But the caller is responsible for keeping track of the numbers as a list ... and for knowing that we have to call the average method ... and for combining them in the right way.

In the object-oriented world, we would approach the problem by creating a new data type, which we might call a ScoreList. We would then create a new instance of ScoreList.

Even if it's the same data underneath, a ScoreList is more explicitly and specifically connected to our domain than a generic Python list. We could then invoke the appropriate method on the ScoreList object:

```
class ScoreList():
    def __init__(self, scores):
        self.scores = scores

    def average(self):
        return sum(self.scores) / len(self.scores)
scores = ScoreList([85, 95, 98, 87, 80, 92])
print(f'The final score is {scores.average()}.')
```

As you can see, there's no difference from the procedural method in what's actually being calculated, and even what technique we're using to calculate it. But there's an organizational and semantic difference here, one that allows us to think in a different way.

We're now thinking at a higher level of abstraction and can better reason about our code. Defining our own types also allows us to use shorthand when describing concepts. Consider the difference between telling someone that you bought a "bookshelf" and describing "wooden boards held together with nails and screws, stored upright and containing places for storing books." The former is shorter, less ambiguous, and more semantically powerful than the latter.

Another advantage is that if we decide to calculate the average in a new way—for example, some teachers might drop the lowest score—then we can keep the existing interface while modifying the underlying implementation.

So, what are the main reasons for using object-oriented techniques?

- We can organize our code into distinct objects, each of which handles a different aspect of our code. This makes for easier planning and maintenance, as well as allowing us to divide a project among multiple people.
- We can create hierarchies of classes, with each child in the hierarchy inheriting functionality from its parents. This reduces the amount of code we need to write and simultaneously reinforces the relationships among similar data types. Given that many classes are slight modifications of other ones, this saves time and coding.
- By creating data types that work the same way as Python's built-in types, our code feels like a natural extension to the language, rather than bolted on. Moreover,

learning how to use a new class requires learning only a tiny bit of syntax, so you can concentrate on the underlying ideas and functionality.

- While Python doesn't hide code or make it private, you're still likely to hear about the difference between an object's implementation and its interface. If I'm using an object, then I care about its interface—that is, the methods that I can call on it and what they do. How the object is implemented internally is not a priority for me and doesn't affect my day-to-day work. This way, I can concentrate on the coding I want to do, rather than the internals of the class I'm using, taking advantage of the abstraction that I've created via the class.

Object-oriented programming isn't a panacea; over the years, we've found that, as with all other paradigms, it has both advantages and disadvantages. For example, it's easy to create monstrously large objects with huge numbers of methods, effectively creating a procedural system disguised as an object-oriented one. It's possible to abuse inheritance, creating hierarchies that make no sense. And by breaking the system into many small pieces, there's the problem of testing and integrating those pieces, with so many possible lines of communication.

Nevertheless, the object paradigm has helped numerous programmers to modularize their code, to focus on specific aspects of the program on which they're working, and to exchange data with objects written by other people.

In Python, we love to say that "everything is an object." At its heart, this means that the language is consistent; the types (such as `str` and `dict`) that come with the language are defined as classes, with methods. Our objects work just like the built-in objects, reducing the learning curve for both those implementing new classes and those using them.

Consider that when you learn a foreign language, you discover that nouns and verbs have all sorts of rules. But then there are the inevitable inconsistencies and exceptions to those rules. By having one consistent set of rules for all objects, Python removes those frustrations for non-native speakers—giving us, for lack of a better term, the Esperanto of programming languages. Once you've learned a rule, you can apply it throughout the language.

> **NOTE** One of the hallmarks of Python is its consistency. Once you learn a rule, it applies to the entire language, with no exceptions. If you understand variable lookup (LEGB, described in chapter 6) and attribute lookup (ICPO, described later in this chapter), you'll know the rules that Python applies all of the time, to all objects, without exception—both those that you create and those that come baked into the language.

At the same time, Python doesn't force you to write everything in an object-oriented style. Indeed, it's common to combine paradigms in Python programs, using an amalgam of procedural, functional, and object-oriented styles. Which style you choose, and where, is left up to you. But at the end of the day, even if you're not writing in an object-oriented style, you're still using Python's objects.

If you're going to code in Python, you should understand Python's object system—the ways objects are created, how classes are defined and interact with their parents, and how we can influence the ways classes interact with the rest of the world. Even if you write in a procedural style, you'll still be using classes defined by other people, and knowing how those classes work will make your coding easier and more straightforward.

This chapter contains exercises aimed at helping you to feel more comfortable with Python's objects. As you go through these exercises, you'll create classes and methods, create attributes at the object and class levels, and work with such concepts as composition and inheritance. When you're done, you'll be prepared to create and work with Python objects, and thus both write and maintain Python code.

NOTE The previous chapter, about modules, was short and simple. This chapter is the opposite—long, with many important ideas that can take some time to absorb. This chapter will take time to get through, but it's worth the effort. Understanding object-oriented programming won't just help you in writing your own classes; it'll also help you to understand how Python itself is built, and how the built-in types work.

Table 9.1 What you need to know

Concept	What is it?	Example	To learn more
`class`	Keyword for creating Python classes	`class Foo`	http://mng.bz/1zAV
`__init__`	Method invoked automatically when a new instance is created	`def __init__(self):`	http://mng.bz/PAa9
`__repr__`	Method that returns a string containing an object's printed representation	`def __repr__(self):`	http://mng.bz/JyvO
super built-in	Returns a proxy object on which methods can be invoked; typically used to invoke a method on a parent class	`super().__init__()`	http://mng.bz/wB0q
`dataclasses.dataclass`	A decorator that simplifies the definition of classes	`@dataclass`	http://mng.bz/qMew

EXERCISE 38 ■ Ice cream scoop

If you're going to be programming with objects, then you'll be creating classes—lots of classes. Each class should represent one type of object and its behavior. You can think of a class as a factory for creating objects of that type—so a Car class would create cars, also known as "car objects" or "instances of Car." Your beat-up sedan would be a car object, as would a fancy new luxury SUV.

In this exercise, you'll define a class, Scoop, that represents a single scoop of ice cream. Each scoop should have a single attribute, flavor, a string that you can initialize when you create the instance of Scoop.

Once your class is created, write a function (create_scoops) that creates three instances of the Scoop class, each of which has a different flavor (figure 9.1). Put these three instances into a list called scoops (figure 9.2). Finally, iterate over your scoops list, printing the flavor of each scoop of ice cream you've created.

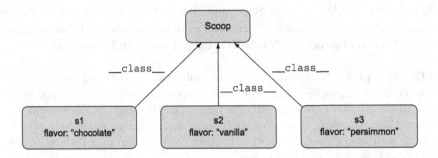

Figure 9.1   Three instances of Scoop, each referring to its class

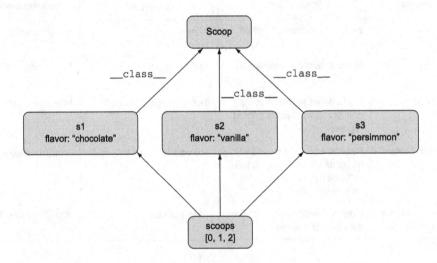

Figure 9.2   Our three instances of Scoop in a list

Working it out

The key to understanding objects in Python—and much of the Python language—is attributes. Every object has a type and one or more attributes. Python itself defines some of these attributes; you can identify them by the __ (often known as *dunder* in the Python world) at the beginning and end of the attribute names, such as __name__ or __init__.

When we define a new class, we do so with the class keyword. We then name the class (Scoop, in this case) and indicate, in parentheses, the class or classes from which our new class inherits.

Our __init__ method is invoked after the new instance of Scoop has been created, but before it has been returned to whoever invoked Scoop('flavor'). The new object is passed to __init__ in self (i.e., the first parameter), along with whatever arguments were passed to Scoop(). We thus assign self.flavor = flavor, creating the flavor attribute on the new instance, with the value of the flavor parameter.

Talking about your "self"

The first parameter in every method is traditionally called self. However, self isn't a reserved word in Python; the use of that word is a convention and comes from the Smalltalk language, whose object system influenced Python's design.

In many languages, the current object is known as this. Moreover, in such languages, this isn't a parameter, but rather a special word that refers to the current object. Python doesn't have any such special word; the instance on which the method was invoked will always be known as self, and self will always be the first parameter in every method.

In theory, you can use any name you want for that first parameter, including this. (But, really, what self-respecting language would do so?) Although your program will still work, all Python developers and tools assume that the first parameter, representing the instance, will be called self, so you should do so too.

Just as with regular Python functions, there isn't any enforcement of types here. The assumption is that flavor will contain a str value because the documentation will indicate that this is what it expects.

NOTE If you want to enforce things more strictly, then consider using Python's type annotations and Mypy or a similar type-checking tool. You can find more information about Mypy at http://mypy-lang.org/. Also, you can find an excellent introduction to Python's type annotations and how to use them at http://mng.bz/mByr.

To create three scoops, I use a list comprehension, iterating over the flavors and creating new instances of Scoop. The result is a list with three Scoop objects in it, each with a separate flavor:

```
scoops = [Scoop(flavor)
          for flavor in ('chocolate', 'vanilla', 'persimmon')]
```

If you're used to working with objects in another programming language, you might be wondering where the "getter" and "setter" methods are, to retrieve and set the value of the flavor attribute. In Python, because everything is public, there's no real need for getters and setters. And indeed, unless you have a really good reason for it, you should probably avoid writing them.

> **NOTE**   If and when you find yourself needing a getter or setter, you might want to consider a Python *property*, which hides a method call behind the API of an attribute change or retrieval. You can learn more about properties here: http://mng.bz/5aWB.

I should note that even our simple `Scoop` class exhibits several things that are common to nearly all Python classes. We have an `__init__` method, whose parameters allow us to set attributes on newly created instances. It stores state inside `self`, and it can store any type of Python object in this way—not just strings or numbers, but also lists and dicts, as well as other types of objects.

> **NOTE**   Don't make persimmon ice cream. Your family will never let you forget it.

Solution

```
class Scoop():
    def __init__(self, flavor):    ←   Every method's first parameter is
        self.flavor = flavor       ←   always going to be "self," representing
                                        the current instance.

                                        Sets the "flavor"
                                        attribute to the value in
                                        the parameter "flavor"
def create_scoops():
    scoops = [Scoop('chocolate'),
              Scoop('vanilla'),
              Scoop('persimmon')]
    for scoop in scoops:
        print(scoop.flavor)

create_scoops()
```

You can work through a version of this code in the Python Tutor at http://mng.bz/8pMZ.

Screencast solution

Watch this short video walkthrough of the solution: https://livebook.manning.com/video/python-workout.

Beyond the exercise

If you're coding in Python, you'll likely end up writing classes on a regular basis. And if you're doing that, you'll be writing many `__init__` methods that add attributes to objects of various sorts. Here are some additional, simple classes that you can write to practice doing so:

- Write a `Beverage` class whose instances will represent beverages. Each beverage should have two attributes: a name (describing the beverage) and a temperature.

Create several beverages and check that their names and temperatures are all handled correctly.

▪ Modify the Beverage class, such that you can create a new instance specifying the name, and not the temperature. If you do this, then the temperature should have a default value of 75 degrees Celsius. Create several beverages and double-check that the temperature has this default when not specified.

▪ Create a new LogFile class that expects to be initialized with a filename. Inside of __init__, open the file for writing and assign it to an attribute, file, that sits on the instance. Check that it's possible to write to the file via the file attribute.

What does __init__ do?

A simple class in Python looks like this:

```
class Foo():
    def __init__(self, x):
        self.x = x
```

And sure enough, with the Foo class in place, we can say

```
f = Foo(10)
print(f.x)
```

This leads many people, and particularly those who come from other languages, to call __init__ a *constructor*, meaning the method that actually creates a new instance of Foo. But that's not quite the case.

When we call Foo(10), Python first looks for the Foo identifier in the same way as it looks for every other variable in the language, following the LEGB rule. It finds Foo as a globally defined variable, referencing a class. Classes are *callable*, meaning that they can be invoked with parentheses. And thus, when we ask to invoke it and pass 10 as an argument, Python agrees.

But what actually executes? The constructor method, of course, which is known as __new__. Now, you should almost never implement __new__ on your own; there are some cases in which it might be useful, but in the overwhelming majority of cases, you don't want to touch or redefine it. That's because __new__ creates the new object, something we don't want to have to deal with.

The __new__ method also returns the newly created instance of Foo to the caller. But before it does that, it does one more thing: it looks for, and then invokes, the __init__ method. This means that __init__ is called after the object is created but before it's returned.

And what does __init__ do? Put simply, it adds new attributes to the object.

(continued)

Whereas other programming languages talk about "instance variables" and "class variables," Python developers have only one tool, namely the attribute. Whenever you have a.b in code, we can say that b is an attribute of a, meaning (more or less) that b references an object associated with a. You can think of the attributes of an object as its own private dict.

The job of __init__ is thus to add one or more attributes to our new instance. Unlike languages such as C# and Java, we don't just declare attributes in Python; we must actually create and assign to them, at runtime, when the new instance is created.

In all Python methods, the self parameter refers to the instance. Any attributes we add to self will stick around after the method returns. And so it's natural, and thus preferred, to assign a bunch of attributes to self in __init__.

Let's see how this works, step by step. First, let's define a simple Person class, which assigns a name to the object:

```
class Person:
    def __init__(self, name):
        self.name = name
```

Then, let's create a new instance of Person:

```
p = Person('myname')
```

What happens inside of Python? First, the __new__ method, which we never define, runs behind the scenes, creating the object, as shown in figure 9.3.

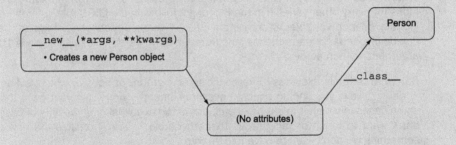

Figure 9.3 **When we create an object, __new__ is invoked.**

It creates a new instance of Person and holds onto it as a local variable. But then __new__ calls __init__. It passes the newly created object as the first argument to __init__, then it passes all additional arguments using *args and **kwargs, as shown in figure 9.4.

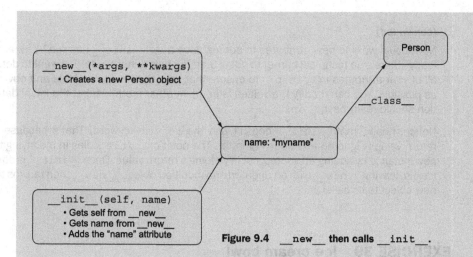

Figure 9.4   `__new__` then calls `__init__`.

Now `__init__` adds one or more attributes to the new object, as shown in figure 9.5, which it knows as `self`, a local variable.

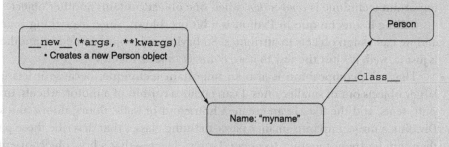

Figure 9.5   `__init__` adds attributes to the object.

Finally, `__new__` returns the newly created object to its caller, with the attribute that was added, as shown in figure 9.6.

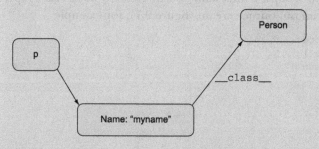

Figure 9.6   Finally, `__init__` exits, and the object in `__new__` is returned to the caller.

(continued)

Now, could we add new attributes to our instance after __init__ has run? Yes, absolutely—there's no technical barrier to doing that. But as a general rule, you want to define all of your attributes in __init__ to ensure that your code is as readable and obvious as possible. You can *modify* the values later on, in other methods, but the initial definition should really be in __init__.

Notice, finally, that __init__ doesn't use the return keyword. That's because its return value is ignored and doesn't matter. The point of __init__ lies in modifying the new instance by adding attributes, not in yielding a return value. Once __init__ is done, it exits, leaving __new__ with an updated and modified object. __new__ then returns this new object to its caller.

EXERCISE 39 ■ Ice cream bowl

Whenever I teach object-oriented programming, I encounter people who've learned it before and are convinced that the most important technique is inheritance. Now, inheritance is certainly important, and we'll look into it momentarily, but a more important technique is *composition*, when one object contains another object.

Calling it a technique in Python is a bit overblown, since everything is an object, and we can assign objects to attributes. So having one object owned by another object is just … well, it's just the way that we connect objects together.

That said, composition is also an important technique, because it lets us create larger objects out of smaller ones. I can create a car out of a motor, wheels, tires, gearshift, seats, and the like. I can create a house out of walls, floors, doors, and so forth. Dividing a project up into smaller parts, defining classes that describe those parts, and then joining them together to create larger objects—that's how object-oriented programming works.

In this exercise, we're going to see a small-scale version of that. In the previous exercise, we created a Scoop class that represents one scoop of ice cream. If we're really going to model the real world, though, we should have another object into which we can put the scoops. I thus want you to create a Bowl class, representing a bowl into which we can put our ice cream (figure 9.7); for example

```
s1 = Scoop('chocolate')
s2 = Scoop('vanilla')
s3 = Scoop('persimmon')

b = Bowl()
b.add_scoops(s1, s2)
b.add_scoops(s3)
print(b)
```

Figure 9.7 A new instance of Bowl, with an empty list of scoops

The result of running print (b) should be to display the three ice cream flavors in our bowl (figure 9.8). Note that it should be possible to add any number of scoops to the bowl using Bowl.add_scoops.

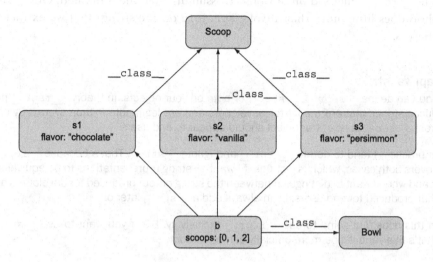

Figure 9.8 Three Scoop objects in our bowl

Working it out

The solution doesn't involve any changes to our Scoop class. Rather, we create our Bowl such that it can contain any number of instances of Scoop.

First of all, we define the attribute self.scoops on our object to be a list. We could theoretically use a dict or a set, but given that there aren't any obvious candidates for keys, and that we might want to preserve the order of the scoops, I'd argue that a list is a more logical choice.

Remember that we're storing instances of Scoop in self.scoops. We aren't just storing the string that describes the flavors. Each instance of Scoop will have its own flavor attribute, a string containing the current scoop's flavor.

We create the self.scoops attribute, as an empty list, in __init__.

Then we need to define add_scoops, which can take any number of arguments—which we'll assume are instances of Scoop—and add them to the bowl. This means, almost by definition, that we'll need to use the splat operator (*) when defining our *new_scoops parameter. As a result, new_scoops will be a tuple containing all of the arguments that were passed to add_scoops.

NOTE There's a world of difference between the variable new_scoops and the attribute self.scoops. The former is a local variable in the function, referring to the tuple of Scoop objects that the user passed to add_scoops. The latter is an attribute, attached to the self local variable, that refers to the object instance on which we're currently working.

We can then iterate over each element of scoops, adding it to the self.scoops attribute. We do this in a for loop, invoking list.append on each scoop.

Finally, to print the scoops, we simply invoke print(b). This has the effect of calling the __repr__ method on our object, assuming that one is defined. Our __repr__ method does little more than invoke str.join on the strings that we extract from the flavors.

repr vs. str

You can define __repr__, __str__, or both on your objects. In theory, __repr__ produces strings that are meant for developers and are legitimate Python syntax. By contrast, __str__ is how your object should appear to end users.

In practice, I tend to define __repr__ and ignore __str__. That's because __repr__ covers both cases, which is just fine if I want all string representations to be equivalent. If and when I want to distinguish between the string output produced for developers and that produced for end users, I can always add a __str__ later on.

In this book, I'm going to use __repr__ exclusively. But if you want to use __str__, that's fine—and it'll be more officially correct to boot.

Notice, however, that we're not invoking str.join on a list comprehension, because there are no square brackets. Rather, we're invoking it on a *generator expression*, which you can think of as a lazy-evaluating version of a list comprehension. True, in a case like this, there's really no performance benefit. My point in using it was to demonstrate that nearly anywhere you can use a list comprehension, you can use a generator expression instead.

is-a vs. has-a

If you have any experience with object-oriented programming, then you might have been tempted to say here that Scoop inherits from Bowl, or that Bowl inherits from Scoop. Neither is true, because inheritance (which we'll explore later in this chapter) describes a relationship known in computer science as "is-a." We can say that an employee is-a person, or that a car is-a vehicle, which would point to such a relationship.

In real life, we can say that a bowl contains one or more scoops. In programming terms, we'd describe this as Bowl has-a Scoop. The "has-a" relationship doesn't describe inheritance, but rather composition.

I've found that relative newcomers to object-oriented programming are often convinced that if two classes are involved, one of them should probably inherit from the other. Pointing out the "is-a" rule for inheritance, versus the "has-a" rule for composition, helps to clarify the two different relationships and when it's appropriate to use inheritance versus composition.

Solution

```
class Scoop():
    def __init__(self, flavor):
        self.flavor = flavor

class Bowl():
    def __init__(self):
        self.scoops = []

    def add_scoops(self, *new_scoops):
        for one_scoop in new_scoops:
            self.scoops.append(one_scoop)

    def __repr__(self):
        return '\n'.join(s.flavor for s in self.scoops)

s1 = Scoop('chocolate')
s2 = Scoop('vanilla')
s3 = Scoop('persimmon')

b = Bowl()
b.add_scoops(s1, s2)
b.add_scoops(s3)
print(b)
```

Initializes self.scoops
with an empty list

*new_scoops is just like
*args. You can use whatever
name you want.

Creates a string
via str.join and
a generator
expression

You can work through a version of this code in the Python Tutor at http://mng.bz/
EdWo.

Screencast solution

Watch this short video walkthrough of the solution: https://livebook.manning.com/
video/python-workout.

Beyond the exercise

You've now seen how to create an explicit "has-a" relationship between two classes.
Here are some more opportunities to explore this type of relationship:

- Create a Book class that lets you create books with a title, author, and price.
  Then create a Shelf class, onto which you can place one or more books with an
  add_book method. Finally, add a total_price method to the Shelf class, which
  will total the prices of the books on the shelf.
- Write a method, Shelf.has_book, that takes a single string argument and
  returns True or False, depending on whether a book with the named title
  exists on the shelf.
- Modify your Book class such that it adds another attribute, width. Then add a
  width attribute to each instance of Shelf. When add_book tries to add books
  whose combined widths will be too much for the shelf, raise an exception.

Reducing redundancy with dataclass

Do you feel like your class definitions repeat themselves? If so, you're not alone. One of the most common complaints I hear from people regarding Python classes is that the __init__ method basically does the same thing in each class: taking arguments and assigning them to attributes on self.

As of Python 3.7, you can cut out some of the boilerplate class-creation code with the dataclass decorator, focusing on the code you actually want to write. For example, here's how the Scoop class would be defined:

```
@dataclass
class Scoop():
    flavor : str
```

Look, there's no __init__ method! You don't need it here; the @dataclass decorator used writes it for you. It also takes care of other things, such as comparisons and a better version of __repr__. Basically, the whole point of data classes is to reduce your workload.

Notice that we used a type annotation (str) to indicate that our flavor attribute should only take strings. Type annotations are normally optional in Python, but if you're declaring attributes in a data class, then they're mandatory. Python, as usual, ignores these type annotations; as mentioned earlier in this chapter, type checking is done by external programs such as Mypy.

Also notice that we define flavor at the class level, even though we want it to be an attribute on our instances. Given that you almost certainly don't want to have the same attribute on both instances and classes, this is fine; the dataclass decorator will see the attribute, along with its type annotation, and will handle things appropriately.

How about our Bowl class? How could we define it with a data class? It turns out that we need to provide a bit more information:

```
from typing import List
from dataclasses import dataclass, field

@dataclass
class Bowl():
    scoops: List[Scoop] = field(default_factory=list)

    def add_scoops(self, *new_scoops):
        for one_scoop in new_scoops:
            self.scoops.append(one_scoop)

    def __repr__(self):
        return '\n'.join(s.flavor for s in self.scoops)
```

Let's ignore the methods add_scoops and __repr__ and concentrate on the start of our class. First, we again use the @dataclass decorator. But then, when we define our scoops attribute, we give not just a type but a default value.

Notice that the type that we provide, List[int], has a capital "L". This means that it's distinct from the built-in list type. It comes from the typing module, which comes with Python and provides us with objects meant for use in type annotations. The List type, when used by itself, represents a list of any type. But when combined with square brackets, we can indicate that all elements of the list scoops will be objects of type Scoop.

Normally, default values can just be assigned to their attributes. But because scoops is a list, and thus mutable, we need to get a little fancier. When we create a new instance of Bowl, we don't want to get a reference to an existing object. Rather, we want to invoke list, returning a new instance of list and assigning it to scoops. To do this, we need to use default_factory, which tells dataclass that it shouldn't reuse existing objects, but should rather create new ones.

This book uses the classic, standard way of defining Python classes—partly to support people still using Python 3.6, and partly so that you can understand what's happening under the hood. But I wouldn't be surprised if dataclass eventually becomes the default way to create Python classes, and if you want to use them in your solutions, you should feel free to do so.

How Python searches for attributes

In chapter 6, I discussed how Python searches for variables using LEGB—first searching in the local scope, then enclosing, then global, and finally in the builtins namespace. Python adheres to this rule consistently, and knowing that makes it easier to reason about the language.

Python similarly searches for attributes along a standard, well-defined path. But that path is quite different from the LEGB rule for variables. I call it ICPO, short for "instance, class, parents, and object." I'll explain how that works.

When you ask Python for a.b, it first asks the a object whether it has an attribute named b. If so, then the value associated with a.b is returned, and that's the end of the process. That's the "I" of ICPO—we first check on the instance.

But if a doesn't have a b attribute, then Python doesn't give up. Rather, it checks on a's class, whatever it is. Meaning that if a.b doesn't exist, we look for type(a).b. If that exists, then we get the value back, and the search ends. That's the "C" of ICPO.

Right away, this mechanism explains why and how methods are defined on classes, and yet can be called via the instance. Consider the following code:

```
s = 'abcd'
print(s.upper())
```

Here, we define s to be a string. We then invoke s.upper. Python asks s if it has an attribute upper, and the answer is no. It then asks if str has an attribute upper, and the answer is *yes*. The method object is retrieved from str and is then invoked. At the same time, we can talk about the method as str.upper because it is indeed defined on str, and is eventually located there.

(continued)

What if Python can't find the attribute on the instance or the class? It then starts to check on the class's parents. Until now, we haven't really seen any use of that; all of our classes have automatically and implicitly inherited from `object`. But a class can inherit from any other class—and this is often a good idea, since the subclass can take advantage of the parent class's functionality.

Here's an example:

```
class Foo():
    def __init__(self, x):
        self.x = x
    def x2(self):
        return self.x * 2


class Bar(Foo):
    def x3(self):
        return self.x * 3


b = Bar(10)
print(b.x2())        ◄───  **Prints 20**
print(b.x3())        ◄───  **Prints 30**
```

In this code, we create an instance of `Bar`, a class that inherits from `Foo` (figure 9.9). When we create the instance of `Bar`, Python looks for `__init__`. Where? First on the instance, but it isn't there. Then on the class (`Bar`), but it isn't there. Then it looks at `Bar`'s parent, `Foo`, and it finds `__init__` there. That method runs, setting the attribute x, and then returns, giving us b, an instance of `Bar` with x equal to 10 (figure 9.10).

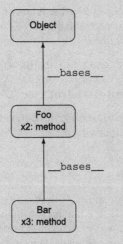

Figure 9.9 `Bar` inherits from `Foo`, which inherits from `object`.

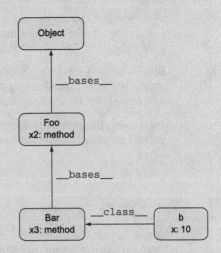

Figure 9.10 b is an instance of `Bar`.

The same thing happens when we invoke x2. We look on b and can't find that method. We then look on type(b), or Bar, and can't find the method. But when we check on Bar's parent, Foo, we find it, and that method executes. If we had defined a method of our own named x2 on Bar, then that would have executed instead of Foo.x2.

Finally, we invoke x3. We check on b and don't find it. We check on Bar and do find it, and that method thus executes.

What if, during our ICPO search, the attribute doesn't exist on the instance, class, or parent? We then turn to the ultimate parent in all of Python, object. You can create an instance of object, but there's no point in doing so; it exists solely so that other classes can inherit from it, and thus get to its methods.

As a result, if you don't define an __init__ method, then object.__init__ will run. And if you don't define __repr__, then object.__repr__ will run, and so forth.

The final thing to remember with the ICPO search path is that the first match wins. This means that if two attributes on the search path have the same name, Python won't ever find the later one. This is normally a good thing in that it allows us to override methods in subclasses. But if you're not expecting that to happen, then you might end up being surprised.

EXERCISE 40 ■ Bowl limits

We can add an attribute to just about any object in Python. When writing classes, it's typical and traditional to define data attributes on instances and method attributes on classes. But there's no reason why we can't define data attributes on classes too.

In this exercise, I want you to define a class attribute that will function like a constant, ensuring that we don't need to hardcode any values in our class.

What's the task here? Well, you might have noticed a flaw in our Bowl class, one that children undoubtedly love and their parents undoubtedly hate: you can put as many Scoop objects in a bowl as you like.

Let's make the children sad, and their parents happy, by capping the number of scoops in a bowl at three. That is, you can add as many scoops in each call to Bowl.add_scoops as you want, and you can call that method as many times as you want—but only the first three scoops will actually be added. Any additional scoops will be ignored.

Working it out

We only need to make two changes to our original Bowl class for this to work.

First, we need to define a class attribute on Bowl. We do this most easily by making an assignment within the class definition (figure 9.11). Setting max_scoops = 3 within the class block is the same as saying, afterwards, Bowl.max_scoops = 3.

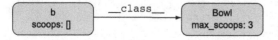

Figure 9.11 max_scoops **sits on the class, so even an empty instance has access to it.**

But wait, do we really need to define max_scoops on the Bowl class? Technically, we have two other options:

- Define the maximum on the instance, rather than the class. This will work (i.e., add self.max_scoops = 3 in __init__), but it implies that every bowl has a different maximum number of scoops. By putting the attribute on the class (figure 9.12), we indicate that every bowl will have the same maximum.
- We could also hardcode the value 3 in our code, rather than use a symbolic name such as max_scoops. But this will reduce our flexibility, especially if and when we want to use inheritance (as we'll see later). Moreover, if we decide to change the maximum down the line, it's easier to do that in one place, via the attribute assignment, rather than in a number of places.

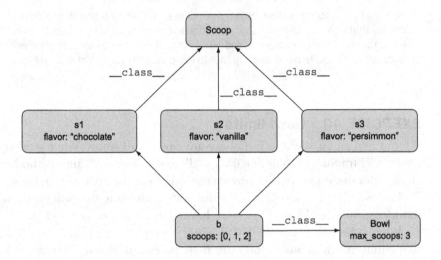

Figure 9.12   A Bowl instance containing scoops, with max_scoops defined on the class

Second, we need to change Bowl.add_scoops, adding an if statement to make the addition of new scoops conditional on the current length of self.scoops and the value of Bowl.max_scoops.

Are class attributes just static variables?

If you're coming from the world of Java, C#, or C++, then class attributes look an awful lot like static variables. But they aren't static variables, and you shouldn't call them that.

Here are a few ways class attributes are different from static variables, even though their uses might be similar:

First, class attributes are just another case of attributes on a Python object. This means that we can and should reason about class attributes the same as all others, with the ICPO lookup rule. You can access them on the class (as `ClassName.attrname`) or on an instance (as `one_instance.attrname`). The former will work because you're using the class, and the latter will work because after checking the instance, Python checks its class.

In the solution for this exercise, `Bowl.max_scoops` is an attribute on the `Bowl` class. We could, in theory, assign `max_scoops` to each individual instance of `Bowl`, but it makes more sense to say that all `Bowl` objects have the same maximum number of scoops.

Second, static variables are shared among the instances and class. This means that assigning to a class variable via an instance has the same effect as assigning to it via the class. In Python, there's a world of difference between assigning to the class variable via the instance and doing so via the class; the former will add a new attribute to the instance, effectively blocking access to the class attribute.

That is, if we assign to `Bowl.max_scoops`, then we're changing the maximum number of scoops that all bowls can have. But if we assign to `one_bowl.max_scoops`, we're setting a new attribute on the instance `one_bowl`. This will put us in the terrible situation of having `Bowl.max_scoops` set to one thing, and `one_bowl.max_scoops` set to something else. Moreover, asking for `one_bowl.max_scoops` would (by the ICPO rule) stop after finding the attribute on the instance and never look on the class.

Third, methods are actually class attributes too. But we don't think of them in that way because they're defined differently. Whatever we may think, methods are created using `def` inside of a class definition.

When I invoke `b.add_scoops`, Python looks on `b` for the attribute `add_scoops` and doesn't find it. It then looks on `Bowl` (i.e., b's class) and finds it—and retrieves the method object. The parentheses then execute the method. This only works if the method is actually defined on the class, which it is. Methods are almost always defined on a class, and thanks to the ICPO rule, Python will look for them there.

Finally, Python doesn't have constants, but we can simulate them with class attributes. Much as I did with `max_scoops` earlier, I often define a class attribute that I can then access, by name, via both the class and the instances.

For example, the class attribute `max_scoops` is being used here as a sort of constant. Instead of storing the hardcoded number 3 everywhere I need to refer to the maximum scoops that can be put in a bowl, I can refer to `Bowl.max_scoops`. This both adds clarity to my code and allows me to change the value in the future in a single place.

Solution

```
class Scoop():
    def __init__(self, flavor):
        self.flavor = flavor

class Bowl():
    max_scoops = 3        <-- 
```
max_scoops is not a variable—it's an attribute of the class Bowl.

```
    def __init__(self):
        self.scoops = []

    def add_scoops(self, *new_scoops):
        for one_scoop in new_scoops:
            if len(self.scoops) < Bowl.max_scoops:
                self.scoops.append(one_scoop)

    def __repr__(self):
        return '\n'.join(s.flavor for s in self.scoops)
```

> Uses Bowl.max_scoops to get the maximum per bowl, set on the class

```
s1 = Scoop('chocolate')
s2 = Scoop('vanilla')
s3 = Scoop('persimmon')
s4 = Scoop('flavor 4')
s5 = Scoop('flavor 5')

b = Bowl()
b.add_scoops(s1, s2)
b.add_scoops(s3)
b.add_scoops(s4, s5)
print(b)
```

You can work through a version of this code in the Python Tutor at http://mng.bz/ NK6N.

Screencast solution

Watch this short video walkthrough of the solution: https://livebook.manning.com/ video/python-workout.

Beyond the exercise

As I've indicated, you can use class attributes in a variety of ways. Here are a few additional challenges that can help you to appreciate and understand how to define and use class attributes:

- Define a Person class, and a population class attribute that increases each time you create a new instance of Person. Double-check that after you've created five instances, named p1 through p5, Person.population and p1.population are both equal to 5.
- Python provides a __del__ method that's executed when an object is garbage collected. (In my experience, deleting a variable or assigning it to another object triggers the calling of __del__ pretty quickly.) Modify your Person class such that when a Person instance is deleted, the population count decrements by 1. If you aren't sure what *garbage collection* is, or how it works in Python, take a look at this article: http://mng.bz/nP2a.
- Define a Transaction class, in which each instance represents either a deposit or a withdrawal from a bank account. When creating a new instance of Transaction,

you'll need to specify an amount—positive for a deposit and negative for a withdrawal. Use a class attribute to keep track of the current balance, which should be equal to the sum of the amounts in all instances created to date.

Inheritance in Python

The time has come for us to use inheritance, an important idea in object-oriented programming. The basic idea reflects the fact that we often want to create classes that are quite similar to one another. We can thus create a *parent* class, in which we define the general behavior. And then we can create one or more *child* classes, or *subclasses*, each of which inherits from the parent class:

- If I already have a `Person` class, then I might want to create an `Employee` class, which is identical to `Person` except that each employee has an ID number, department, and salary.
- If I already have a `Vehicle` class, then I can create a `Car` class, a `Truck` class, and a `Bicycle` class.
- If I already have a `Book` class, then I can create a `Textbook` class, as well as a `Novel` class.

As you can see, the idea of a subclass is that it does everything the parent class does, but then goes a bit further with more specific functionality. Inheritance allows us to apply the DRY principle to our classes, and to keep them organized in our heads.

How does inheritance work in Python? Define a second class (i.e., a subclass), naming the parent class in parentheses on the first line:

```
class Person():
    def __init__(self, name):
        self.name = name

    def greet(self):
        return f'Hello, {self.name}'
class Employee(Person)
    def __init__(self, name, id_number):
        self.name = name
        self.id_number = id_number
```

This is how we tell Python that "Employee" is-a "Person," meaning it inherits from "Person."

Does this look funny to you? It should—more soon.

With this code in place, we can now create an instance of `Employee`, as per usual:

```
e = Employee('empname', 1)
```

But what happens if we invoke `e.greet`? By the ICPO rule, Python first looks for the attribute `greet` on the instance `e`, but it doesn't find it. It then looks on the class `Employee` and doesn't find it. Python then looks on the parent class, `Person`, finds it, retrieves the method, and invokes it. In other words, inheritance is a powerful idea—but in Python, it's a natural outgrowth of the ICPO rule.

(continued)

There's one weird thing about my implementation of `Employee`, namely that I set `self.name` in `___init___`. If you're coming from a language like Java, you might be wondering why I have to set it at all, since `Person.__init__` already sets it. But that's just the thing: in Python, `__init__` really needs to execute for it to set the attribute. If we were to remove the setting of `self.name` from `Employee.__init__`, the attribute would never be set. By the ICPO rule, only one method would ever be called, and it would be the one that's closest to the instance. Since `Employee.__init__` is closer to the instance than `Person.__init__`, the latter is never called.

The good news is that the code I provided works. But the bad news is that it violates the DRY rule that I've mentioned so often.

The solution is to take advantage of inheritance via `super`. The `super` built-in allows us to invoke a method on a parent object without explicitly naming that parent. In our code, we could thus rewrite `Employee.__init__` as follows:

```
class Employee(Person)
    def __init__(self, name, id_number):
        super().__init__(name)          Implicitly invoking
        self.id_number = id_number      Person.__init__ via super
```

EXERCISE 41 ▪ A bigger bowl

While the previous exercise might have delighted parents and upset children, our job as ice cream vendors is to excite the children, as well as take their parents' money. Our company has thus started to offer a `BigBowl` product, which can take up to five scoops.

Implement `BigBowl` for this exercise, such that the only difference between it and the `Bowl` class we created earlier is that it can have five scoops, rather than three. And yes, this means that you should use inheritance to achieve this goal.

You can modify `Scoop` and `Bowl` if you must, but such changes should be minimal and justifiable.

> **NOTE** As a general rule, the point of inheritance is to add or modify functionality in an existing class without modifying the parent. Purists might thus dislike these instructions, which allow for changes in the parent class. However, the real world isn't always squeaky clean, and if the classes are both written by the same team, it's possible that the child's author can negotiate changes in the parent class.

Working it out

This is, I must admit, a tricky one. It forces you to understand how attributes work, and especially how they interact between instances, classes, and parent classes. If you really get the ICPO rule, then the solution should make sense.

In our previous version of `Bowl.add_scoops`, we said that we wanted to use `Bowl.max _scoops` to keep track of the maximum number of scoops allowed. That was fine, as long as every subclass would want to use the same value.

But here, we want to use a different value. That is, when invoking `add_scoops` on a `Bowl` object, the maximum should be `Bowl.max_scoops`. And when invoking `add_scoops` on a `BigBowl` object, the maximum should be `BigBowl.max_scoops`. And we want to avoid writing `add_scoops` twice.

The simplest solution is to change our reference in `add_scoops` from `Bowl.max _scoops`, to `self.max_scoops`. With this change in place, things will work like this:

- If we ask for `Bowl.max_scoops`, we'll get 3.
- If we ask for `BigBowl.max_scoops`, we'll get 5.
- If we invoke `add_scoops` on an instance of `Bowl`, then inside the method, we'll ask for `self.max_scoops`. By the ICPO lookup rule, Python will look first on the instance and then on the class, which is `Bowl` in this case, and return `Bowl.max-_scoops`, with a value of 3.
- If we invoke `add_scoops` on an instance of `BigBowl`, then inside the method we'll ask for `self.max_scoops`. By the iCPO lookup rule, Python will first look on the instance, and then on the class, which is `BigBowl` in this case, and return `BigBowl.max_scoops`, with a value of 5.

In this way, we've taken advantage of inheritance and the flexibility of `self` to use the same interface for a variety of classes. Moreover, we were able to implement `BigBowl` with a minimum of code, using what we'd already written for `Bowl`.

Solution

```
class Scoop():
    def __init__(self, flavor):
        self.flavor = flavor


class Bowl():
    max_scoops = 3          ← Bowl.max_scoops
                              remains 3.

    def __init__(self):
        self.scoops = []
                              Uses self.max_scoops, rather
    def add_scoops(self, *new_scoops):    than Bowl.max_scoops, to
        for one_scoop in new_scoops:      get the attribute from the
            if len(self.scoops) < self.max_scoops:  ←  correct class
                self.scoops.append(one_scoop)

    def __repr__(self):
        return '\n'.join(s.flavor for s in self.scoops)


class BigBowl(Bowl):       BigBowl.max_scoops
    max_scoops = 5    ←    is set to 5.
```

```
s1 = Scoop('chocolate')
s2 = Scoop('vanilla')
s3 = Scoop('persimmon')
s4 = Scoop('flavor 4')
s5 = Scoop('flavor 5')

bb = BigBowl()
bb.add_scoops(s1, s2)
bb.add_scoops(s3)
bb.add_scoops(s4, s5)
print(bb)
```

You can work through a version of this code in the Python Tutor at http://mng.bz/ D2gn.

Screencast solution

Watch this short video walkthrough of the solution: https://livebook.manning.com/ video/python-workout.

Beyond the exercise

As I've already indicated in this chapter, I think that many people exaggerate the degree to which they should use inheritance in object-oriented code. But that doesn't mean I see inheritance as unnecessary or even worthless. Used correctly, it's a powerful tool that can reduce code size and improve its maintenance. Here are some more ways you can practice using inheritance:

- Write an Envelope class, with two attributes, weight (a float, measuring grams) and was_sent (a Boolean, defaulting to False). There should be three methods: (1) send, which sends the letter, and changes was_sent to True, but only after the envelope has enough postage; (2) add_postage, which adds postage equal to its argument; and (3) postage_needed, which indicates how much postage the envelope needs total. The postage needed will be the weight of the envelope times 10. Now write a BigEnvelope class that works just like Envelope except that the postage is 15 times the weight, rather than 10.

- Create a Phone class that represents a mobile phone. (Are there still nonmobile phones?) The phone should implement a dial method that dials a phone number (or simulates doing so). Implement a SmartPhone subclass that uses the Phone.dial method but implements its own run_app method. Now implement an iPhone subclass that implements not only a run_app method, but also its own dial method, which invokes the parent's dial method but whose output is all in lowercase as a sign of its coolness.

- Define a Bread class representing a loaf of bread. We should be able to invoke a get_nutrition method on the object, passing an integer representing the number of slices we want to eat. In return, we'll receive a dict whose key-value pairs will represent calories, carbohydrates, sodium, sugar, and fat, indicating the nutritional statistics for that number of slices. Now implement two new classes that inherit from Bread, namely WholeWheatBread and RyeBread. Each class should implement the same get_nutrition method, but with different nutritional information where appropriate.

EXERCISE 42 ■ FlexibleDict

I've already said that the main point of inheritance is to take advantage of existing functionality. There are several ways to do this and reasons for doing this, and one of them is to create new behavior that's similar to, but distinct from, an existing class. For example, Python comes not just with dict, but also with Counter and defaultdict. By inheriting from dict, those two classes can implement just those methods that differ from dict, relying on the original class for the majority of the functionality.

In this exercise, we'll also implement a subclass of dict, which I call FlexibleDict. Dict keys are Python objects, and as such are identified with a type. So if you use key 1 (an integer) to store a value, then you can't use key '1' (a string) to retrieve that value. But FlexibleDict will allow for this. If it doesn't find the user's key, it will try to convert the key to both str and int before giving up; for example

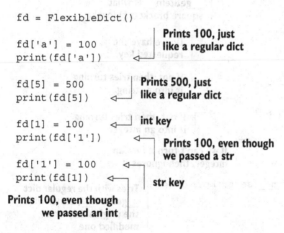

```
fd = FlexibleDict()

fd['a'] = 100
print(fd['a'])          Prints 100, just
                        like a regular dict

fd[5] = 500
print(fd[5])            Prints 500, just
                        like a regular dict

fd[1] = 100             int key
print(fd['1'])
                        Prints 100, even though
                        we passed a str

fd['1'] = 100           str key
print(fd[1])

Prints 100, even though
we passed an int
```

Working it out

This exercise's class, FlexibleDict, is an example of where you might just want to inherit from a built-in type. It's somewhat rare, but as you can see here, it allows us to create an alternative type of dict.

The specification of FlexibleDict indicates that everything should work just like a regular dict, except for retrievals. We thus only need to override one method, the __getitem__ method that's always associated with square brackets in Python. Indeed, if you've ever wondered why strings, lists, tuples, and dicts are defined in different ways but all use square brackets, this method is the reason.

Because everything should be the same as dict except for this single method, we can inherit from dict, write one method, and be done.

This method receives a key argument. If the key isn't in the dict, then we try to turn it into a string and an integer. Because we might encounter a ValueError trying to turn a key into an integer, we trap for ValueError along the way. At each turn, we check to see if a version of the key with a different type might actually work—and, if so, we reassign the value of key.

At the end of the method, we call our parent __getitem__ method. Why don't we just use square brackets? Because that will lead to an infinite loop, seeing as square brackets are defined to invoke __getitem__. In other words, a[b] is turned into a.__getitem__(b). If we then include self[b] inside the definition of __getitem__, we'll end up having the method call itself. We thus need to explicitly call the parent's method, which in any event will return the associated value.

> **NOTE** While FlexibleDict (and some of the "Beyond the exercise" tasks) might be great for teaching you Python skills, building this kind of flexibility into Python is very un-Pythonic and not recommended. One of the key ideas in Python is that code should be unambiguous, and in Python it's also better to get an error than for the language to guess.

Solution

```
class FlexibleDict(dict):
    def __getitem__(self, key):
        try:
            if key in self:
                pass
            elif str(key) in self:
                key = str(key)
            elif int(key) in self:
                key = int(key)
        except ValueError:
            pass

        return dict.__getitem__(self, key)

fd = FlexibleDict()

fd['a'] = 100
print(fd['a'])

fd[5] = 500
print(fd[5])

fd[1] = 100
print(fd['1'])

fd['1'] = 100
print(fd[1])
```

__getitem__ is what square brackets [] invoke.

Do we have the requested key?

If not, then tries turning it into a string

If not, then tries turning it into an integer

If we can't turn it into an integer, then ignores it

Tries with the regular dict __getitem__, either with the original key or a modified one

You can work through a version of this code in the Python Tutor at http://mng.bz/ lGx6.

Screencast solution

Watch this short video walkthrough of the solution: https://livebook.manning.com/ video/python-workout.

Beyond the exercise

We've now seen how to extend a built-in class using inheritance. Here are some more exercises you can try, in which you'll also experiment with extending some built-in classes:

- With `FlexibleDict`, we allowed the user to use any key, but were then flexible with the retrieval. Implement `StringKeyDict`, which converts its keys into strings as part of the assignment. Thus, immediately after saying `skd[1] = 10`, you would be able to then say `skd['1']` and get the value of 10 returned. This can come in handy if you'll be reading keys from a file and won't be able to distinguish between strings and integers.

- The `RecentDict` class works just like a `dict`, except that it contains a user-defined number of key-value pairs, which are determined when the instance is created. In a `RecentDict(5)`, only the five most recent key-value pairs are kept; if there are more than five pairs, then the oldest key is removed, along with its value. Note: your implementation could take into account the fact that modern dicts store their key-value pairs in chronological order.

- The `FlatList` class inherits from `list` and overrides the append method. If append is passed an iterable, then it should add each element of the iterable separately. This means that `fl.append([10, 20, 30])` would not add the list `[10, 20, 30]` to fl, but would rather add the individual integers 10, 20, and 30. You might want to use the built-in `iter` function (http://mng.bz/Qy2G) to determine whether the passed argument is indeed iterable.

EXERCISE 43 ■ Animals

For the final three exercises in this chapter, we're going to create a set of classes that combine all of the ideas we've explored in this chapter: classes, methods, attributes, composition, and inheritance. It's one thing to learn about and use them separately, but when you combine these techniques together, you see their power and understand the organizational and semantic advantages that they offer.

For the purposes of these exercises, you are the director of IT at a zoo. The zoo contains several different kinds of animals, and for budget reasons, some of those animals have to be housed alongside other animals.

We will represent the animals as Python objects, with each species defined as a distinct class. All objects of a particular class will have the same species and number of legs, but the color will vary from one instance to another. We can thus create a white sheep:

```
s = Sheep('white')
```

I can similarly get information about the animal back from the object by retrieving its attributes:

```
                          │ Prints "sheep"
print(s.species)       ◄──┘
print(s.color)         ◄──┘ Prints "white"
print(s.number_of_legs)   ◄──┐
                          │ Prints "4"
```

If I convert the animal to a string (using str or print), I'll get back a string combining all of these details:

```
                     │ Prints "White
print(s)          ◄──┤ sheep, 4 legs"
```

We're going to assume that our zoo contains four different types of animals: sheep, wolves, snakes, and parrots. (The zoo is going through some budgetary difficulties, so our animal collection is both small and unusual.) Create classes for each of these types, such that we can print each of them and get a report on their color, species, and number of legs.

Working it out

The end goal here is somewhat obvious: we want to have four different classes (Wolf, Sheep, Snake, and Parrot), each of which takes a single argument representing a color. The result of invoking each of these classes is a new instance with three attributes: species, color, and number_of_legs.

A naive implementation would simply create each of these four classes. But of course, part of the point here is to use inheritance, and the fact that the behavior in each class is basically identical means that we can indeed take advantage of it. But what will go into the Animal class, from which everyone inherits, and what will go into each of the individual subclasses?

Since all of the animal classes will have the same attributes, we can define __repr__ on Animal, the class from which they'll all inherit. My version uses an f-string and grabs the attributes from self. Note that self in this case will be an instance not of Animal, but of one of the classes that inherits from Animal.

So, what else should be in Animal, and what should be in the subclasses? There's no hard-and-fast rule here, but in this particular case, I decided that Animal.__init__ would be where the assignments all happen, and that the __init__ method in each subclass would invoke Animal.__init__ with a hardcoded number of legs, as well as the color designated by the user (figure 9.13).

In theory, __init__ in a subclass could call Animal.__init__ directly and by name. But we also have access to super, which returns the object on which our method

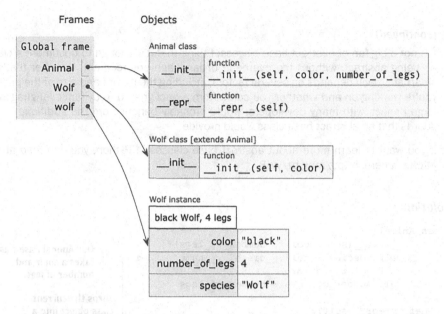

Figure 9.13   `Wolf` **inherits from** `Animal`**. Notice which methods are defined where.**

should be called. In other words, by calling `super().__init__`, we know that the right method will be called on the right object, and can just pass along the `color` and `number_of_legs` arguments.

But wait, what about the `species` attribute? How can we set that without input from the user?

My solution to this problem was to take advantage of the fact that Python classes are very similar to modules, with similar behavior. Just as a module has a `__name__` attribute that reflects what module was loaded, so too classes have a `__name__` attribute, which is a string containing the name of the current class. And thus, if I invoke `self.__class__` on an object, I get its class—and if I invoke `self.__class__.__name__`, I get a string representation of the class.

Abstract base classes

The `Animal` class here is what other languages might call an *abstract base class*, namely one that we won't actually instantiate, but from which other classes will inherit. In Python, you don't have to declare such a class to be abstract, but you also won't get the enforcement that other languages provide. If you really want, you can import ABC-Meta from the `abc` (abstract base class) module. Following its instructions, you'll be able to declare particular methods as *abstract*, meaning that they must be overridden in the child.

(continued)

I'm not a big fan of abstract base classes; I think that it's enough to document a class as being abstract, without the overhead or language enforcement. Whether that's a smart approach depends on several factors, including the nature and size of the project you're working on and whether you come from a background in dynamic languages. A large project, with many developers, would probably benefit from the additional safeguards that an abstract base class would provide.

If you want to learn more about abstract base classes in Python, you can read about `ABCMeta` here: http://mng.bz/yyJB.

Solution

```python
class Animal():
    def __init__(self, color, number_of_legs):
        self.species = self.__class__.__name__
        self.color = color
        self.number_of_legs = number_of_legs

    def __repr__(self):
        return f'{self.color} {self.species}, \
{self.number_of_legs} legs'

class Wolf(Animal):
    def __init__(self, color):
        super().__init__(color, 4)

class Sheep(Animal):
    def __init__(self, color):
        super().__init__(color, 4)

class Snake(Animal):
    def __init__(self, color):
        super().__init__(color, 0)

class Parrot(Animal):
    def __init__(self, color):
        super().__init__(color, 2)


wolf = Wolf('black')
sheep = Sheep('white')
snake = Snake('brown')
parrot = Parrot('green')

print(wolf)
print(sheep)
print(snake)
print(parrot)
```

Our Animal base class takes a color and number of legs.

Turns the current class object into a string

Uses an f-string to produce appropriate output

You can work through a version of this code in the Python Tutor at http://mng.bz/B2Z0.

Screencast solution

Watch this short video walkthrough of the solution: https://livebook.manning.com/video/python-workout.

Beyond the exercise

In this exercise, we put a few classes in place as part of a hierarchy. Here are some additional ways you can work with inheritance and think about the implications of the design decisions we're making. I should note that these questions, as well as those following in this chapter, are going to combine hands-on practice with some deeper, philosophical questions about the "right" way to work with object-oriented systems:

- Instead of each animal class inheriting directly, from `Animal`, define several new classes, `ZeroLeggedAnimal`, `TwoLeggedAnimal`, and `FourLeggedAnimal`, all of which inherit from `Animal`, and dictate the number of legs on each instance. Now modify `Wolf`, `Sheep`, `Snake`, and `Parrot` such that each class inherits from one of these new classes, rather than directly from `Animal`. How does this affect your method definitions?

- Instead of writing an `__init__` method in each subclass, we could also have a class attribute, `number_of_legs`, in each subclass—similar to what we did earlier with `Bowl` and `BigBowl`. Implement the hierarchy that way. Do you even need an `__init__` method in each subclass, or will `Animal.__init__` suffice?

- Let's say that each class's `__repr__` method should print the animal's sound, as well as the standard string we implemented previously. In other words, `str(sheep)` would be Baa—white sheep, 4 legs. How would you use inheritance to maximize code reuse?

EXERCISE 44 ■ Cages

Now that we've created some animals, it's time to put them into cages. For this exercise, create a `Cage` class, into which you can put one or more animals, as follows:

```
c1 = Cage(1)
c1.add_animals(wolf, sheep)

c2 = Cage(2)
c2.add_animals(snake, parrot)
```

When you create a new `Cage`, you'll give it a unique ID number. (The uniqueness doesn't need to be enforced, but it'll help us to distinguish among the cages.) You'll then be able to invoke `add_animals` on the new cage, passing any number of animals that will be put in the cage. I also want you to define a `__repr__` method so that printing a cage prints not just the cage ID, but also each of the animals it contains.

Working it out

The solution's definition of the Cage class is similar in some ways to the Bowl class that we defined earlier in this chapter.

When we create a new cage, the __init__ method initializes self.animals with an empty list, allowing us to add (and even remove) animals as necessary. We also store the ID number that was passed to us in the id_number parameter.

Next, we implement Cage.add_animals, which uses similar techniques to what we did in Bowl.add_scoops. Once again, we use the splat (*) operator to grab all arguments in a single tuple (animals). Although we could use list.extend to add all of the new animals to list.animals, I'll still use a for loop here to add them one at a time. You can see how the Python Tutor depicts two animals in a cage in figure 9.14.

The most interesting part of our Cage definition, in my mind, is our use of __repr__ to produce a report. Given a cage c1, saying print(c1) will print the ID of the cage, followed by all of the animals in the cage, using their printed representations. We do this by first printing a basic header, which isn't a huge deal. But then we take each animal in self.animals and use a generator expression (i.e., a lazy form of list comprehension) to return a sequence of strings. Each string in that sequence will consist of a tab followed by the printed representation of the animal. We then feed the result of our generator expression to str.join, which puts newline characters between each animal.

Solution

```python
class Animal():
    def __init__(self, color, number_of_legs):
        self.species = self.__class__.__name__
        self.color = color
        self.number_of_legs = number_of_legs

    def __repr__(self):
        return f'{self.color} {self.species}, {self.number_of_legs} legs'

class Wolf(Animal):
    def __init__(self, color):
        super().__init__(color, 4)


class Sheep(Animal):
    def __init__(self, color):
        super().__init__(color, 4)


class Snake(Animal):
    def __init__(self, color):
        super().__init__(color, 0)


class Parrot(Animal):
    def __init__(self, color):
        super().__init__(color, 2)
```

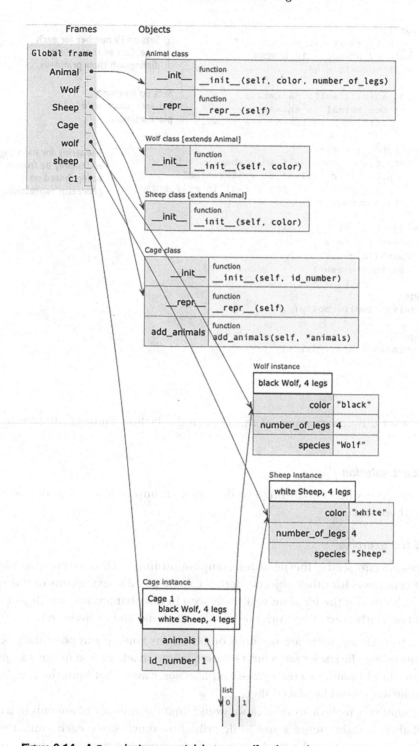

Figure 9.14 A Cage instance containing one wolf and one sheep

```
class Cage():
    def __init__(self, id_number):
        self.id_number = id_number
        self.animals = []

    def add_animals(self, *animals):
        for one_animal in animals:
            self.animals.append(one_animal)

    def __repr__(self):
        output = f'Cage {self.id_number}\n'
        output += '\n'.join('\t' + str(animal)
                            for animal in self.animals)
        return output
wolf = Wolf('black')
sheep = Sheep('white')
snake = Snake('brown')
parrot = Parrot('green')

c1 = Cage(1)
c1.add_animals(wolf, sheep)

c2 = Cage(2)
c2.add_animals(snake, parrot)

print(c1)
print(c2)
```

Annotations:
- Sets an ID number for each cage, just so that we can distinguish their printouts
- Sets up an empty list, into which we'll place animals
- The string for each cage will mainly be from a string, based on a generator expression.

You can work through a version of this code in the Python Tutor at http://mng.bz/dyeN.

Screencast solution

Watch this short video walkthrough of the solution: https://livebook.manning.com/video/python-workout.

Beyond the exercise

We're once again seeing the need for composition in our classes—creating objects that are containers for other objects. Here are some possible extensions to this code, all of which draw on the ideas we've already seen in this chapter, and which you'll see repeated in nearly every object-oriented system you build and encounter:

- As you can see, there are no limits on how many animals can potentially be put into a cage. Just as we put a limit of three scoops in a Bowl and five in a BigBowl, you should similarly create Cage and BigCage classes that limit the number of animals that can be placed there.
- It's not very realistic to say that we would limit the number of animals in a cage. Rather, it makes more sense to describe how much space each animal needs and to ensure that the total amount of space needed per animal isn't greater

than the space in each cage. You should thus modify each of the `Animal` sub-classes to include a `space_required` attribute. Then modify the `Cage` and `Big-Cage` classes to reflect how much space each one has. Adding more animals than the cage can contain should raise an exception.

■ Our zookeepers have a macabre sense of humor when it comes to placing animals together, in that they put wolves and sheep in the first cage, and snakes and birds in the other cage. (The good news is that with such a configuration, the zoo will be able to save on food for half of the animals.) Define a dict describing which animals can be with others. The keys in the dict will be classes, and the values will be lists of classes that can compatibly be housed with the keys. Then, when adding new animals to the current cage, you'll check for compatibility. Trying to add an animal to a cage that already contains an incompatible animal will raise an exception.

EXERCISE 45 ■ Zoo

Finally, the time has come to create our `Zoo` object. It will contain cage objects, and they in turn will contain animals. Our `Zoo` class will need to support the following operations:

■ Given a zoo z, we should be able to print all of the cages (with their ID numbers) and the animals inside simply by invoking `print(z)`.

■ We should be able to get the animals with a particular color by invoking the method `z.animals_by_color`. For example, we can get all of the black animals by invoking `z.animals_by_color('black')`. The result should be a list of `Animal` objects.

■ We should be able to get the animals with a particular number of legs by invoking the method `z.animals_by_legs`. For example, we can get all of the four-legged animals by invoking `z.animals_by_legs(4)`. The result should be a list of `Animal` objects.

■ Finally, we have a potential donor to our zoo who wants to provide socks for all of the animals. Thus, we need to be able to invoke `z.number_of_legs()` and get a count of the total number of legs for all animals in our zoo.

The exercise is thus to create a `Zoo` class on which we can invoke the following:

```
z = Zoo()
z.add_cages(c1, c2)

print(z)
print(z.animals_by_color('white'))
print(z.animals_by_legs(4))
print(z.number_of_legs())
```

Working it out

In some ways, our Zoo class here is quite similar to our Cage class. It has a list attribute, self.cages, in which we'll store the cages. It has an add_cages method, which takes *args and thus takes any number of inputs. Even the __repr__ method is similar to what we did with Cage.__repr__. We'll simply use str.join on the output from running str on each of the cages, just as the cages run str on each of the animals. We'll similarly use a generator expression here, which will be slightly more efficient than a list comprehension.

But then, when it comes to the three methods we needed to create, we'll switch direction a little bit. In both animals_by_color and animals_by_legs, we want to get the animals with a certain color or a certain number of legs. Here, we take advantage of the fact that the zoo contains a list of cages, and that each cage contains a list of animals. We can thus use a nested list comprehension, getting a list of all of the animals.

But of course, we don't want all of the animals, so we have an if statement that filters out those that we don't want. In the case of animals_by_color, we only include those animals that have the right color, and in animals_by_legs, we only keep those animals with the requested number of legs.

But then we also have number_of_legs, which works a bit differently. There, we want to get an integer back, reflecting the number of legs that are in the entire zoo. Here, we can take advantage of the built-in sum method, handing it the generator expression that goes through each cage and retrieves the number of legs on each animal. The method will thus return an integer.

Although the object-oriented and functional programming camps have been fighting for decades over which approach is superior, I think that the methods in this Zoo class show us that each has its strengths, and that our code can be short, elegant, and to the point if we combine the techniques. That said, I often get pushback from students who see this code and say that it's a violation of the object-oriented principle of *encapsulation*, which ensures that we can't (or shouldn't) directly access the data in other objects.

Whether this is right or wrong, such violations are also fairly common in the Python world. Because all data is public (i.e., there's no private or protected), it's considered a good and reasonable thing to just scoop the data out of objects. That said, this also means that whoever writes a class has a responsibility to document it, and to keep the API alive—or to document elements that may be deprecated or removed in the future.

Solution

This is the longest and most complex class definition in this chapter—and yet, each of the methods uses techniques that we've discussed, both in this chapter and in this book:

```
class Zoo():
    def __init__(self):
        self.cages = []
```

Sets up the self.cages attribute, a list where we'll store cages

```
        def add_cages(self, *cages):
            for one_cage in cages:
                self.cages.append(one_cage)

        def __repr__(self):
            return '\n'.join(str(one_cage)
                             for one_cage in self.cages)

        def animals_by_color(self, color):          ◄──────    Defines the method
            return [one_animal                                  that'll return animal
                    for one_cage in self.cages                  objects that match
                    for one_animal in one_cage.animals          our color
                    if one_animal.color == color]

        def animals_by_legs(self, number_of_legs):   ◄──────    Defines the method
            return [one_animal                                  that'll return animal
                    for one_cage in self.cages                  objects that match
                    for one_animal in one_cage.animals          our number of legs
                    if one_animal.number_of_legs ==
                        number_of_legs]

        def number_of_legs(self):                    ◄──────    Returns the
            return sum(one_animal.number_of_legs                number of legs
                       for one_cage in self.cages
                       for one_animal in one_cage.animals)

wolf = Wolf('black')
sheep = Sheep('white')
snake = Snake('brown')
parrot = Parrot('green')

print(wolf)
print(sheep)
print(snake)
print(parrot)

c1 = Cage(1)
c1.add_animals(wolf, sheep)

c2 = Cage(2)
c2.add_animals(snake, parrot)

z = Zoo()
z.add_cages(c1, c2)

print(z)
print(z.animals_by_color('white'))
print(z.animals_by_legs(4))
print(z.number_of_legs())
```

You can work through a version of this code in the Python Tutor at http://mng.bz/
lGMB.

Screencast solution

Watch this short video walkthrough of the solution: https://livebook.manning.com/video/python-workout.

Beyond the exercise

Now that you've seen how all of these elements fit together in our Zoo class, here are some additional exercises you might want to try out, to extend what we've done—and to better understand object-oriented programming in Python:

- Modify `animals_by_color` such that it takes any number of colors. Animals having any of the listed colors should be returned. The method should raise an exception if no colors are passed.
- As things currently stand, we're treating our Zoo class almost as if it's a *singleton* object—that is, a class that has only one instance. What a sad world that would be, with only one zoo! Let's assume, then, that we have two instances of Zoo, representing two different zoos, and that we would like to transfer an animal from one to the other. Implement a `Zoo.transfer_animal` method that takes a `target_zoo` and a subclass of `Animal` as arguments. The first animal of the specified type is removed from the zoo on which we've called the method and inserted into the first cage in the target zoo.
- Combine the `animals_by_color` and `animals_by_legs` methods into a single `get_animals` method, which uses `kwargs` to get names and values. The only valid names would be `color` and `legs`. The method would then use one or both of these keywords to assemble a query that returns those animals that match the passed criteria.

Summary

Object-oriented programming is a set of techniques, but it's also a mindset. In many languages, object-oriented programming is forced on you, such that you're constantly trying to fit your programming into its syntax and structure. Python tries to strike a balance, offering all of the object-oriented features we're likely to want or use, but in a simple, nonconfrontational way. In this way, Python's objects provide us with structure and organization that can make our code easier to write, read, and (most importantly) maintain.

Iterators and generators

10

Have you ever noticed that many Python objects know how to behave inside of a
for loop? That's not an accident. Iteration is so useful, and so common, that
Python makes it easy for an object to be iterable. All it has to do is implement a
handful of behaviors, known collectively as *the iterator protocol*.

In this chapter, we'll explore that protocol and how we can use it to create iterable objects. We'll do this in three ways:

1 We'll create our own iterators via Python classes, directly implementing the
   protocol ourselves.

2 We'll create *generators*, objects that implement the protocol, based on something
   that looks very similar to a function. Not surprisingly, these are known
   as *generator functions*.

3 We'll also create generators using *generator expressions*, which look quite a bit
   like list comprehensions.

Even newcomers to Python know that if you want to iterate over the characters in a
string, you can write

```
for i in 'abcd':
    print(i)
```
**Prints a, b, c, and d,
each on a separate line**

This feels natural, and that's the point. What if you just want to execute a chunk of
code five times? Can you iterate over the integer 5? Many newcomers to Python
assume that the answer is yes and write the following:

```
for i in 5:
    print(i)
```
**This doesn't
work.**

197

This code produces an error:

```
TypeError: 'int' object is not iterable
```

From this, we can see that while strings, lists, and dicts are iterable, integers aren't. They aren't because they don't implement the iterator protocol, which consists of three parts:

- The __iter__ method, which returns an iterator
- The __next__ method, which must be defined on the iterator
- The StopIteration exception, which the iterator raises to signal the end of the iterations

Sequences (strings, lists, and tuples) are the most common form of iterables, but a large number of other objects, such as files and dicts, are also iterable. Best of all, when you define your own classes, you can make them iterable. All you have to do is make sure that the iterator protocol is in place on your object.

Given those three parts, we can now understand what a for loop really does:

- It asks an object whether it's iterable using the iter built-in function (http:// mng.bz/jgja). This function invokes the __iter__ method on the target object. Whatever __iter__ returns is called the *iterator*.
- If the object is iterable, then the for loop invokes the next built-in function on the iterator that was returned. That function invokes __next__ on the iterator.
- If __next__ raises a StopIteration exception, then the loop exits.

This protocol explains a couple things that tend to puzzle newcomers to Python:

1 Why don't we need any indexes? In C-like languages, we need a numeric index for our iterations. That's so the loop can go through each of the elements of the collection, one at a time. In those cases, the loop is responsible for keeping track of the current location. In Python, the object itself is responsible for producing the next item. The for loop doesn't know whether we're on the first item or the last one. But it does know when we've reached the end.

2 How is it that different objects behave differently in for loops? After all, strings return characters, but dicts return keys, and files return lines. The answer is that the iterator object can return whatever it wants. So string iterators return characters, dict iterators return keys, and file iterators return the lines in a file.

If you're defining a new class, you can make it iterable as follows:

- Define an __iter__ method that takes only self as an argument and returns self. In other words, when Python asks your object, "Are you iterable?" the answer will be, "Yes, and I'm my own iterator."
- Define a __next__ method that takes only self as an argument. This method should either return a value or raise StopIteration. If it never returns Stop-Iteration, then any for loop on this object will never exit.

There are some more sophisticated ways to do things, including returning a separate, different object from __iter__. I demonstrate and discuss that later in this chapter.

Here's a simple class that implements the protocol, wrapping itself around an iterable object but indicating when it reaches each stage of iteration:

```
class LoudIterator():
    def __init__(self, data):
        print('\tNow in __init__')      ┐  Stores the data in an
        self.data = data             ◄──┘  attribute, self.data
        self.index = 0    ◄───┐  Creates an index
                              │  attribute, keeping track
    def __iter__(self):       │  of our current position
        print('\tNow in __iter__')
        return self    ◄───┐  Our __iter__ does the simplest
                           │  thing, returning self.
    def __next__(self):
        print('\tNow in __next__')
        if self.index >= len(self.data):   ◄──┐  Raises StopIteration if our
            print(                            │  self.index has reached the end
                f'\tself.index ({self.index}) is too big; exiting')
            raise StopIteration
                                     ┐  Grabs the current value,
                                     │  but doesn't return it yet
        value = self.data[self.index]  ◄──┘
        self.index += 1
        print('\tGot value {value}, incremented index to {self.index}')
        return value
```

Increments self.index points to the line `self.index += 1`.

```
for one_item in LoudIterator('abc'):
    print(one_item)
```

If we execute this code, we'll see the following output:

```
Now in __init__
        Now in __iter__
        Now in __next__
        Got value a, incremented index to 1
a
        Now in __next__
        Got value b, incremented index to 2
b
        Now in __next__
        Got value c, incremented index to 3
c
        Now in __next__
        self.index (3) is too big; exiting
```

This output walks us through the iteration process that we've already seen, starting with a call to __iter__ and then repeated invocations of __next__. The loop exits when the iterator raises StopIteration.

Adding such methods to a class works when you're creating your own new types. There are two other ways to create iterators in Python:

1 You can use a generator expression, which we've already seen and used. As you might remember, generator expressions look and work similarly to list comprehensions, except that you use round parentheses rather than square brackets. But unlike list comprehensions, which return lists that might consume a great deal of memory, generator expressions return one element at a time.

2 You can use a *generator function*—something that looks like a function, but when executed acts like an iterator; for example

```
def foo():
    yield 1
    yield 2
    yield 3
```

When we execute `foo`, the function's body doesn't execute. Rather, we get a generator object back—that is, something that implements the iterator protocol. We can thus put it in a `for` loop:

```
g = foo()
for one_item in g:
    print(one_item)
```

This loop will print 1, 2, and 3. Why? Because with each iteration (i.e., each time we call `next` on g), the function executes through the next `yield` statement, returns the value it got from `yield`, and then goes to sleep, waiting for the next iteration. When the generator function exits, it automatically raises `StopIteration`, thus ending the loop.

Iterators are pervasive in Python because they're so convenient—and in many ways, they've been made convenient because they're pervasive. In this chapter, you'll practice writing all of these types of iterators and getting a feel for when each of these techniques should be used.

iterable vs. iterator

The two terms *iterable* and *iterator* are very similar but have different meanings:

- An iterable object can be put inside a `for` loop or list comprehension. For something to be iterable, it must implement the __iter__ method. That method should return an iterator .
- An iterator is an object that implements the __next__ method.

In many cases, an iterable is its own iterator. For example, file objects are their own iterators. But in many other cases, such as strings and lists, the iterable object returns a separate, different object as an iterator.

Table 10.1 What you need to know

Concept	What is it?	Example	To learn more
`iter`	A built-in function that returns an object's iterator	`iter('abcd')`	http://mng.bz/jgja
`next`	A built-in function that requests the next object from an iterator	`next(i)`	http://mng.bz/WPBg
`StopIteration`	An exception raised to indicate the end of a loop	`raise StopIteration`	http://mng.bz/8p0K
`enumerate`	Helps us to number elements of iterables	`for i, c in enumerate('ab'):` `print(f'{i}: {c}')`	http://mng.bz/qM1K
Iterables	A category of data in Python	Iterables can be put in `for` loops or passed to many functions.	http://mng.bz/EdDq
`itertools`	A module with many classes for implementing iterables	`import itertools`	http://mng.bz/NK4E

`range`	Returns an iterable sequence of integers	`# every 3rd integer, from 10`
		`# to (not including) 50`
		`range(10, 50, 3)`
			http://mng.bz/B2DJ

`os.listdir`	Returns a list of files in a directory	`os.listdir('/etc/')`	http://mng.bz/YreB
`os.walk`	Iterates over the files in a directory	`os.walk('/etc/')`	http://mng.bz/D2Ky
`yield`	Returns control to the loop temporarily, optionally returning a value	`yield 5`	http://mng.bz/lG9j
`os.path.join`	Returns a string based on the path components	`os.path.join('etc',` `'passwd')`	http://mng.bz/oPPM
`time.perf_counter`	Returns the number of elapsed seconds (as a float) since the program was started	`time.perf_counter()`	http://mng.bz/B21v

`zip`	Takes n iterables as arguments and returns an iterator of tuples of length n	`# returns [('a', 10),`
		`# ('b', 20), ('c', 30)]`
		`zip('abc',`
		`[10, 20, 30])`
			http://mng.bz/Jyzv

EXERCISE 46 ▪ MyEnumerate

The built-in enumerate function allows us to get not just the elements of a sequence, but also the index of each element, as in

```
for index, letter in enumerate('abc'):
    print(f'{index}: {letter}')
```

Create your own MyEnumerate class, such that someone can use it instead of enumerate. It will need to return a tuple with each iteration, with the first element in the tuple being the index (starting with 0) and the second element being the current element from the underlying data structure. Trying to use MyEnumerate with a noniterable argument will result in an error.

Working it out

In this exercise, we know that our MyEnumerate class will take a single iterable object. With each iteration, we'll get back not one of that argument's elements, but rather a two-element tuple.

This means that at the end of the day, we're going to need a __next__ method that will return a tuple. Moreover, it'll need to keep track of the current index. Since __next__, like all methods and functions, loses its local scope between calls, we'll need to store the current index in another place. Where? On the object itself, as an attribute.

Thus, our __init__ method will initialize two attributes: self.data, where we'll store the object over which we're iterating, and self.index, which will start with 0 and be incremented with each call to __next__. Our implementation of __iter__ will be the standard one that we've seen so far, namely return self.

Finally __next__ checks to see if self.index has gone past the length of self.data. If so, then we raise StopIteration, which causes the for loop to exit.

Multiclass iterators

So far, we've seen that our __iter__ method should consist of the line return self and no more. This is often a fine way to go. But you can get into trouble. For example, what happens if I use our MyEnumerate class in the following way?

```
e = MyEnumerate('abc')

print('** A **')
for index, one_item in e:
    print(f'{index}: {one_item}')

print('** B **')
for index, one_item in e:
    print(f'{index}: {one_item}')
```

We'll see the following printout:

```
** A **
0: a
1: b
2: c
** B **
```

Why didn't we get a second round of a, b, and c? Because we're using the same iterator object each time. The first time around, its `self.index` goes through 0, 1, and 2, and then stops. The second time around, `self.index` is already at 2, which is greater than `len(self.data)`, and so it immediately exits from the loop.

Our `return self` solution for `__iter__` is fine if that's the behavior you want. But in many cases, we need something more sophisticated. The easiest solution is to use a second class—a helper class, if you will—which will be the iterator for our class. Many of Python's built-in classes do this already, including strings, lists, tuples, and dicts. In such a case, we implement `__iter__` on the main class, but its job is to return a new instance of the helper class:

```
# in MyEnumerate

def __iter__(self):
    return MyEnumerateIterator(self.data)
```

Then we define `MyEnumerateIterator`, a new and separate class, whose `__init__` looks much like the one we already defined for `MyIterator` and whose `__next__` is taken directly from `MyIterator`.

There are two advantages to this design:

1 As we've already seen, by separating the iterable from the iterator, we can put our iterable in as many `for` loops as we want, without having to worry that it'll lose the iterations somehow.

2 The second advantage is organizational. If we want to make a class iterable, the iterations are a small part of the functionality. Thus, do we really want to clutter the class with a `__next__`, as well as attributes used only when iterating? By delegating such problems to a helper iterator class, we separate out the iterable aspects and allow each class to concentrate on its role.

Many people think that we can solve the problem in a simpler way, simply by resetting `self.index` to 0 whenever `__iter__` is called. But that has some flaws too. It means that if we want to use the same iterable in two different loops simultaneously, they'll interfere with one another. Such problems won't occur with a helper class.

Solution

```
class MyEnumerate():
    def __init__(self, data):
        self.data = data
        self.index = 0
```

Initializes MyEnumerate with an iterable argument, "data"

Stores "data" on the object as self.data

Initializes self.index with 0

```
    def __iter__(self):
        return self
```
Because our object will be its own iterator, returns self

```
    def __next__(self):
        if self.index >= len(self.data):
            raise StopIteration
```
Are we at the end of the data? If so, then raises StopIteration.

```
        value = (self.index, self.data[self.index])
```
Sets the value to be a tuple, with the index and value

```
        self.index += 1
```
Increments the index

Returns the tuple
```
        return value
```

```
for index, letter in MyEnumerate('abc'):
    print(f'{index} : {letter}')
```

You can work through a version of this code in the Python Tutor at http://mng.bz/JydQ.

Note that the Python Tutor sometimes displays an error message when StopIteration is raised.

Screencast solution

Watch this short video walkthrough of the solution: https://livebook.manning.com/video/python-workout.

Beyond the exercise

Now that you've created a simple iterator class, let's dig in a bit deeper:

- Rewrite MyEnumerate such that it uses a helper class (MyEnumerateIterator), as described in the "Discussion" section. In the end, MyEnumerate will have the __iter__ method that returns a new instance of MyEnumerateIterator, and the helper class will implement __next__. It should work the same way, but will also produce results if we iterate over it twice in a row.
- The built-in enumerate method takes a second, optional argument—an integer, representing the first index that should be used. (This is particularly handy when numbering things for nontechnical users, who believe that things should be numbered starting with 1, rather than 0.)
- Redefine MyEnumerate as a generator function, rather than as a class.

EXERCISE 47 ▪ Circle

From the examples we've seen so far, it might appear as though an iterable simply goes through the elements of whatever data it's storing and then exits. But an iterator can do anything it wants, and can return whatever data it wants, until the point when it raises StopIteration. In this exercise, we see just how that works.

Define a class, Circle, that takes two arguments when defined: a sequence and a number. The idea is that the object will then return elements the defined number of times. If the number is greater than the number of elements, then the sequence repeats as necessary. You should define the class such that it uses a helper (which I call `CircleIterator`). Here's an example:

```
c = Circle('abc', 5)
print(list(c))          ⟵─┘  Prints a, b, c, a, b
```

Working it out

In many ways, our `Circle` class is a simple iterator, going through each of its values. But we might need to provide more outputs than we have inputs, circling around to the beginning one or more times.

The trick here is to use the modulus operator (`%`), which returns the integer remainder from a division operation. Modulus is often used in programs to ensure that we can wrap around as many times as we need.

In this case, we're retrieving from `self.data`, as per usual. But the element won't be `self.data[self.index]`, but rather `self.data[self.index % len(self.data)]`.

Since `self.index` will likely end up being bigger than `len(self.data)`, we can no longer use that as a test for whether we should raise `StopIteration`. Rather, we'll need to have a separate attribute, `self.max_times`, which tells us how many iterations we should execute.

Once we have all of this in place, the implementation becomes fairly straightforward. Our `Circle` class remains with only `__init__` and `__iter__`, the latter of which returns a new instance of `CircleIterator`. Note that we have to pass both `self.data` and `self.max_times` to `CircleIterator`, and thus need to store them as attributes in our instance of `Circle`.

Our iterator then uses the logic we described in its `__next__` method to return one element at a time, until we have `self.max_times` items.

Another solution

Oliver Hach and Reik Thormann, who read an earlier edition of this book, shared an elegant solution with me:

```
class Circle():

    def __init__(self, data, max_times):
        self.data = data
        self.max_times = max_times

    def __iter__(self):
        n = len(self.data)
        return (self.data[x % n] for x in range(self.max_times))
```

This version of `Circle` takes advantage of the fact that an iterating class may return *any* iterator, not just `self`, and not just an instance of a helper class. In this case, they returned a generator expression, which is an iterator by all standards.

(continued)

The generator expression iterates a particular number of times, as determined by self.max_times, feeding that to range. We can then iterate over range, returning the appropriate element of self.data with each iteration.

In this way, we see there are multiple ways to answer the question, "What should __iter__ return?" As long as it returns an iterator object, it doesn't matter whether it's an iterable self, an instance of a helper class, or a generator.

Solution

```
class CircleIterator():
    def __init__(self, data, max_times):
        self.data = data
        self.max_times = max_times
        self.index = 0

    def __next__(self):
        if self.index >= self.max_times:
            raise StopIteration
        value = self.data[self.index % len(self.data)]
        self.index += 1
        return value


class Circle():
    def __init__(self, data, max_times):
        self.data = data
        self.max_times = max_times

    def __iter__(self):
        return CircleIterator(self.data,
                              self.max_times)

c = Circle('abc', 5)
print(list(c))
```

You can work through a version of this code in the Python Tutor at http://mng.bz/wBjg.

Screencast solution

Watch this short video walkthrough of the solution: https://livebook.manning.com/video/python-workout.

Beyond the exercise

I hope you're starting to see the potential for iterators, and how they can be written in a variety of ways. Here are some additional exercises to get you thinking about what those ways could be:

- Rather than write a helper, you could also define iteration capabilities in a class and then inherit from it. Reimplement `Circle` as a class that inherits from `CircleIterator`, which implements `__init__` and `__next__`. Of course, the parent class will have to know what to return in each iteration; add a new attribute in `Circle`, `self.returns`, a list of attribute names that should be returned.
- Implement `Circle` as a generator function, rather than as a class.
- Implement a `MyRange` class that returns an iterator that works the same as range, at least in `for` loops. (Modern range objects have a host of other capabilities, such as being subscriptable. Don't worry about that.) The class, like range, should take one, two, or three integer arguments.

EXERCISE 48 ▪ All lines, all files

File objects, as we've seen, are iterators; when we put them in a `for` loop, each iteration returns the next line from the file. But what if we want to read through a number of files? It would be nice to have an iterator that goes through each of them.

In this exercise, I'd like you to create just such an iterator, using a generator function. That is, this generator function will take a directory name as an argument. With each iteration, the generator should return a single string, representing one line from one file in that directory. Thus, if the directory contains five files, and each file contains 10 lines, the generator will return a total of 50 strings—each of the lines from file 0, then each of the lines from file 1, then each of the lines from file 2, until it gets through all of the lines from file 4.

If you encounter a file that can't be opened—because it's a directory, because you don't have permission to read from it, and so on—you should just ignore the problem altogether.

Working it out

Let's start the discussion by pointing out that if you really wanted to do this the right way, you would likely use the `os.walk` function (http://mng.bz/D2Ky), which goes through each of the files in a directory and then descends into its subdirectories. But we'll ignore that and work to understand the `all_lines` generator function that I've created here.

First, we run `os.listdir` on `path`. This returns a list of strings. It's important to remember that `os.listdir` only returns the filenames, not the full path of the file. This means that we can't just open the filename; we need to combine `path` with the filename.

We could use `str.join`, or even just + or an f-string. But there's a better approach, namely `os.path.join` (http://mng.bz/oPPM), which takes any number of parameters (thanks to the `*args`) and then joins them together with the value of `os.sep`, the directory-separation character for the current operating system. Thus, we don't need to think about whether we're on a Unix or Windows system; Python can do that work for us.

What if there's a problem reading from the file? We then trap that with an except OSError clause, in which we have nothing more than pass. The pass keyword means that Python shouldn't do anything; it's needed because of the structure of Python's syntax, which requires something indented following a colon. But we don't want to do anything if an error occurs, so we use pass.

And if there's no problem? Then we simply return the current line using yield. Immediately after the yield, the function goes to sleep, waiting for the next time a for loop invokes next on it.

> **NOTE** Using except without specifying which exception you might get is generally frowned upon, all the more so if you pair it with pass. If you do this in production code, you'll undoubtedly encounter problems at some point, and because you haven't trapped specific exceptions or logged the errors, you'll have trouble debugging the problem as a result. For a good (if slightly old) introduction to Python exceptions and how they should be used, see: http://mng.bz/VgBX.

Solution

```
import os


def all_lines(path):
    for filename in os.listdir(path):          Gets a list of files in path
        full_filename = os.path.join(path,      Uses os.path.join to create a full filename
                                 filename)       that we'll open
        try:
            for line in open(full_filename):     Opens and iterates over each line in full_filename
                yield line                       Returns the line using yield, needed in iterators
        except OSError:
            pass                                 Ignores file-related problems silently
```

The Python Tutor site doesn't work with files, so there's no link to it. But you could see all of the lines from all files in the /etc/ directory on your computer with

```
for one_line in all_lines('/etc/'):
    print(one_line)
```

Screencast solution

Watch this short video walkthrough of the solution: https://livebook.manning.com/video/python-workout.

Beyond the exercise

If something you want to do as an iterator doesn't align with an existing class but can be defined as a function, then a generator function will likely be a good way to implement it. Generator functions are particularly useful in taking potentially large quantities of data, breaking them down, and returning their output at a pace that won't overwhelm the system. Here are some other problems you can solve using generator functions:

- Modify all_lines such that it doesn't return a string with each iteration, but rather a tuple. The tuple should contain four elements: the name of the file, the current number of the file (from all those returned by os.listdir), the line number within the current file, and the current line.
- The current version of all_lines returns all of the lines from the first file, then all of the lines from the second file, and so forth. Modify the function such that it returns the first line from each file, and then the second line from each file, until all lines from all files are returned. When you finish printing lines from shorter files, ignore those files while continuing to display lines from the longer files.
- Modify all_lines such that it takes two arguments—a directory name, and a string. Only those lines containing the string (i.e., for which you can say s in line) should be returned. If you know how to work with regular expressions and Python's re module, then you could even make the match conditional on a regular expression.

NOTE In generator functions, we don't need to explicitly raise StopIteration. That happens automatically when the generator reaches the end of the function. Indeed, raising StopIteration from within the generator is something that you should not do. If you want to exit from the function prematurely, it's best to use a return statement. It's not an error to use return with a value (e.g., return 5) from a generator function, but the value will be ignored. In a generator function, then, yield indicates that you want to keep the generator going and return a value for the current iteration, while return indicates that you want to exit completely.

EXERCISE 49 ▪ Elapsed since

Sometimes, the point of an iterator is not to change existing data, but rather to provide data in addition to what we previously received. Moreover, a generator doesn't necessarily provide all of its values in immediate succession; it can be queried on occasion, whenever we need an additional value. Indeed, the fact that generators retain all of their state while sleeping between iterations means that they can just hang around, as it were, waiting until needed to provide the next value.

In this exercise, write a generator function whose argument must be iterable. With each iteration, the generator will return a two-element tuple. The first element in the tuple will be an integer indicating how many seconds have passed since the previous iteration. The tuple's second element will be the next item from the passed argument.

Note that the timing should be relative to the previous iteration, not when the generator was first created or invoked. Thus the timing number in the first iteration will be 0.

You can use `time.perf_counter`, which returns the number of seconds since the program was started. You could use `time.time`, but `perf_counter` is considered more reliable for such purposes.

Working it out

The solution's generator function takes a single piece of data and iterates over it. However, it returns a two-element tuple for each item it returns, in which the first element is the time since the previous iteration ran.

For this to work, we need to always know when the previous iteration was executed. Thus, we always calculate and set `last_time` before we `yield` the current values of `delta` and `item`.

However, we need to have a value for `delta` the first time we get a result back. This should be 0. To get around this, we set `last_time` to `None` at the top of the function. Then, with each iteration, we calculate `delta` to be the difference between `current_time` and `last_time` or `current_time`. If `last_time` is `None`, then we'll get the value of `current_time`. This should only occur once; after the first iteration, `last_time` will never be zero.

Normally, invoking a function multiple times means that the local variables are reset with each invocation. However, a generator function works differently: it's only invoked once, and thus has a single stack frame. This means that the local variables, including parameters, retain their values across calls. We can thus set such values as `last_time` and use them in future iterations.

Solution

```python
import time

def elapsed_since(data):
    last_time = None                        # Initializes last_time with None
    for item in data:
        current_time = time.perf_counter()  # Gets the current time
        delta = current_time - (last_time
                    or current_time)         # Calculates the delta between the last time and now
        last_time = time.perf_counter()
        yield (delta, item)                  # Returns a two-element tuple

for t in elapsed_since('abcd'):
    print(t)
    time.sleep(2)
```

You can work through a version of this code in the Python Tutor at http://mng.bz/qMjz.

Screencast solution

Watch this short video walkthrough of the solution: https://livebook.manning.com/video/python-workout.

Beyond the exercise

In this exercise, we saw how we can combine user-supplied data with additional information from the system. Here are some more exercises you can try to get additional practice writing such generator functions:

- The existing function elapsed_since reported how much time passed between iterations. Now write a generator function that takes two arguments—a piece of data and a minimum amount of time that must elapse between iterations. If the next element is requested via the iterator protocol (i.e., next), and the time elapsed since the previous iteration is greater than the user-defined minimum, then the value is returned. If not, then the generator uses time.sleep to wait until the appropriate amount of time has elapsed.

- Write a generator function, file_usage_timing, that takes a single directory name as an argument. With each iteration, we get a tuple containing not just the current filename, but also the three reports that we can get about a file's most recent usage: its access time (atime), modification time (mtime), and creation time (ctime). Hint: all are available via the os.stat function.

- Write a generator function that takes two elements: an iterable and a function. With each iteration, the function is invoked on the current element. If the result is True, then the element is returned as is. Otherwise, the next element is tested, until the function returns True. Alternative: implement this as a regular function that returns a generator expression.

EXERCISE 50 ■ MyChain

As you can imagine, iterator patterns tend to repeat themselves. For this reason, Python comes with the itertools module (http://mng.bz/NK4E), which makes it easy to create many types of iterators. The classes in itertools have been optimized and debugged across many projects, and often include features that you might not have considered. It's definitely worth keeping this module in the back of your mind for your own projects.

One of my favorite objects in itertools is called chain. It takes any number of iterables as arguments and then returns each of their elements, one at a time, as if they were all part of a single iterable; for example

```
from itertools import chain

for one_item in chain('abc', [1,2,3], {'a':1, 'b':2}):
    print(one_item)
```

This code would print:

```
a
b
c
```

```
1
2
3
a
b
```

The final `'a'` and `'b'` come from the dict we passed, since iterating over a dict returns its keys.

While `itertools.chain` is convenient and clever, it's not that hard to implement. For this exercise, that's precisely what you should do: implement a generator function called `mychain` that takes any number of arguments, each of which is an iterable. With each iteration, it should return the next element from the current iterable, or the first element from the subsequent iterable—unless you're at the end, in which case it should exit.

Working it out

It's true that you could create this as a Python class that implements the iterator protocol, with `__iter__` and `__call__`. But, as you can see, the code is so much simpler, easier to understand, and more elegant when we use a generator function.

Our function takes `*args` as a parameter, meaning that `args` will be a tuple when our function executes. Because it's a tuple, we can iterate over its elements, no matter how many there might be.

We've stated that each argument passed to `mychain` should be iterable, which means that we should be able to iterate over those arguments as well. Then, in the inner `for` loop, we simply `yield` the value of the current line. This returns the current value to the caller, but also holds onto the current place in the generator function. Thus, the next time we invoke `__next__` on our iteration object, we'll get the next item in the series.

Solution

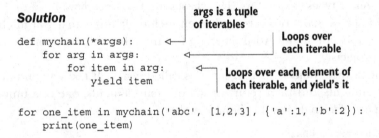

```
def mychain(*args):            ←  args is a tuple
    for arg in args:              of iterables
        for item in arg:       ←  Loops over
            yield item            each iterable

                               ←  Loops over each element of
                                  each iterable, and yield's it

for one_item in mychain('abc', [1,2,3], {'a':1, 'b':2}):
    print(one_item)
```

You can work through a version of this code in the Python Tutor at http://mng.bz/7Xv4.

Screencast solution

Watch this short video walkthrough of the solution: https://livebook.manning.com/video/python-workout.

Beyond the exercise

In this exercise, we saw how we can better understand some built-in functionality by reimplementing it ourselves. In particular, we saw how we can create our own version of itertools.chain as a generator function. Here are some additional challenges you can solve using generator functions:

- The built-in zip function returns an iterator that, given iterable arguments, returns tuples taken from those arguments' elements. The first iteration will return a tuple from the arguments' index 0, the second iteration will return a tuple from the arguments' index 1, and so on, stopping when the shortest of the arguments ends. Thus zip('abc', [10, 20, 30]) returns the iterator equivalent of [('a', 10), ('b', 20), ('c', 30)]. Write a generator function that reimplements zip in this way.
- Reimplement the all_lines function from exercise 49 using mychain.
- In the "Beyond the exercise" section for exercise 48, you implemented a MyRange class, which mimics the built-in range class. Now do the same thing, but using a generator expression.

Summary

In this chapter, we looked at the iterator protocol and how we can both implement and use it in a variety of ways. While we like to say that there's only one way to do things in Python, you can see that there are at least three different ways to create an iterator:

- Add the appropriate methods to a class
- Write a generator function
- Use a generator expression

The iterator protocol is both common and useful in Python. By now, it's a bit of a chicken-and-egg situation—is it worth adding the iterator protocol to your objects because so many programs expect objects to support it? Or do programs use the iterator protocol because so many programs support it? The answer might not be clear, but the implications are. If you have a collection of data, or something that can be interpreted as a collection, then it's worth adding the appropriate methods to your class. And if you're not creating a new class, you can still take advantage of iterables with generator functions and expressions.

After doing the exercises in this chapter, I hope that you can see how to do the following:

- Add the iterator protocol to a class you've written
- Add the iterator protocol to a class via a helper iterator class
- Write generator functions that filter, modify, and add to iterators that you would otherwise have created or used
- Use generator expressions for greater efficiency than list comprehensions

Conclusion

Congratulations! You've reached the end of the book, which (if you're not peeking ahead) means that you've finished a large number of Python exercises. As a result, your Python has improved in a few ways.

First, you're now more familiar with Python syntax and techniques. Like someone learning a foreign language, you might previously have had the vocabulary and grammar structures in place, but now you can express yourself more fluently. You don't need to think quite as long when deciding what word to choose. You won't be using constructs that work but are considered un-Pythonic.

Second, you've seen enough different problems, and used Python to solve them, that you now know what to do when you encounter new problems. You'll know what questions to ask, how to break the problems down into their elements, and what Python constructs will best map to your solutions. You'll be able to compare the trade-offs between different options and then integrate the best ones into your code.

Third, you're now more familiar with Python's way of doing things and the vocabulary that the language uses to describe them. This means that the Python documentation, as well as the community's ecosystem of blogs, tutorials, articles, and videos, will be more understandable to you. The descriptions will make more sense, and the examples will be more powerful.

In short, being more fluent in Python means being able to write better code in less time, while keeping it readable and Pythonic. It also means being able to learn more as you continue on your path as a developer.

I wish you the best of success in your Python career and hope that you'll continue to find ways to practice your Python as you move forward.

index